# Professional Praise

"*Secrets of the Young & Successful* gives you the best road map to develop your own game plan for a successful career and meaningful life."
—Jim Davis, former VP Marketing & New Business Initiatives, eBay

"I have had the chance to work closely with Jennifer and I was extremely impressed with her ability to intimately connect with young people in transition. It's clear why so many forward thinking companies have turned to her for her insight on the young adult market. Her gift of inspiration transcends all ages."
—John Raj, VP Advertising, VISA

"Not just instructions, this book is an entire tool box! When used with the online companion tools this is a powerful guide of self-discovery, planning and step-by-step process that any young person can use to take hold of their passions and steer them to success."
—Alvin Rohrs, President & CEO, Students In Free Enterprise (SIFE)

"I've spent the last 10 years hunting down the most talented women entrepreneurs, coaching them and introducing them to funders who can make their dreams of building billion dollar businesses come true. Now armed with Jen and Scott's *Secrets of the Young & Successful*, we now have a powerful handbook that will give our women a true advantage."
—Amy Millman, President, Springboard Enterprises

"Youths would be wise to head her advice."
—USA Today

"Jen embodies the spirit and passion of her personal crusade to empower her generation's ability to 'live the dream.' What makes her guidance even more remarkable is the simplicity with which anyone regardless of age or experience can achieve success in however they define the term. This isn't about boardrooms and financial titans; this is about making an investment in yourself."
—Robert M. Cohen, Assistant Director,
Harvard University Office of Career Services

"A roadmap to finding what you love and figuring out a plan to make your dreams happen."
—Ryan Seacrest, Host, American Idol

"Having studied young people for over 15 years, information on how to get ahead, what to do, and how to be a success is always desperately needed. This book offers the best tips, information and guidance I've seen for young people today. It will not only motivate and inspire the most confused young person, but offer them real world practical advice in a tone that understands the issues they are dealing with."
—Jane Buckingham, President, Youth Intelligence

"The practical strategies set forth in this book are relevant to aspiring young leaders in every country. Jennifer and Scott succinctly and engagingly address many of the critical challenges that keep young people around the world from achieving their dreams. By studying the principles described in *Secrets of the Young & Successful* and applying them to your life, you will greatly improve your chances of succeeding anywhere in the world."
—Bruce Rector, 58th President of JCI (Junior Chamber International) and author of Monday Morning Messages:
Teaching, Inspiring and Motivating to Lead

"*Secrets of the Young & Successful* imparts universal truths, values and ideas that are important to every young person in the world today."
—Steve Mariotti, Founder and President, The National Foundation for Teaching Entrepreneurship (NFTE)

"Jennifer and Scott are today's motivational gurus for young people who are in search of finding success and meaning in their careers. *Secrets of the Young & Successful* helped me immensely in finding the right career and will do the same for you!"
—Jennifer Egan, Director, Gen Art Los Angeles

 # Reader Praise

"I just wanted to thank you so much for getting my butt in gear in making me go after my dream (and showing me how easy it really is). It may seem really silly, but I feel like my whole life has changed, and I have so much more faith in my capabilities and my future now."

Molly – Cambridge, MA

"You Can Do It! I saw this book this weekend and had to pick it up. I couldn't put the book down once I started reading it. I am so motivated now to go out and conquer the world, and to not let anything or anyone hold me back. I checked out the website and was so impressed to find out that I could connect with other young entrepreneurs from around the world. How cool is that? Now I can email these people and maybe we can even swap stories and share ideas and have a network of support of other people trying to do the same thing. I strongly recommend this book to anyone with big dreams that wants to take the next step to change their lives. I am 32 years old and I know there is still time and a way for me and there certainly is for all of you."

Sharon – Orlando, FL

"It wasn't until I received your book from my grandparents, on my 18th birthday, and read the first chapter of your book that I felt compelled to get up and start working. This summer, thanks to you, I made more money than any other summer before. Your 'grand plan' really helped me finally organize my thoughts and efforts and I've finally started to make my move. I've already told every one of my friends about your book and several have really taken an interest."

Hanson – Holland

"The authors of this book did an incredible job of profiling some of the country's hottest twenty and thirty-somethings. It is so cool to read about my peers going out and rising to the top of their industries at such a young age. Maybe now, people will stop claiming our generation is full of lazy people. How could you EVER think that after reading this book? It made me put down my TV remote and actually sit down to begin writing the business plan that I have been putting off for the last 6 months. Thanks for the motivation and inspiration. You guys ROCK!"

Chase – San Francisco, CA

"You must buy this book! Being a recent college grad and trying to make the difficult transition from college to the real world is extremely frustrating. But, after reading this wonderful book, I feel so much more at ease, to say the least. This book teaches you the REAL thing, not what we are taught in school. This is the kind of material we should be taught in the classroom! This book really motivates you. This is definitely a book worth reading...and I am buying it for all of my friends!!! Kudos to Jennifer and Scott!!!"

Stacey – New York, NY

"I just finished reading your book *Secrets of the Young & Successful*. It is wonderful, I must say. I am a Nigerian and I find this book very inspiring, especially for struggling African youth like me. You wrote this book for people in the states, but I can tell you that it addresses issues everywhere."

Ojo – Nigeria

"You have been able to speak the language of a generation of people that many have considered lazy, uneducated and useless, having been able to awaken something in their hearts, minds, and spirits that they may have only dreamed about."

Karrianna – Atlanta, GA

"This is exactly the book I needed! I've always known I would make it, I've always wanted to make it, I just didn't know how; now I do! Thank you Jennifer and Scott for showing us the way!"

Peter – Los Angeles, CA

"The book has inspired me to get excited about life and it's possibilities, instead of being stressed about what I was going to do and how I was going to do it. Thank you for all of your guidance and insight."

Rachael – Raleigh, NC

"I must say it's an explosive book as it really exposes and introduces young readers like me to stuff like money matters of the young and successful, which is very useful as it helps in setting up good money habits from the start. And enables us to start young!"

Wang – Singapore

"Your book has been an inspiration to me. In fact, it has been my bible for the past several months. I take it with me most places, and read it often. I love the energy, ideas, stories, and most of all the motivation it has given me."

Julia – Toledo, OH

"It was the day that changed my life. Jennifer Kushell took me by storm.

She visited Harvard, where I am a student, and in an informal setting, asked fifteen of us to question what we were doing with our lives, with our career goals, with our passions. None of us could readily tell her WHAT we intended. Most definitely we'd thought about it, but no one had ever challenged us like she did, telling us it was our responsibility to ourselves, our future families and to the rest of our lives to think about it NOW. She caught me by surprise, made me question what I was doing, took me out of my comfort zone in a bewildering, yet amazingly constructive way. She asked each of us to stand up for ourselves and our futures, to combat our preconceptions and those of our generation, and to map out the steps we could and should be taking at that moment and every moment to build our careers.

As an ambitious, motivated student, what some might call an "over-achiever", I was used to being told to "live in the moment", not to plan, and to "worry about it later." Kushell told me the facts: thinking about it later is often too late and I shouldn't let anyone convince me otherwise. The time to act, to explore, to question and to search is NOW. Take risks now. Do what makes me happy now.

I have unbridled enthusiasm for her and her teachings. She counseled me that it was okay to explore, okay to take risks, and okay to question my relationship to "the system." She moved me to be more proactive and to create, then act, on my dream. In her very magical way, she inspired me more profoundly than anyone ever had before."

Tiffany – Cambridge, MA

secrets of the
young &
successful ®

how to get everything you want
without waiting a lifetime

JENNIFER KUSHELL
SCOTT M. KAUFMAN

published by ys media corp.
los angeles

YS Media Corp.
4712 Admiralty Way #530
Marina del Rey, CA 90292
www.ysn.com/ysmedia

Published by YS Media Corp. in association with YS Interactive Corp.

Young & Successful® is a registered trademark of YS Media Corp. The YS logo mark, Secrets of the Young & Successful™, Bio Builder™, Your Personal Balance Sheet™, Your Ideal Life™, Ideal Life Monument™, The Grand Plan™, Grand Plan Development System™, Master Your Universe™, Take A Taste™, Real World University™, Personal Fire Drill™, TAPPS™, REST™, POP – Power of People™, and The House on the Hill™ are trademarks of YS Media Corp.

YSN™, Your Success Network™ and YSN.com are trademarks of YS Interactive Corp.

All other referenced trademarks are property of their respective companies.

This publication is designed to provide accurate and authoritative information in regard to the subject matter covered. It is sold with the understanding that the Authors and Publisher is not engaged in rendering personalized legal, accounting, financial planning or other professional services. If you require legal advice or other expert assistance, you should seek the services of a competent professional. The Authors and Publisher specifically disclaim any liability, loss, or risk, which is incurred as a consequence, directly or indirectly, of the use and application of any of the contents of this work.

YS Media books, audios, videos and other content may be purchased in bulk at special discounts for educational, business, fundraising, or sales promotional use. Unique premium editions, including personalized covers, excerpts, and corporate imprints, can be created in large quantities for special needs. For more information, please email: **SpecialMarkets@ysn.com**

First Edition: June 2003

Publisher's Cataloging-in-Publication Data
Kushell, Jennifer.

Secrets of the young & successful : how to get everything you want without waiting a lifetime / Jennifer Kushell ; Scott M. Kaufman. – Marina del Rey, CA : YS Media Corp., 2006.

p. ; cm.
Includes index.
ISBN: 1-933956-00-3
ISBN13: 978-1-933956-00-8

1. Success—Psychological aspects. 2. Job satisfaction. I.Title.
HF5381.5.K87 2006
153.94—dc22   2006924754

Printed in the United States of America
10 09 08 07 06 • 5 4 3 2 1

To all those who are different—

the overachievers,
the misunderstood,
the underappreciated,
the diamonds in the rough.

This book is for you.

Acknowledgments

WE ARE SO LUCKY TO HAVE BEEN SURROUNDED by many inspiring and supportive people—not just in putting this book together, but in sculpting our lives and careers.

First and foremost, we must thank our families for believing in us and in what we could do, even when our drive and grand aspirations seemed crazy. Growing up around so many entrepreneurs—five businesses in mine, four in Scott's—we were exposed to the concept of taking ownership and control of our lives at an early age. Not only did our families teach us the true meaning of a solid work ethic, responsibility, diligence, perseverance, and passion, but they also showed us how to take pride in our endeavors and ourselves. Most importantly, they gave us the courage to fail, the humility to succeed, and all along, helped us get the most out of every experience. We will never forget their support and generosity both in the best of times, and when we struggled the most.

Next to family, Scott and I have to thank the people who stood close by us and cheered us along every step of the way: Ben Kyan, Curtis and Kristi Estes, Jonathan and Niva Kilman, Jen and Barry Gribbon, Keith Wagner, Harold Wrobel, Spencer Proffer, Mark & Maura Rampolla, Brad & Shariae Dugdale, Julie Joncas, Jennifer Iannolo, Bob Cohen, Jeff and Mark Bloom, Jay Gleason, Lee and Jon Weisner, Jordan and Sheri Levy, Brad Kesler, Larry Angrisani, JC Shardo, Layne

Britton, Ken Deckinger, Steve Mariotti, Maureen Ford, Kathy Allen, Rieva Lesonsky, Fred DeLuca, and Jane Rinzler-Buckingham.

Thank you to those who believed in our vision, jumped on board, rolled up their sleeves, and shared their invaluable expertise and support: Ken Browning, Rick Frishman, David Hahn, Dee Steine, Pam Jennings, Jim Jennings, Barry Felsen, Bruce and Caroline Somers, Jennifer Fiscus, Nancy Mamann, Cortney Sellers, Ian Young, Jim Davis, Art Insana, Chris Lutz, Anna Mongayt, Candy Ibarra, Kelly Barash, Grace Han, Ron Warner, Chuck Meyer, Beth Broday, Amber Cordero, Steve Harrision, Yanik Silver, Joanna Katz, Carol Schotz, John Kovarek, Tracy Hoffman, Ian Murrogh, Jessica Stevens, Deborah Granger, Randy Gordon, Jake Phillips, Brian Rock, Bob Kahan, Ramsey Hanna, Russ Watson, Bob Keim, Randy Bort, Jamie Resin, Todd Gitlin, and Jerry Jenkins. We'd also like to thank our original publishing team at Simon & Schuster for supporting our initial vision for this book to take flight. And finally, thank you to Bob Mecoy, a true gem in the publishing world and the kind of editor and advisor with whom every writer hopes to work. It was an absolute privilege and pleasure.

Secrets of the Young & Successful is a by-product of a lifetime of work and dreams. We are so grateful to have this opportunity to share what we've seen, heard, studied, and marveled at for years in a way that would enable others to experience and benefit from it, too. For that privilege we thank *you*.

Contents

 # Preface: The Evolution

From *Secrets of the Young & Successful* to ysn.com

WAKING UP IN MY CAMBRIDGE HOTEL ROOM, a sudden thought pierced through my early morning fog: Today was a big day. I rose early to review my notes, because later that morning I was keynoting Harvard's Spring Career Conference. I reached the window and pulled the curtains back to let some sunlight in, discovering the Charles River glistening below and a collegiate crew team gliding by. I smiled, thinking about the day ahead, and suddenly found myself staring across the river at another familiar site: the dorm I called "home" as a Boston University freshman. I remembered what it was like to see that building for the first time, and realized this would actually be my ten-year anniversary of leaving home to venture across the country in my first major act of independence. Leaving my friends and family more than 3,000 miles away, I had no idea what I was getting myself into; I was every bit as uncertain about my future as the thousands of people I now work with each year. Today, however, would be far different from that first day in Boston; this time, I was a guest of one of the most prestigious institutions in the world. The idea that Harvard students were looking for my guidance to help them figure out their next steps after graduation was still sinking in. Then again, a lot had happened in the past few years.

Like most people, I assumed that if you made it to Harvard, you probably had your life pretty well figured out. When I met the students, however, they confided that wasn't exactly the case. Despite their world-class education and stellar academic careers, they were confused and frustrated about their post-graduation existence. They all knew that their futures would be bright, and they were well-equipped to find success somehow in life, but the real question was: "Success according to whom?" What *I* wanted to know was what would make them most happy. What I heard instead were a lot of people telling me what they *should* be doing. "I know I *should* go into . . . consulting . . . banking . . . medicine . . ." Fill in the blank. The menu of options they saw for themselves seemed pretty limited. The most glaring omission from their collective vocabulary, however, was a simple word: want. For many, it wasn't even a thought—it just didn't seem "practical."

I spent almost four hours answering questions after my speech— definitely a record for me. We talked through their individual scenarios and worked out simple solutions and next steps. First we figured out what they were most passionate about—even if it had nothing to do with what they were studying, planning to do for the summer, or the job they had lined up after graduation. Then we talked through a series of different real-world opportunities and how to start capitalizing on those opportunities right away. One by one, the confused, frustrated looks turned to smiles and outright joy in their faces. One girl even said she felt like it was Christmas.

Somewhere in the middle, I was struck with déjà vu. These conversations were just like the ones we'd had with young people in Australia, El Salvador, Japan, Austria, Denmark, Italy, Spain, Belize, Canada, Thailand, China, Mexico, etc. Geography and personal experiences varied, but the overall issues were universal: Young adults around the world are being educated for the future, theoretically, but most haven't taken the time to think about the futures they most want to build for themselves. And no one has shown them how.

When we first set out to write *Secrets*, we knew a lot of people were struggling to make this big transition—but we honestly didn't realize how many. We certainly did not understand how global the phenomenon had become. We discovered the magnitude of this trend in 2003, right around when Scott and I got the call that the first edition of this book had hit the New York Times Bestseller list. All the years of hard work had paid off. The response was overwhelming, and the feedback humbling and incredibly validating all at once. We'd written a book to help teach young people how to harness their energy, passions, talents and drive, and turn those characteristics into a career and lifestyle they could not just live with, but would truly *love*. We wanted to help people who had struggled, just like us, to figure out how to find that sweet spot where their lives could be filled with passion and purpose—and most importantly, happiness.

It was working. Letters poured in from young people around the world; they thanked us for helping them to discover the direction they'd been so desperate to find, and for giving them the confidence and tools to change course, take a leap of faith, and commit to pursuing what was most important to *them*. We also discovered that the *Secrets of the Young & Successful* were not only important tools for those just starting out in the real world, but for anyone looking to make a big transition or catapult to the next level in his or her career—at any age. While this book is a great start, we learned that there is a need for even more intimate ongoing support—from us and from people just like you who are experiencing the same challenges, questions, and frustrations on the road to success and fulfillment. It's funny how things work though. It seemed *our* dreams had come true in the process. Or had they?

We soon realized this book was only the beginning. When we raised our own expectations and imagined the possibilities without limits, we knew the scope of this project and our original vision had the potential to reach far beyond these printed pages. This need is what spawned the creation of:

ysn.com—your success network™

Ironically, the steps we've outlined for you in this book are the ones that led us to transform our original vision into ysn.com–a robust, global online environment created to help you learn what you *really* need to know to excel in today's rapidly changing world. Key features at ysn.com include a comprehensive (yet fun!) online self-assessment, an interactive professional social networking community, and rich multimedia career profiles from every walk of life. You'll also find trade secrets, newsletters, tips, articles, one-of-a-kind software, collaboration tools, and connections to a vast array of people, organizations and companies that might be looking for someone just like you to help fulfill *their* dreams. You'll have the opportunity to take the tools you have learned from this book and immediately put them to work for you out in the real world: Read it here, do it there, then reap the rewards. Every step outlined in this book will be taken to the next level: Learn the most effective way to write your "bio" and resume; how to network with people in the fields you find most interesting or intriguing; then put all of it into action by creating your personal profile and portfolio, and join our global community of others with common aspirations. Learn how to explore various career options, gain invaluable real-world experience, then find the next great opportunity that's calling your name at ysn.com.

One of the most amazing advancements since this book was first released is the development of our online self-assessment system at ysn.com. For a limited time, with the purchase of this book you'll get a special complimentary code for this innovative assessment as our gift to you for taking this step to invest in yourself.

> Check out the special postcard included in the back of this book for more details about how you can take your FREE YSN Self-Assessment TODAY (a $30.00 retail value!) at ysn.com.

Rest assured though, this is not in any way related to those boring standardized tests you've probably been forced to take at some point in your life. This is very different. HOW? This was specially designed for your current needs, and examines your personality traits, your values, your likes and dislikes, and suggests the best working environments and industries to showcase your talents and passions. This unique assessment is your first step in discovering your ideal life path. If you're curious to find out more about yourself right now, then go ahead and turn to the last page of this book, yank out that postcard, and get started today! It may be the best 30 minutes you could spend to ensure a future where success in life and work is properly aligned with your personal passions and desires. Do it today. (Let's get real: If you put it off you may never come back to it.) Next, get registered at ysn.com and sign up for our YSN Weekly Newsletter so we can stay in close contact and be sure you get your weekly dose of inspiration, ideas, resources, tips and profiles to keep you motivated and moving in the right direction.

Are you ready to take that fire in your belly and channel it into a rich, fulfilling career and life? Read the book to learn the *Secrets of the Young & Successful*. Then go to ysn.com and use the network to make *your success* happen now. Read on. Log on. Your future is waiting.

 # Introduction

GIVE IT TIME.

Be patient.

Enjoy yourself.

You have the rest of your life ahead of you, so don't worry.

Give me a break! I've heard it all before—and I know you have, too.

But what if you're not content with being like everyone else? What if you're done trying to play by the rules and ready to do things your way?

Most of us have been taught that we should follow a methodical path to success: Go to school and get good grades. Earn your degree. Get to work on your résumé so you can land a great job. Act like an adult. Work hard so you can make good money and support yourself. Find someone nice so you can settle down and have kids. Be responsible, faithful and patient, and you'll retire happy. Make your family proud.

So we try to fit in. We stay on the clearly marked roads; but after a while, that gets old and boring. Sometimes traditional strategies are ineffective. Roads dead-end. At some point, many of us discover that the path that's been laid out for us, or the route we've stumbled onto ourselves, isn't exactly what we want. Perhaps we're even heading in the wrong direction altogether; or worse, we know exactly what we want, but just can't figure out how to get it.

That's when you know it's time to shake up the plan a bit.

You want to be successful. The big question is how, isn't it? And what if you're not interested in waiting a lifetime to get what you want?

Well, we come with good news: You don't have to wait, struggle, or be confused anymore. After years of searching for answers to these same questions, we've uncovered some of the biggest secrets on how to achieve extraordinary things at an early age, and they don't have to be a mystery to anyone anymore. Best of all, they consist of simple solutions that you can implement right away, and reap the benefits of almost immediately.

Want to know how to make some seriously impressive and impactful things happen with your life? Whether that means landing your dream job, dedicating your days and nights to a startup or nonprofit, rising to the top of an industry, pursuing something totally out of the ordinary, or having the option to retire really early, there's much to be done—today. And if you have grand aspirations for yourself, your life, your loved ones and your community, you'd better get with the program because the rules have changed.

The world is a very different place than it ever has been—not just from when our parents grew up, but even just a few years ago. Technology, media, and modern communications have given us so many wonderful gifts while making the world a much smaller, more accessible place. However, the resulting explosion of options and opportunities (open to younger people, nonetheless), can be totally overwhelming. You're not alone though. Millions of others are in the same boat questioning how this new world really works, and how to find the best place for themselves in it. Travel the globe like we have, and you'll see that these frustrations are universal, too.

Despite how dazed you may be by all this, it doesn't have to scare you. Adopt the Y&S perspective and you'll soon realize that it has actually never been a more exciting time to be alive. Our career options have never offered more potential for us to explore our passions, carve out new paths, and do what we love, both for work and for fun. Ideally, the two can become indistinguishable for you, too. Sometimes it just takes a fresh new perspective, and a better understanding of what's really possible.

There are people out there—many of them your peers—who are capitalizing on the ever-changing landscape in a big way. They have developed powerful strategies and acquired unique insight early that has enabled them to conquer the challenges most people face repeatedly throughout a lifetime. Not surprisingly, these people are achieving remarkable goals, finding tremendous personal and professional satisfaction, and absolutely loving their lives.

We call them the Young & Successful.

So how can you be one of them? This book will show you how.

We'll give you an all-access pass to this very different world of thought, action, and achievement. Here, we promise to share with you the strategies, tools, and knowledge that these incredible people use to get ahead in record time. These are the *Secrets of the Young & Successful.*

Implementing these secrets in your own life is easy, too. For example:

- Take the right risks and reap the rewards.
- Ask the right questions and get the answers you're seeking.
- Step out of your comfort zone and discover a whole new world.
- Discover your true passion and everything else can fall into place quickly.
- Surround yourself with people who understand your ambitions and truly support your quest to find your own way and you'll never be alone again.
- Find your fans and mentors and keep them close because they will become your biggest allies in the world.
- Put yourself and your aspirations out there and fascinating new opportunities will emerge over and over again.

Sound too simple? It is. Now get over it and keep reading. When it comes to finding success, most people just get in their own way and make things more complicated than they need to be. We've seen it happen a million times, both in our lives and in those of our readers. What we offer is a different perspective that we hope you'll connect with, because not only have we "been there," but we really do understand what you're up against as someone who's establishing your own sense of self and your place in the world—all while you're still at the beginning of your career or making a transition into an entirely new career path or industry. This is supposed to be one of the most exciting times of your life, but odds are it's not turning out to be quite what you expected. We'll show you how it can be, and more. This book will give you the tools to adopt a new mindset and create a road map to follow to *your success.*

Like many of you, Scott and I started out trying to fit in with everyone else and play by the rules. It didn't last for long though. If being raised around so many entrepreneurs taught us anything, it was that sometimes blazing your own path is the best route. Personally, we've always done that through entrepreneurship. I can't say we always knew what we were doing, or what we were getting ourselves into, but it was clear that we wanted to do things our way: live our lives according to *our* ideas, dreams and convictions, not those of other people. We tried to be just like everyone else for a while, then just gave up, accepted what made us different, learned to run with it . . . and never looked back. It certainly hasn't been the easy route at times, but we wouldn't trade it for the world.

Scott and I have both been drawn to successful people our whole lives. Typically, he gravitates to industry titans, I to entrepreneurs and young people just starting out. I track people who started very early, follow their progress, and watch as they make great successes of themselves. Scott usually works from the other direction, studying the biggest moguls, then researching their careers to trace back to when they were younger. We are both constantly analyzing their decisions, milestones, and strategies, retracing their steps through meticulous research. We joined forces to share what we had found, and this book is our first step.

We've made a career out of doing things that we were *theoretically* too young to be doing, didn't have enough experience in, weren't smart enough to do, and didn't have any credibility or background for. So can you. I've hit the ten-year mark in my career as a public activist of sorts—writing, speaking, consulting, teaching, and, I'll confess, a little preaching, too—about how people can capitalize on untraditional opportunities and achieve unheard-of success at any stage of their life. Now, you are about to learn the *Secrets of the Young & Successful.*

We truly hope this book touches your life and speaks to you and your personal journey and dreams in a very special way.

We believe that extraordinary things are possible. And we hope you do, too.

Part
One

Meet the Young & Successful

IMAGINE WHAT YOUR LIFE WOULD BE LIKE if everything always seemed to go your way. How would you feel if all those haunting questions about your future just vanished? What if you could transform your biggest challenges into your greatest advantages and do everything you've always dreamed about? If you could sculpt the Ideal Life for yourself, what would it look like?

Well, we all know nobody really has a *perfect* life, but there are people out there—you've seen them . . . maybe you're even one of them—who have figured out how to turn their lives into something wonderful and outrageous, and their wildest dreams into reality. What's more, many of these people are *young*. Sometimes *really* young, too. And while they've already accomplished so much, they're not in the middle or at the end of their careers, they're just getting warmed up. They've taken control and ownership of their lives and, best of all, have figured out for themselves how to get everything they want, without waiting a lifetime. We call them the Young & Successful.

Who Are the Young & Successful?

The Young & Successful are a diverse group of passionate people whose achievements can be seen in all industries, cultures, and countries.

They include the twenty-eight-year-old who's the managing director of an investment bank, the sixteen-year-old whose second small business employs three adults twice his age, the nineteen-year-old who represents his country at a global youth employment conference, the thirty-three-year-old who is a frequent speaker before Congress, and the thirty-year-old who convinced thousands of her peers to teach needy children. These people are all around us—in business, the arts, education, politics, medicine, law . . . you name it.

The Young & Successful are action-oriented and proactive. They have an exhilarating aura of freedom and independence. They do what most of us just talk and dream about. They create a stir—make the world sit up and take notice. They always seem to land the best jobs, get the most coveted opportunities, and make money doing the things they love. They make the biggest impact on the lives of others.

Want to know how? Well, don't worry. Soon you will too.

The first Young & Successful person I knew was Lisa Lazar. Lisa wasn't the prettiest, the coolest, or the most popular girl in school, but she was the student body president and seemed to be at the center of everything. I always noticed and admired her confidence and character, and although I never knew her well, Lisa's example helped me realize that I could be much more than another face in the crowd. A few years later, I realized that I, too, had some interesting ideas to share, and soon, I was president. Just watching Lisa keep her eye on the ball, take charge, and motivate an entire school with her words and actions taught me that I could set for myself the same seemingly unrealistic goal and achieve it. In what turned out to be a profound turn of events in my life, I finally stood up . . . and was heard. I found my voice. And it was stronger than I'd ever imagined.

In college, one of my closest friends was Alidad Khayami. He was born in Iran, grew up in France, lived in London, and was probably one of the most worldly, sophisticated people I'd ever met. From his finesse in orchestrating unforgettable get-togethers to the way he could hold the attention of people twice his age and captivate any crowd, no one ever doubted that he could have or do anything he wanted in life. I may have been just nineteen, but with Alidad, I learned how to carry myself like an adult and present myself with sophistication and class. After spending so much time with Alidad in *his* world, I was no longer a kid in mine.

When I started getting involved with entrepreneurs, I began to meet many more people in the Young & Successful crowd. I remember when my friend Alan Ezeir invited me over to see his new house. Just a few years older than me, Alan and a few friends (six to be exact) had moved into a big, beautiful house in exclusive Bel Air the year after they graduated from UCLA. I'll never forget walking into Alan's room upstairs and seeing my first high-tech home office. His single bed was in the far left corner, and to the right of that a long set of desks stretched along two walls and offered about twenty feet of counter space. A neatly organized assortment of the latest technology—a computer, a fax machine, stationery boxes, business card holders, phones, a voice-mail system, a pager, and a brick-size cell phone (it's been a few years)—filled the entire surface. The technology was, for that day and age, very cool, but that wasn't what mattered. Alan managed a network of hundreds of contacts, and he worked hard to turn these people into customers for his growing telecom company.

Back then, who knew that meeting great people could be such an art form? I learned it in Alan's room that day, and I went on to build relationships with more people in the next few years than I had ever dreamed of meeting in a lifetime.

In my first few years out in the working world I came across another young woman who would completely change my perspective on business and my opportunities. Her name was Jane Rinzler-Buckingham. At twenty-four, I was just starting to get involved in big industry conferences, like "Targeting the Growing College Market" and "Reaching Generation X." For me, being asked to be a featured speaker in front of hundreds of executives from Fortune 500 companies was pretty unreal. I've got to admit, too, that as I prepared my presentations on how big companies and organizations could better meet the needs of young entrepreneurs—a population they had never given much thought to—I did have a few doubts about whether anyone would really listen. I was so young, and my whole company could easily fit in one of their executive washrooms.

As the conferences began to open up, I saw Jane warmly welcoming the sea of familiar faces—to her at least—introducing powerful marketing directors to each other left and right. I quickly discovered that anyone who was anyone in the business of youth marketing knew who Jane was, because she was the source of some of the best data and insight on that demographic. It turns out that Jane spent her twenties building her own company, aptly named Youth Intelligence, and was now the center of attention. Jane had paved the way for others like me, who were still young but had valuable insights to share. She had demonstrated that her age could actually be an advantage.

More on Jane soon.

The Young & Successful were as much a mystery to me then as they might be to you now. I constantly wanted to know "Who are these people?" and "How did they get so far *so* fast?" I've spent years learning the answers—that it's a process—of learning about yourself, creating a vivid picture of what you want, mapping out a plan, strategizing your moves and major decisions, conquering new worlds, harnessing the power of people and relationships, earning credibility and respect, and gaining access.

I asked a lot of people a lot of questions. And I learned that many of the Young & Successful are just like you and me except they've figured out a few things that made all the difference.

The Young & Successful of Yesterday and Today

Before we tell you about the Young & Successful and introduce you to some people who are making amazing things happen today, let's look back for a moment. The Young & Successful have always managed to blaze interesting new trails. Here are a few of the most popular (and inspiring) Young & Successful people in history.

. Temba Tsheri, at fifteen, became the youngest person to reach the summit of Mount Everest.

. Fred DeLuca started Subway, the second largest restaurant chain in the world, at seventeen.

. Edgar Allan Poe published his first book of poetry at eighteen.

. Scott Olsen, a Canadian hockey player, started Rollerblade, Inc. at twenty.

. Caresse Crosby patented the first ladies' bra at twenty-two (crafted from two handkerchiefs and a piece of ribbon).

. Charlie Chaplin had already been in thirty-five films by age twenty-five.

. John D. Rockefeller built the Standard Oil Company, the largest oil refinery, by age twenty-five.

. Charles Lindbergh, at twenty-five, was the first pilot to fly across the Atlantic Ocean alone.

· Harold Ford, Jr., became the youngest person elected to the U.S. Congress at twenty-six.

- Napoleon was only twenty-six when he conquered Italy.

- Fred Smith started FedEx at twenty-seven.

- Michael Dell became the youngest Fortune 500 company owner at thirty.

- Bill Gates became the youngest billionaire in history at thirty.

- Dr. Martin Luther King, Jr., became the youngest person to win the Nobel Peace Prize at thirty-five.

While it's unlikely that we're going to have anyone conquering Italy in our generation, young people are nonetheless achieving great things in practically every city and town around the world.

Curtis Estes is one of the best examples of a Young & Successful person around today. However, if you looked at how things started for him, this probably isn't the outcome you'd have predicted.

Curtis spent his first few years growing up in your average middle-class home in a small Kansas town. But one Christmas day, when he was eleven, his life took a devastating turn. Returning from a visit to an aunt in a nearby town, Curtis's family found their home in flames. Not only were all their newly opened presents inside, but everything they owned was destroyed—their clothes, their furniture, their pictures, their toys. Everything.

That night, the Estes family slept at a friend's house and after that, at a local shelter. With no insurance and little money to rebuild their life and move on, new clothes had to come from the Salvation Army, and the entire family—Curtis, his younger sister Deb, and his mom—went to work at McDonald's. It was then that Curtis began to formulate his big picture plans. He knew then and there that this was not a life he wanted to get used to. While attending the University of Kansas (a campus that was three times the size of his hometown) he realized how much opportunity existed in the outside world.

Curtis always dreamed of moving to Los Angeles and making it big. So right after college, he picked himself up and did just that. Because of his dedication and drive, the first job he took ended up guiding him down the path to getting everything he ever wanted and more. He became a financial representative with Northwestern Mutual Financial Network—widely recognized as the top life insurance company in the country and named eighteen years in a row as the "most admired" company in *Forbes* annual survey of corporate reputations. Insurance is not typically known as a glamorous or easy career path. Curtis worked hard, but more important, he worked smart. Within eight years he had climbed to the top of the company.

Last year, Curtis was ranked in the top 20 of the company's eight thousand agents! Not bad for a small-town Midwestern boy who's barely turned thirty. But being a top performer in one of the leading companies in the world is only a part of what makes Curtis Young & Successful.

Jane Rinzler-Buckingham is another prime Young & Successful example. What distinguishes Jane from her peers is how fast she got out of the gate. Jane was only sixteen when she and her mother teamed up to write a book, *Teens Speak Out*. Jane had a lot to say about her generation then, but she couldn't have had any idea what was in store for her from there. Ten years later, she convinced the ad agency where she was working to let her start a new division focused on youth marketing. And that's where the magic happened. The division was so successful and the industry buzz so great that Jane ended up spinning off the group into her own company, Youth Intelligence. Today, her research company produces market data and reports on trends, and conducts comprehensive studies for companies like MTV, Nike, AT&T, and American Express—special insight that they pay tens and even hundreds of thousands of dollars for.

Curtis and Jane exemplify what we mean when we say Young & Successful. They have taken full ownership and control of their lives and carefully sculpted their paths to success. Either of them could have sat on the sidelines and settled for just getting by in their lives and at work, but there was something inside that told them they could do more. They had a vision of what might be possible and an intuitive sense of what success would mean for them. With that vision as a starting point, they started early on their journey working toward their goals. As a result, they've created the life of their dreams and, best of all, they still have *a whole lifetime ahead of them* to enjoy the rewards and build upon their early success.

What Makes the Young & Successful Different?

The Young & Successful manage to figure out what they want early on, or at least choose a path that makes sense for them, and pursue it aggressively. The Young & Successful don't waste time. They try things, do things, and then make decisions. When they realize that they've made a wrong choice, they pick up and move on, always taking what they've learned with them when they go. It's because of this ethic that the Young & Successful accomplish so much in their early years and position themselves to pursue bigger and better opportunities as they grow older. In the first twenty or thirty years of their lives, the Young & Successful enjoy experiences and opportunities that most will never see in a lifetime.

So what makes them different? The big X factor is their ability to turn what everyone calls their greatest *dis*-advantages into their most powerful motivators—and often even their greatest *advantages*.

Add a Little Spin

Have you ever been on a job interview where they brushed you off with "If you just had some experience . . ." Or has someone responded to an idea of yours with "That's not the way things are done here?" Well, that's sweet music to the Young & Successful. They use their youth, lack of experience, readiness to try new things, and passion as their competitive advantages. Their age gifts them with the energy to face any challenge head-on and the time to learn from their mistakes. Their lack of experience means that they're not weighed down by history, that they're ready to think outside the box because they don't even *see* the box.

BREAKING TRADITION

More and more industries welcome that competitive advantage today—even the most conservative ones. In many ways, there's no business more conservative than the automobile industry. A new car model can take years to develop and cost billions of dollars to manufacture. Usually only the most senior designers get a shot when a company starts with a blank sheet of paper, but that's not how it went on two of the most exciting and successful designs of the last few years. Craig Kember says that when he was in high school, "I didn't even know you could do this for a living." His relationship with Toyota began when he accepted an internship while still in college. A few years later, he saw a Toyota Matrix—his design—on the street for the first time. "It felt awesome," he says. "I could recognize it from a half a mile away."

Craig is twenty-eight and one of the industry's youngest lead designers ever. He embodies the Toyota Motor Corporation's commitment to transforming itself.

Bryan Nesbitt, also in his late twenties, is a lead designer for another one of the top car companies. He scored big time with his first blank-sheet design—the Chrysler PT Cruiser, one of the most successful new car launches since the Ford Mustang.

When companies want out-of-the-box thinking, even the most conservative realize that they may have to hunt for a little touch of the X factor. When they came looking, Bryan and Craig were ready.

But what if you're not *quite* ready? Or the world doesn't seem to think you are . . .

When the Young & Successful are still a work in progress and still negotiating their own uncharted path, they can be called a lot of things: "scattered," "unfocused," "unrealistic," "dreamer" (yeah, that last one is pretty popular).

To join the ranks of the Young & Successful, the first thing you have to learn is how to turn a deaf ear to the criticism, the naysayers, and the labels, and just keep going. People may characterize you as they see fit, but it's your definition of yourself that often makes you who you really are. Forge your own path and work toward the vision *you* have of the life and the career that you desire. Instead of giving in to all the skepticism out there, describe yourself as the self-affirming Young & Successful do: "hard-working," "adventurous," "curious," "creative," "proactive," "insightful," "unafraid," "unique," "different." It all starts with how you perceive yourself.

This kind of optimism and confidence, coupled with a certain amount of preparation and the right tools, ensures the Young & Successful are well equipped for their journeys.

They possess vision and passion in their dreams and convictions.
They're highly resourceful, creative, and inventive.
They seize opportunities and create their own whenever possible.
They know what motivates them.
They have a strong sense of their own identity.
They have spent a substantial amount of time on introspection and self-discovery.
They refuse to let other people dictate how they should live.
They take responsibility for their happiness.

Most important, the Young & Successful are different because they own their lives and their careers. They take control early on, and never let go.

What Motivates the Young & Successful?

We all know that we have it in us to be successful, given the right conditions. But too often, if someone asks us what's standing in our way, we yank out our laundry list: "I don't have enough time." "I don't have any experience." "I don't know the right people." "I haven't found the right opportunity." "I don't have what I need." "I'm not sure what I want yet." Go on—I'm sure you can add a few more to this pile of excuses.

The Young & Successful take these cries as a call to action. The challenges, fears, and insecurities that shut everyone else down are often the very things that drive the Young & Successful through the long days and the sleepless nights that creating success requires. For the Young & Successful, adversity is the impetus to spring into action.

On the surface, the Young & Successful face the same challenges that everyone else does. Their motivations are not unique. It's their reactions that make them different. It's that X factor again—being able to take challenges and turn them on their heads. Creating advantages where others see only disadvantages.

If you don't believe me, consider this: the Young & Successful react similarly—and are ultimately motivated—by a combination of a few major challenges. In fact, we've found six hot-button motivators. Any of these sound familiar to you?

1. The Mere Words "No" or "You Can't"

Accepting that you can't do something or that you don't have any choices or options in a given situation is the kiss of death for anyone striving to break away from the pack and defy the odds. If you tend to accept these kinds of debilitating comments, then you are probably someone who is quick to accept the status quo, and you settle.

The Young & Successful have a lot of trouble accepting the word "no" and, even more so, the suggestion that "they can't" do something—anything, for that matter. Perhaps the greatest way to launch a Young & Successful person into action is by challenging his or her ability to do something.

2. A Cry for Help or Blatant Injustice

The Young & Successful see injustice, inequity, or oppression and take action. They know that on their own, their impact may be limited but likewise realize that they can make waves and build consensus. On one recent occasion you could clearly see this tendency in action. When New York City cut the school budgets, dozens of stars—young musicians, hip-hop artists, rappers, anchors, and entertainment executives—turned out to protest on the steps of City Hall. What started with a few phone calls quickly turned into a demonstration with tens of thousands of people calling for more money for education. Almost instantly, a few emotional conversations were transformed into a collective demand for justice.

In cases like this, many will criticize, argue, or debate important issues at hand, but most tend to just complain a lot rather than join the fight and confront the evil head-on. The Young & Successful, like activists, adopt a cause, join a battle, and sometimes even become obsessed with finding a solution. For many, the experience defines them, and that label can say "I'm oppressed" or "I'm a fighter." In almost any given situation, leaders will rise to lead the pack. This is the root of where many Young & Successful get their motivation.

3. The Repressed Eventually Rebel

A lot of people find their true inner power after it's been repressed or stymied for a long time. I'd venture to guess that millions are afflicted by jobs they hate, misguided career paths, unsupportive environments, bad relationships, and an overall sense of being trapped—situations that can lead to depression and spiral downward from there. The Young & Successful spin on this: When external forces hold you down and make you feel small and insignificant, you *have to* find an outlet to get out and free yourself.

Feelings of helplessness are not acceptable to the Young & Successful. When faced with adversity, they take responsibility for sculpting a more perfect environment for themselves that can better serve them. They turn challenges into powerful motivators.

4. It's All in the Family

When the term "dysfunctional family" took root a few years ago, it soon became part of the chic psychobabble most of us adopted as we illustrated for people in the outside world the outrageous characters that made up our families. Now, few can claim a Brady Bunch–like upbringing, but it's not uncommon for people to let their childhood baggage control their success as adults. We need to grow up and move beyond whatever may have hampered our success up until now. If we need to come to grips with our past and confront old demons (like divorce, disagreements, debilitating debt, emotional security, estrangements, or other entanglements) there are plenty of therapists and other advisors who can help. But allowing our past to get in the way of our future opportunities is about as tragic as it gets.

The Young & Successful realize early on that we all have issues about how we were raised. Of course life is considerably easier when you have parents who are attentive, a family that's loving, teachers who are motivating and positive or mentors who are inspiring, and a prevailing sense that you can in fact do anything you want to in life.

But not everyone is so lucky. The key is in finding your motivations and supporters wherever you can.

5. Tragedy or Adversity Strikes

Lance Armstrong, one of the greatest professional cyclists in history, is a textbook example of how the Young & Successful respond to misfortune. At twenty-eight, Lance was an aggressive, determined athlete with a strong future and, as he puts it, a sizable ego to go along with it. But then a trip to the doctor revealed he had cancer, which was followed by treatments of chemotherapy and radiation at such high levels that most people would not have survived.

Lance not only beat the disease twice, but he defied the pessimistic experts and pledged that he would race again. Dropped by his former team, he built a new team. And when he came back to attempt the Tour de France, the longest, toughest bicycle race in the world, he didn't just ride, he won—four years in a row. Today, he is considered the greatest racer in the world.

6. *The Money Is Oh, So Sweet*

All right, I don't want you to get the impression right off the bat that the Young & Successful do what they do because of money, because most of the time that's simply not true. They do, however, have very deep-seated motivations for pursuing success with such fervor. I'd be lying if I didn't admit that a few more toys and a little extra cash don't hurt their overall motivation.

What's interesting about the pursuit of material wealth, though, is that it makes some people act strangely. Instead of motivating people to work harder, it causes some to develop self-defeating prophecies. If they want something that they think is out of their reach (a house, a boat, a car, a plane), they instantly convince themselves that it's a worthless or pointless pursuit, to justify why they're not taking part in it. This protects them from failing in the eyes of others, although they sulk and often become resentful of those who have what they want. Envy has never been the best form of motivation.

Instead, the Young & Successful have something to teach us

here yet again. Learn to celebrate the successes of others around you and you'll not only gain more successful friends, mentors, and peers but you'll also learn that much more about what it takes to earn some of the more material rewards yourself. And that doesn't sound like such a bad thing, does it?

Motivation is the critical ingredient for achieving anything and everything you want in life. And take full advantage of the X factor. Get used to spinning challenges, and, instead of allowing them to pull you down, use them to compel you to achieve greater things.

Can You Be Young & Successful?

I'm supremely confident that that answer is "*yes!*" There's no question that many of the Young & Successful I've talked to do seem to have some inborn drive or talent that would make them a success no matter what they did. But the more people I talked to, the more I have come to believe that there's an approach and a skill set that can enable anyone to live the life of their dreams very early on in life, if not *right now!*

But before we go any further, I have to ask you to level with yourself. Just how strong are your passion and drive to succeed? Are they strong enough to carry you where you want to go? Are you willing to do everything necessary to get there? If you are, the incredibly rewarding, yet highly challenging life of the Young & Successful can be yours. While you *will* experience failure, uncertainty, and frequent challenges that will test what you are really made of, you won't ever torture yourself with thoughts of dreams and passions unrealized. Whatever may happen, I can assure you you'll never experience the regret of "what if?"

Young & Successful people have a deep-seated desire to be successful. It's as fundamental a need for them, just as having enough food or a place to live is a basic need for everyone else. The Young & Successful pursue their dreams as if they have nothing to lose. They maintain a tight focus on their future and open themselves up for subtle clues and more profound ah-ha moments that offer direction as powerful as beacons of light in the fog.

In this book we'll guide you through a two-part process designed to show you how anyone can become, or learn from, the *Secrets of the Young & Successful*. Part One (Chapters One through Four) calls for some personal introspection and will help you

1   gain a greater sense of who you are today and why

2   identify or clarify what will make you most happy and fulfilled

3   guide you in creating a solid plan of action to get you there

With your new Grand Plan in hand, Part Two (Chapters Five through Eleven) will reveal the greatest success stimulators used by the Young & Successful. These secrets will help you

1   master any world or industry you want to play in

2   show you how to sample the life and experiences that you most desire

3   teach you how to gain the real-world knowledge and expertise you need to excel in all areas

4   ensure that you can weather life's grestest challenges while strategically making your most critical decisions

5   guide you in dealing with your personal money matters and developing a strong financial foundation

6   show you how to build powerful and rewarding relationships

7   tie everything together to give you access to the most exclusive circles of power and influence, ensuring that you know what it takes to successfully execute even your grandest plans

When put to work in your life, these stimulators will help catapult you down the path to success faster than you ever imagined.

So, come along. Take a leap of faith and make the greatest investment of your life—bet on yourself. I guarantee that you will never be sorry for making your life—and probably a few others around you—better than ever.

2

What's Your Story?

RECENTLY I HAD TO CALL A BIG-TIME attorney whom I'd never met. I wanted to talk to him about a project I was working on. Our company was putting on a conference for young people looking for insight on how to climb to the top of their industry and we wanted him to speak about his work in representing some famous clients. While I had a great referral from a mutual friend, I was a bit nervous because everyone had told me the guy was a powerhouse. So, when he picked up the phone, I was all ready to lay my pitch on him, but he wasn't ready to hear it. As soon as I said "Hello," he jumped out with, "Hey, Jennifer! How are you? Tell me what you're up to. What's your story?"

For a second, I froze, uncertain exactly what to tell him. *What is my story?*

We All Have a Story to Tell

Asking someone to tell his or her story is a loaded question. Your story is made up of a lot of things—where you come from, who you are, what your aspirations are, your mission. If you can answer these questions, odds are you're pretty far ahead of the game. If you can't, you're probably missing out on some great opportunities.

Every day, for instance, incredible people slip in and out of our lives unnoticed. The trick is to identify them, meet them, then draw them into our lives, even if just for a few precious moments. How well we capitalize on these opportunities, especially the unexpected ones, has a lot to do with how well we can tell our own story. Telling our story well is what baits them to engage with us.

The Young & Successful are always ready to sell themselves and what they're working on. Let's face it, whether our career defines us as such or not, we're all in sales. In some way, or some form, we all have to sell ourselves every day.

A twentysomething guy named Tyson once told me a funny story that illustrates this point perfectly. On the way to a big meeting with a prospective client, Tyson stepped into a big corporate office building with his firm's two senior sales managers. While Tyson had done most of the research in preparing for the meeting, his responsibility here was simply to back up his bosses if they needed more background info. Frustrated with these orders, he went along, hoping he'd get a chance to do something more than just sit and nod along for an hour. So just as they all pushed through a crowd of rushed executives in the lobby, his two bosses managed to elbow their way through the closing doors of the first available elevator. Tyson didn't make it, though.

Left behind and slightly irritated, Tyson waited for the next available elevator to show up. When it did, he pressed the button for the thirty-second floor and began to adjust his collar and smooth out his hair. Well, it turns out an older guy behind Tyson was peering over his shoulder checking out the cover of the glossy presentation he had painstakingly put together. "Are you coming in for the big presentation today?" the gentleman inquired. Tyson nodded and asked him if he'd be there, but the man looked disappointed and said, "I'd really like to hear what you have to show us, but I'm afraid I have another meeting I can't get out of. What's it all about anyway?" Surprised at the interest, Tyson gave the guy a quick pitch, pulling facts and figures out of his head at an astonishing pace. The more impressed the guy looked, the further Tyson continued.

He was anxious for the chance to share the ideas he'd come up with, which his bosses were about to pass off as their own. A couple minutes and a few stops later, the door opened to the thirty-second floor and they stepped out into the reception area only to find Tyson's bosses waiting and smirking at having left their young associate behind. The man then tapped Tyson on the shoulder, told him that he enjoyed their chat, and wished him good luck in the meeting.

An hour later, the meeting ended and the three got back in the elevator to leave. The mood this time was very different. The presentation hadn't gone too smoothly and they doubted they'd get the business. But back at the office, there was a message waiting for them. A secretary explained that the people they'd just met with had already called to let them know that they'd won the account because the CEO was so impressed with Tyson's presentation. Thoroughly confused, they looked at each other in disbelief. *The CEO wasn't even at the meeting.* And besides, Tyson hadn't managed to get a word in the whole time. Then it hit them. The guy in the elevator! After everything, Tyson had landed the account with his little elevator pitch, in a totally random encounter with the number-one decision maker, the CEO. You can be sure that was the last time Tyson was ever told to stay quiet in a meeting.

To be successful, we all have to be able to sell ourselves quickly and clearly. Just think: How can other people buy into your vision and what you're all about if they don't know what you have to offer in the first place? One of the most remarkable things about the Young & Successful is that they almost always have a story to tell that defines them. When asked what they're up to, they never utter the useless response, "Uh, nothing much."

If you want to join the ranks of the Young & Successful, get your story down and have it ready. You'll need it soon, and often at some pretty unexpected times.

Don't worry if you're not quite certain what your story is right now. In this chapter, we're going to show you a process that will help you better understand and express who you are (even if you're not entirely certain who that is right now).

Go Ahead, Introduce Yourself

A few years ago I was teaching a workshop on advanced small business issues to a bunch of students from the National Foundation for Teaching Entrepreneurship (NFTE). On this particular afternoon, a bunch of wealthy and influential community leaders were coming to the school to observe the students. Throughout the day I watched the well-dressed group enter classes in progress and quietly move to the back of the rooms, hoping to catch a glimpse of what really went on behind closed doors. The problem was, in many cases, the students were so pre-occupied checking out the people who were there to check *them* out that the class discussions quickly became very quiet. Seeing this over and over, I got an idea.

I ran back to my class and asked everyone if they'd noticed the group of people moving slowly throughout the building. They all said yes, then shifted awkwardly in their seats when I informed them we were the next stop on the tour. "Listen," I said, "I have an idea. Let's take control of this situation here." They had no idea where I was heading, but they certainly liked the direction. "I know these people seem kind of intimidating and it's a little strange to have them scrutinizing everything you say and do. But they're actually here for an important reason. These people are investors, and without them, this organization wouldn't exist, you wouldn't have had an all-expenses-paid trip here, and none of us would have the opportunity to spend all this time creating businesses that may one day make you all rich and famous." The smiles came fast. I had their attention.

"So I was thinking, we owe it to NFTE to impress these investors with just how smart you all are. But at the same time, I have a feeling that you might be able to make some pretty incredible connections yourself if we're smart here. How about this—when the group comes in, instead of just continuing with the lesson plan, why don't we welcome them as a class, let them know what we've been working on all this time, and then we'll go around the room and you can all introduce yourselves. But none of this, 'Hi, my name is Kenisha,' then diving back into your seat. I really want you to be outgoing. Greet them warmly, tell them your full name, where you come from, what your company is called, and what your concept is. Then tell them what you're still missing, what you need help with, or what you'd like to learn more about while you're here . . . just in case any one of the visitors has any ideas for you. I have a feeling they'll be really interested to hear what you have to say. Then we'll ask them to go around and introduce themselves to us. While they're talking, take a mental note of anyone who might be interesting to meet and I'll give you some time to go mingle afterward. Just be bold and confident. Walk up to whomever you want to meet, smile, introduce yourself again, and shake his hand firmly while looking him squarely in the eyes. Show him you are confident. Ask him to tell you more about what he does or what he's hoping to learn during his visit here, and who knows what will happen from there."

Well, it worked. The organization leaders couldn't have been happier to see their students and the investors chatting away and enjoying themselves together. Likewise, the investors were blown away by the reception, fascinated with the students, happy to sit and talk to them one-on-one, and afterward, my students had collected more business cards and offers of help and friendship in those few minutes than ever before.

The better you can learn to articulate your story and the bolder you are in telling it to the right people, the more you'll see that opportunities are all around us. Sometimes we just have to reach out a bit and help open those doors ourselves.

Knowing our story, who we are, what we're made of, and where we're going is critical because it

- Helps define us to ourselves and others.

- Gives us a solid sense of purpose.

- Conveys to others what we're about and why they should support us.

- Prompts us to spell out our goals and dreams.

- Gives us a sense of pride in ourselves and our history.

- Reminds us of how much we've already accomplished.

- Puts into context both the good and the bad from our past.

- Let's us see where we're going.

- Provides us with incentives for moving forward and reaching higher.

- Makes us confident and capable and gives us a real sense of power and control.

Building Your Bio

In business, once you achieve a certain level of success—once you're being asked to make presentations or speeches or you're the one called on when the media needs an expert opinion—one of the first things you're asked for is a "bio." This is a summary of your story—of who you are and what you've accomplished. It's kind of like a résumé but richer and more interesting. In fact, it's kind of the first step toward transforming yourself into a high-profile player. What I like best about it is that it gives you an opportunity to round out your story. Unlike a résumé that just lists job titles, dates, and key responsibilities, a bio becomes a key piece of the image you present to the world.

Renee Warren, co-president of Noelle-Elaine Media, Inc., a public relations and media training firm, believes that we each contribute to our own bio every day through our decisions and actions. Much of what often seems like the mundane (our volunteer efforts, our internships, our odd jobs) quickly adds up to how we present ourselves to the world and helps others formulate their opinions of us. So take some time to think of your bio from the perspective of everyone around you. What story does it tell about you? Do your actions truly illustrate who you are and who you aim to be? Renee advises those seeking success to write down their goals so that they can become part of their bios even before they achieve them. After all, you never know when people will start to tell your story on their own.

I'll give you an example of my own discovery of just how powerful a bio can be. When my story first started getting picked up by the media some years ago, I was suddenly being asked questions I had never before contemplated. People wanted to know what my mission was, what had influenced my work, and who my role models were. As I answered, I got the rare opportunity to see my own story unfold in the pages of magazines and newspapers, before I'd even had the thought to put it all together myself. You know, I've got to admit, it put things in a new context for me. When told by professional journalists, my story was actually starting to sound pretty interesting. But then the word "expert" started to be used to describe me, and I panicked. Who was I to be called an expert? Sure, I had worked with a lot of people and had started a few little businesses, but how was I qualified enough to be called an expert on anything? I decided (after I finished panicking) that creating a solid bio could help me define myself before the media did it for me.

The first thing that I discovered was that a bio is much more than a piece of paper. It told who I was (according to me), where I'd come from (in terms of education, experience, and intent—again, according to me), and where I was planning on going with everything I'd done so far (also, according to me). I appreciated the sense of control that this gave me. Most important, by writing out my story, I learned that I still had a long way to go.

As I wrote about what I had done, it became painfully obvious to me that there was a lot missing—experience, maturity, range, and more. That first draft helped me foresee the tough questions other people— the media, my partners, my clients—would ask, and that meant I would never be caught off guard. From there it was easy to see that in order to build my bio, I needed to build my credentials. So I looked at dozens of other so-called experts whom I admired, and examined their credentials. The patterns emerged quickly. They had written books, built impressive client lists, researched untapped niches, appeared in prominent publications, sat on corporate and nonprofit boards, and spoken at industry events. That was what I needed, too.

By looking at where I had been, I could see where I needed to go. I could see, clearer than ever, what my next steps had to be.

BIO BUILDER™

If you think you're ready to take on the world, then it's time to write a bio for yourself. Even if you're not completely ready, it's time. No matter where you're coming from, once you can see your own story, you'll have a much more lucid picture of what you need to do to understand and benefit from your past and solidify your future.

If you haven't done this already in your career, consider tossing your résumé aside for a while and creating your own bio. Here's a good shell:

1. Start with a snapshot of who you are and what you're doing today.

2. Give a brief overview of your past. What has led you up to here? What accomplishments, special recognitions, and experiences tell your history?

3. Toward the end, provide a statement of purpose. What is your mission, your goal?

4. Mention your educational background and any special degrees you have.

5. End with where you were born and where you live now (and if you want, with whom—spouse, pets, etc.).

When it comes to your average bio length, one to three paragraphs is pretty common, but try to keep it to one page, even if you have a lot of experience to share. Limit yourself to the most impressive, most impactful info. Focus on your accomplishments (especially over the past five to seven years) and your mission, and sprinkle it with your most relevant, unique, or defining interests. If it's too long, people probably won't read it. So make sure your bio packs a punch.

> You can make your bio formal or rather casual, depending on what you're using it for. Do write in the third person, though. (For those of you who forgot everything you learned in English class, that means write about yourself as if you're talking about someone else.) Then consider having some people you trust, and hopefully who write well themselves, look it over to help you improve it. I promise this will be a great thing to have during some of your more prominent moments in life!

Okay, here's the latest version of my bio. Like my life, it is still very much a work in progress.

JENNIFER KUSHELL
President & Co-founder

YS INTERACTIVE CORP.

At 32, Jennifer Kushell has lead a movement inspiring young people to achieve more with their lives for more than a decade. **[MISSION]** As the President and Co-founder of Young & Successful Media Corp. in 2000, and as a relentless advocate for her generation, her efforts have impacted the lives and futures of millions.

Called a "guru" of her generation by *US News & World Report,* Jennifer has worked with thousands of young people and entrepreneurs through her speaking, teaching, workshops, and corporate consulting, and has appeared in front of over 200 million people throughout the world via major media such as CNN, CNBC, FOX News, BBC, NPR, PBS, *The Wall Street Journal, The Los Angeles Times, USA Today, BusinessWeek, Entrepreneur, Cosmopolitan, and Seventeen.* **[ACCOLADES]**

The Founder and President of the Young Entrepreneurs Network, at 19, Jennifer created one of the first online communities—an organization of thousands of young & successful entrepreneurs from over 75 countries. **[ACCOMPLISHMENT]** As author of the New York Times Bestseller *Secrets of the Young & Successful, The Young Entrepreneur's Edge, and Solo Para Emprendedores* she is, today, one of the most widely recognized experts on young professionals, leaders and entrepreneurs.

Jennifer's extensive work within the corporate and non-profit sectors has included projects with Visa, Bank of America, AOL, Business Week, Inc, Ernst & Young, MTV, Oxygen Media, Subway, Staples, Mobil, The Australian Government, and The National Mentoring Coalition. She has also served on the advisory boards of The National Foundation for Teaching Entrepreneurship, Southern California Entrepreneurship Academy, National Mentoring Policy Counsel and Women's Leadership Exchange. **[ACHIEVEMENT]** Jennifer holds a degree in International Management from Boston University's School of Management and today lives in Marina del Rey, California. **[EDUCATION, PERSONAL]**

Regardless of what you have to work with when you sit down to write your bio, understand that we all start from somewhere, and at the outset that's usually nowhere spectacular. Look at your bio as a personal challenge, as a story that is only just beginning. When you think about yourself as a work in progress, you can take great pride in even the simple fact that you're now thinking about your story like this in the first place.

Now get to work on transforming it into something you can be proud to share with anyone. Be sure to celebrate each new accomplishment that adds greater depth to your bio, and soon enough you will marvel at the incredible story it tells.

▶ The History of You

Finding out who we are and what we're really made of often involves some digging into our pasts. It's hard to deny that where we come from has a lot to do with who we are today. Whether we're the perfect products of our environments, or the total antitheses of what we were expected to become, looking back at what has shaped us and our ambitions can offer us valuable insights and enable us to carefully sculpt our futures.

In this chapter we want to look at who you are, not just on paper, but what you're really made of and what made you the person you are today. This is the place where we stop just telling you about the Young & Successful and start showing you how to join their ranks. And if you are already on the path to early success, I want to try to make the road a little smoother, to help you find a few more shortcuts along the way.

One of the key secrets of the Young & Successful is that they have a great sense of who they are because they've spent a good deal of time analyzing themselves and their environments. From that analysis, the Young & Successful gain a keen awareness of their strengths and weakness, and of their deepest desires. But this self-awareness doesn't come easy. For most, it takes time to figure out. For each and every one it involves asking a lot of questions. If I could sit down with you, I'd have a million questions to ask you. But because I can't do that here, I'm going to help you ask yourself some of the questions so you can begin to hear your story taking shape. This will start to reveal where you're strong and where you're vulnerable; what you *want* and what you *need.*

This Is Your Life!

If you really want to see an amazing account of where you come from and what your life looks like so far as a whole, spend a weekend afternoon relaxing with an empty notepad or journal. Tell your story. In one to two sentences, record every significant memory and event, including your most humbling experiences. Work chronologically from birth to today. If you get stuck, you can start by numbering a page vertically from one to your age now. Then use those years as benchmarks to put down where you lived, when you moved, when you traveled, made new friends, experienced your great achievements or even losses. Use different color pens like red or blue so you can clearly identify the good from the bad. (That last part will come in pretty helpful in a minute.) Focus particular attention on your transitions, like home to independence, high school to college to real world, student to executive, intern to employee, frustrated at job to liberation in new career. You get the picture. We all go through phases—especially in our earlier years—and these can often be where the really important stuff happens for us.

What we're looking for are clues that the past has left behind for you. With them in hand, you'll start to see some structure in your own story. Take some time to remember what's gotten you to this point today. Start to look at yourself and your life in a fresh new context. Seeing your whole life down on paper is incredible. It says, "This is me. This is my story."

Tie all your memories together—and consider what significant events happened in your life as a result. What we're looking for here are triggers, or events that happened long ago, that still have an impact on you today. Significant, even life changing events are usually pretty easy to recall, even if we don't choose to think about them frequently. It's an interesting exercise, though, and is certain to uncover some really insightful things about you and your story.

Before we look at who you are today and what you want to achieve in the future, we need to look at your past. Understanding this can help you figure out major career choices or changes and even entrepreneurial decisions, like which business idea is right for you. These days, a lot of employers will have you take a personality assessment test before they hire you so *they* can make the best decisions about you. Why not give yourself that same advantage?

The Grand Slams

When I asked Scott his answer took no less than five seconds to fly out of his mouth. "Sports, definitely." While he absolutely loved basketball and baseball, his most profound skill, and some of his most significant childhood events, involved tennis. His most memorable moment, he says, was beating one of the top-ranked junior players in the country who had badly beaten him time and time again for years. He tried to stop there, but I could tell there was more to this story.

When he was just a kid about seven years old, Scott's grandfather gave him a little red tennis racket. Everytime a tennis game would come on television, Scott would race around the room, pretending he was on the court right there with the athletes. In the summer he'd watch his father and mother play doubles for hours, wanting desperately to play himself. Despite his pleading, he was always told that he was too young, or not good enough to play with the adults. His salvation came at the end of their games, when one of his parents would hit balls with him for about fifteen minutes. It was then that Scott was happiest. Soon it was time to go to camp, and there Scott, for the first time, was allowed to play tennis all he wanted. Apparently, you couldn't pry him away from the courts (unless of course there were girls around . . . but that's another story). After a while, he started to become pretty good. So much so, that when he got home, he started playing with his father. When he started beating his father and eventually his coach—the people who'd once told him he couldn't play—he began to look for more challenging opponents. His hard work was starting to pay off.

The next summer, it was on to tennis camp, for an even more intense training experience. Just like when he was a little kid, Scott played his heart out and never forgot all those times that he just wasn't good enough. There was no way he was going to let inexperience get in his way. A few months later, while on vacation with his family in Mexico, Scott met a woman who invited him to train at a special tennis facility in Kentucky. As an athlete, he was getting better and better. That led to an invitation to visit Belgium and France, to play against top European players.

Scott's greatest tennis moment came when after all those years of playing, training, and competing, he returned home to play. As his father had long since become a big fan of his, the only one left to confront was another kid in the state who was nationally ranked and had never been beaten in high school. This was Scott's nemesis—he had played him for years and lost every single time. (And if he didn't lose to him, Scott says he'd lose to the guy's older sister who was also nationally ranked.) In one of his final high school matches, in front of his principal, coaches, parents, and a crowd of his fellow students, Scott finally got his chance to play him again . . . but this time, he came from behind and won. In his mind, he had conquered one of his biggest childhood challenges. Ultimately, these experiences helped to define him as a person.

Tennis was a game in which Scott had to prove himself, but he was lucky, because once he discovered he had a skill for the game, it was easy to measure his achievements because the benchmarks were always right in front of him. What he loved about the game was what he eventually looked for in his choice of business ventures, ambitions, events, and many other endeavors throughout his life—situations where the game is a challenge but the playing field and the score are easy to define.

To say that Scott is a competitor is an understatement. To this day, he rarely shies away from a challenge, and once told he cannot do something (especially if he really wants to), he will not stop trying until he can rise to the challenge, and exceed expectations.

Think about some of the top experiences that you remember above all else. Try to identify the sources, or root causes of your ambition, enthusiasm, and motivation.

Think about what makes you uncomfortable, too. Often those issues get buried inside of us so fast and so deep that we never confront them and learn to put them in their rightful place. Avoiding even the very topic itself can lead to serious repression and more long-term, far-reaching effects than you can imagine. However, if we can dig up some of these old wounds and confront them once and for all, often we can find many ways to turn them into not only great learning experiences, but even better, amazing internal strength.

Recently, Scott had the opportunity to sit down with Sumner Redstone, chairman of Viacom, the parent company of MTV, VH1, Blockbuster, CBS, Paramount Studios, and many others. While today he's one of the most powerful business moguls, most people don't realize that Redstone also had his fair share of challenges and humbling experiences.

Over sixty years later, for instance, he still cringes at the memory of misspelling "tuberculosis" in a sixth grade competition, en route to becoming the National Spelling Bee champion. The memory of that day still haunts him and pushes him to pay attention to the most minute details, even as he runs a multibillion-dollar empire.

On one particularly painful occasion, Redstone was caught in a hotel fire that nearly cost him his life. With flames blazing through his room, he was forced to crawl out the window and hang by his hands off the balcony for what seemed like an eternity until help arrived. He suffered horrible burns and was told that he might never walk again. Thankfully, he made a near-full recovery after months of grueling rehabilitation. This experience helped him realize that he could persevere through anything.

◢ Making the Best of the Past

Ask yourself some questions about what you were like growing up and what memories continue to impact you to this day:

What significant events had the most profound effect on you?
What were your favorite activities?
What abilities and skills were you most proud of?
What activities did you dislike more than anything?
What abilities and skills were you most lacking?
What experiences were so humbling that you never quite got over them?

What kind of patterns do you see? Were you better in a group or on your own? Did you gravitate toward opportunities to work independently? Were you uncomfortable with ambiguity, when expectations of you were unclear? Look for the connections.

Look at your answers closely, and you'll discover interesting clues about how you became the person you are today. Compare these things that shaped who you were growing up to who you are now. Look for similarities and patterns.

A few years ago I also wanted concrete information to help me explain some challenges I'd grappled with for many years. Here's an example from my life.

The Search for Answers

Okay, I asked you to do it, so it's only fair that I confess some of my weaknesses to you. Growing up I was terrible at numbers, cleaning, confrontations, tests, and competitions. My focus was terrible, and I had a difficult time concentrating on things that didn't interest me. The funny thing was, I did really well at the things that did interest me (writing, speaking, and coming up with something new and different to do every day). So right after I graduated from college, I realized that there might be something more serious going on. So I subjected myself to an eight-hour battery of tests at the Center for Neuropsychology and Learning Disabilities in Rhode Island. And it ended up being a day that changed my life.

First, the doctor who tested me explained that I had a severe case of Attention Deficit and Hyperactivity Disorder (ADHD), which explained why I had always struggled in school. Second, great news—my IQ was actually pretty high. But the best news came when Dr. Elizabeth Leimkuhler complimented me on what she referred to as an extraordinary ability to "compensate beautifully" for my deficiencies. According to her, people with ADHD usually either have a lifelong struggle because of this condition or become overachievers in the areas they *are* comfortable with. And that "comfort zone" often has to do with creative, less regimented or structured environments, and often more entrepreneurial careers. Now it all made sense. On that day I learned to define myself and finally better understand who I was.

Now, not everyone can expect a battery of tests or time spent digging into your personal history to produce such an epiphany, but it does go to show you that what lies beneath can often uncover, oddly enough, your true strengths.

Some of the most powerful men and women in America have endured far more than you or I ever will. One of them dropped out of school at sixteen. One didn't learn to read until he discovered comic books in the third grade (the pictures helped him figure out the words). Another nearly flunked out of college. These men who were once called "losers" are all dyslexic. This group includes Richard Branson, founder of Virgin Records and Airlines: Craig McCaw, the first cell-phone billionaire; Charles Schwab, founder and co-CEO of Charles Schwab brokerage; and Paul Orfalea, founder of Kinko's.

Orfalea actually failed second grade and spent part of third grade in a class for mentally challenged children. He found it almost impossible to learn to read, despite the best efforts of his parents, testers, tutors, therapists, special reading groups, and even eye doctors. In fact, his parents were, at one point, advised to enroll him in a trade school to learn to lay carpet so that he could at least earn a living.

What struggles or weaknesses can you, or have you, ultimately turned into strengths or benefits? While I derived incredible personal insight from my experience in seeking help, you certainly don't need doctors (unless of course you suspect that there's a larger problem that you can't deal with on your own). In most cases, you don't even have to spend any money to make these discoveries. Talk to friends and family members about what tendencies or patterns they've recognized in you over the years. Did you have a favorite teacher or teachers, ones who really made a difference for you? Have you ever had a tutor or someone you'd consider a mentor? Talk to them about what they did or didn't see in you. Try to uncover your own challenges and flip them on their heads—try to turn them to your advantage and make them start to work for you. We all have the chance to make our past—regardless of what it is—work in our favor.

Your Personal Balance Sheet™

Now that you've identified the influential elements from your own history, let's move into your present story to uncover more about who you are and what makes you happiest today. Consider this the first day of your new life. And while you're at it, roll up your sleeves because we're really going to work on you now.

First, we're going to talk about taking all of these skills and abilities, as well as the weaknesses and disadvantages that you've uncovered, and put them to good use. Second, we'll look at how to make sure you stay happy along the way to getting all the things you dream of. To do this, we've developed some tools for you.

One of the major secrets of the Young & Successful is that they have a keen awareness of both their strengths and weaknesses or, as we'll refer to them here, their "assets" and "liabilities." If you've ever studied accounting or finance, you'll know that in business, the process of assessing and balancing your assets and liabilities is done through a common financial statement called a balance sheet. If you try to get a loan or investigate a company you want to invest in, this will be one of the first documents you'll need.

A balance sheet in business essentially provides a snapshot, on any given day, of a company's overall financial health. If there is too much debt (liabilities) and not enough cash (assets), for example, that could be a sign of big trouble. The goal is to keep the assets and liabilities in a healthy balance.

This exercise will tell you volumes about yourself. And I don't know of a more powerful assessment tool than this to figure out exactly where you are today and what you have to work on to get better and smarter, and achieve even greater success.

How Do You Balance Out?

Take a piece of paper and draw a vertical line down the middle of the sheet creating two columns. On the top of the left column write "assets," and on the top of the right column write "liabilities." Now you have the basic format of a balance sheet. From there, create a list of your assets and liabilities in descending order. Try to start with the most prominent or strongest examples at the top, and work your way down to the less significant ones.

Many people at first will undervalue their assets and overexaggerate their liabilities. Just be fair and honest with yourself. Here's an example with a lot of typical issues that we hear.

ASSETS	LIABILITIES
natural sales ability	talk too much
great communicator	work too much
very perceptive	always late
wonderful family	struggle with record keeping
driven by challenges	don't enjoy reading
great skier	grammar needs polishing
independent/self-reliant	have a bad back
handle risk well	can be overly aggressive
outgoing personality	get bored easily
relatively good-looking	short temper
great friend	don't get enough exercise
nice person	$10K in credit card debt
decent cook	not good about saving

Note: Unlike a balance sheet in business, the information here is pretty subjective. What you may call a liability, someone else might see as an actual benefit. For example, if you get bored easily and are concerned about your attention span—someone else might point out that your so-called disadvantage leads you to get a lot more done during the day since you require constant stimulation. It's up to you to decide how you define what. It's also important for you to understand what you're dealing with.

Need some help? Here are a few areas to consider:

BORN WITH · Think of assets and liabilities that you were "gifted" with at birth. What came into your life from your parents, your genes, or was "God given"? (For example, basic senses, appearance, athletic ability, health, disabilities, etc.)

BORN INTO · What factors did you inherit from your family or surrounding environment? What do you have as a sheer result of who you are and how you were raised? (For example, wealth, health of family members, where you live, culture, religion, etc.)

ACQUIRED OR DEVELOPED · What personal assets and liabilities did you pick up during your development and growth? What can you take most of the credit for acquiring or developing on your own? (For example, confidence, social skills, knowledge, responsibility, style, values, etc.)

While this is your personal list, we do want to get all the facts down on paper. Omitting anything important will only make your information less valuable to work with. So consider showing this list to someone who knows you well, and whose opinion and constructive criticism you value most. See if they have anything to add, subtract, or even move into a different position on the list—or to a different column altogether. Now we have all the information we need to check out our personal balance.

Assessing Your Statement

To best capitalize on, or at least utilize the information we uncover, we want to minimize our liabilities and increase our assets so that we can best leverage them.

But not so fast. When we talk about assets, it's easy to just pat ourselves on the back and take them for granted. However, there's more to consider here. Is it possible that we're underutilizing those assets? Often we're just as quick to dismiss our liabilities too. Not just because we don't want to deal with them, but because we actually fail to realize how they might actually work to our advantage.

Consider the following:

Assets

Check out your assets and ask yourself the following questions:

- Am I using these assets to my greatest advantage?
- Could I be relying on one thing or another too much?
- Am I misjudging anything as an asset, when it's really a liability to me?
- Is there anything that could turn into a liability if I'm not careful?
- Have I prioritized them correctly?
- What can I do to make weaker assets stronger?
- Am I steadily and conscientiously increasing my assets or just relying on what I have?

Liabilities

Now consider the following about your liabilities:

- Could I be misjudging anything as a liability when it's really an asset?
- Do any actually allow me to do things that I couldn't otherwise?
- Have any of these liabilities turned into major motivators for me?

- What am I doing to compensate for my liabilities?

- Am I using any as an excuse?

- Have I prioritized them correctly?

- Am I steadily reducing my liabilities or the overall effect they have on my life?

Now go back and make any adjustments you need to. The list above should have given you probing questions to consider, and those will help you better assess your overall situation. You're also sure to find several things on your list that can be easily dealt with—issues that can be overcome simply by being aware of them and making minor changes in your behavior. Most important, keep this as a reference for yourself and update your Personal Balance Sheet periodically so you can track your progress and maximize your personal returns.

Don't mistake this balance sheet for your destiny, though. It should be thought of as only a "snapshot" of this moment. Like you saw with your bio, you are continuously evolving. This is a very simple and easy way to check your balance at any given point. Nothing is set in stone or is permanent. That's why creating one of these assessments offers an incredible opportunity to make some really significant enhancements to your life.

The Incredible Power of Compounding

Albert Einstein was once asked, "What is the miracle of the universe?" His response surprised many when he stated "compound interest." Einstein called compounding "mankind's greatest invention—the eighth wonder of the world—because it allows for the reliable, systematic accumulation of wealth."

The power of compounding allows the Young & Successful to

take advantage of starting earlier than others, resulting in their ability to achieve greater success faster in all areas of life. To illustrate the power of compounding, let's take a look at the effect it can have on your financial life. Say on your twenty-fifth birthday you started investing $100 per month into an investment vehicle that earns you, for example, 9 percent interest per year. You continue to do so each month for ten years until your thirty-fifth birthday, when you decide to stop investing any further. However, having already invested $12,000 so far, you keep the accruing compounded interest in your account for thirty more years. At that time, as a result of the power of compounding, by your sixty-fifth birthday, you will have accumulated a little more than . . . $285,000!

Now let's say you decided to kick into gear a little later in life. You invest the same way, with the same 9 percent annual interest rate, however, you start when you turn thirty-five years old *instead of* twenty-five years old. Even if you kept investing that same $100 each month for the next thirty years, putting in more than $37,000, by your sixty-fifth birthday you would have accumulated only around $196,000 vs. more than $285,000 that you would have if you started just ten years earlier at twenty-five.

**Power of Compounding: Start investing $100/month
at 25 years old and stop at 35 years old**

Your Age	Your Starting Balance	Cumultive Total Invested to Date	Plus (+) Interest at 9% per year
25		$1,200	$1,308
35	$19,872	$12,000	$21,661
45	$47,045	$12,000	$51,279
55	$111,373	$12,000	$121,396
65	$263,660	$12,000	
		$12,000 Total Invested	**$287,389**

Power of Compounding: Start investing $100/month
at 35 years old and stop at 65 years old

Your Age	Your Starting Balance	Cumultive Total Invested to Date	Plus (+) Interest at 9% per year
35		$1,200	$1,308
45	$19,872	$12,000	$22,969
55	$66,917	$24,000	$74,248
65	$178,290	$37,200	
		$37,200 Total Invested	**$195,644**

How can there be such a big difference? Well, because the first person started early and put time on his side, the power of compounding kicked into full effect much sooner for him. *By starting just ten years later, you would have to invest more than three times as much for thirty more years and you still wouldn't catch up to the growth, momentum, and return that starting earlier brings.*

Talk about turning your age into an advantage! The younger you are, the better you can take advantage of the power of compounding. Just imagine how much more you could benefit from starting earlier when it comes to learning about an industry, building relationships, exercising, excelling at your favorite sport, etc.

So why not consider employing Einstein's insight by getting started as early as *you* can? Take the concept of compounding and imagine how it can affect your career, your life, and your story as you learn more, achieve greater things, and gain more insight every year. So keep building, adding mentors, information, and skills. And most important, never forget the power of continually reinvesting in yourself over time.

BUILDING EXPONENTIAL GROWTH

Brad Kesler never realized how powerful compounding could really be until he saw it work for himself. Once his achievements started to build upon one another, his experience, expertise, and success grew exponentially . . . and so did his rewards. First, though, he had to take a serious look at his own story and make some drastic changes in his life.

Growing up in the streets of Baltimore, Maryland, Brad says he was what most people would call a hoodlum. His parents raised him in a hard-working middle-class neighborhood that had two very different worlds on either side, just two blocks away. To the north was an upscale neighborhood of fancy homes and wealthy people. But to the south was the 'hood, the inner city. And that's where Brad chose to spend most of his time. It wasn't uncommon for his friends to get arrested two or three times a year, and by the time they were teens, a number of them had carved out a niche for themselves in the drug trade.

Then one day everything changed. Brad's best friend, Joe, was shot and killed in the middle of a deal. In that instant, Brad pulled away from the "street," decided to stay out of the marginal parts of his neighborhood, and cleaned up his act. Fortunately, he had a safer, more secure life to fall back on, thanks to his parents and the good school they had worked so hard to keep him in. But that doesn't mean it was easy. The school principal knew that Brad had been hanging out with a tough crowd, and he made it clear that if he saw Brad cross the line he'd show him the door.

Brad never crossed that line. In fact, he soon graduated from high school and never looked back. He continued on to college, focused on school, became almost obsessive about nutrition and weight training, and four years later, graduated with honors from the University of Maryland. While he was there, Brad reflected on something he'd discovered as a kid when he was mowing lawns: How was it that some people could buy not one but several homes, rent them out, and have their mortgages and maintenances paid for by other people? Brad learned exactly how that worked by taking some real estate finance classes at school and through his own intensive study of the business. He bought every infomercial program he could find, took advantage of every educational resource he could get his hands on, and built up his own personal library on the subject.

By twenty-three he bought his first house, lived in it for a year, fixed it up himself, and sold it for a $30,000 profit. He then bought a second house and did the same with that. His next investment: four town houses as rental properties. Over the next ten years, Brad expects to buy and sell more than thirty properties and earn more than $700,000 with $125,000 annual residual income. In the meantime, though, he's keeping his job as a supervisor for one of the leading railroad companies, and slowly but surely, he's building the life he always dreamed of having.

So how did Brad reap the benefits of compounding? Let's look at that for a minute in terms of his critical steps:

1. Very early, while mowing lawns, Brad recognized there might be an opportunity for him in real estate one day.

2. Despite the negative influences and tragic situations he encountered, Brad managed to stay in school and surround himself with a more positive set of influences.

3. While in school, he began working construction jobs to stay out of trouble, make some money, and learn some valuable skills.

4. After graduating from high school—an idea that once was low on his priority list—Brad was able to get into a great college and substantially increase his understanding of business and finance.

5. His new experiences led him to explore a long-time curiosity about how the real-estate market worked. And thus Brad's library and self-guided training were started.

6. The basics of business and intellectual polishing enabled him to conduct more comprehensive research on the real-estate business and better assess the exact role that he wanted to play in it.

7. By continuing to work, Brad built up his cash reserves and soon was able to land a well-paying job that would enable him to earn the kind of money that would allow him to make a down payment of his first property within the first year.

8. When he purchased his first house, he acquired his first asset, initial practical experience, learned how

much he could do to improve the value on his own, and built his growth plan.

9. Soon, Brad was able to sell the first house at a sizable profit, which, in turn, gave him the money to buy another property of greater value, build up more equity, and do it all again, this time more easily and with a more lucrative return . . . which, of course, he immediately reinvested again.

I could go on and on here, but I think my point is clear. Every experience of Brad's built a more solid foundation from which he could improve upon, and grow. And if you follow his progression, it's clear to see how his hard work continued to pay off exponentially as time went on.

This concept of compounding is a beautiful thing. And here's the bottom line: Everyone has his own fair share of strengths and weaknesses. Awareness is the key. Understand and put to good use your own unique gifts and commit yourself to constantly reinvesting and continuously building upon your experiences. With the power of compounding working for you, your life will continue to get better and better.

How Happy Are You Right Now?

Now that we've got a good picture of our assets and liabilities, how balanced they all are, and how the power of compounding can maximize our opportunities and experiences, let's move on to the last part of this chapter and to what may ultimately matter most—how happy you are.

There are many benefits to being happy and ensuring that all areas of your life are in balance, the way you want them to be. For instance, when you're happy you:

- Perform better.

- Think clearer and more rationally.

- Handle stress better.

- Clear hurdles that would stop many dead in their tracks.

- Foster greater creativity.

- Engage in the things that you are passionate about.

- Attract other positive, happy people in your life.

- Stay in shape and enjoy increased energy levels and a fortified immune system.

There's no question that the Young & Successful work hard, dream big, and are constantly strategizing and planning. They also often have to make serious sacrifices to get where they want to go early in life. But they, like us, must always keep a few questions in mind:

- Are we putting our efforts in the right places?

- Are we working toward something that really makes us happy?

- Do we have sufficient motivation to do all this hard work?

- Are we enjoying the process, or the fruits of our labor along the way?

- Are we proud of ourselves, confident in our abilities, and looking forward to what the future may bring?

After all, if we're not happy, what's the point? And how can we ever really call ourselves successful without that basic level of satisfaction from what we do? It may sound so simplistic, but what's absurd is the paltry number of people who really give this the weight it is due.

Getting a clear understanding of your own story is a critical step, though all this information isn't going to do us much good without having a clear idea of where we truly want to go, and why, to guide us along the way. So that's our next order of business.

Get ready for something exciting.

It's time for a little departure from reality. Let's take a trip into your future. Now we're going to enhance your goals, your dreams, and your passions, and illustrate them in a unique vision that's all your own. Get ready to experience Your Ideal Life.

3 Welcome to Your Ideal Life™

HAVE YOU EVER BEEN TO A SPA?

It's truly a magical experience. Enter a good one and you're instantly transported to a place far away from your everyday stresses. Inside, the surroundings are soothing and tranquil. There is beautiful music, and the smell of fresh fruits and flowers fill the air.

Imagine slipping into the Jacuzzi and letting its powerful jets of hot water sweep away your tension. Breathe deeply and the eucalyptus-scented steam will fill your lungs. Calm and peace wash over you. Are you visualizing this? Experiencing the utter perfection of it all?

When you feel this peaceful and serene, don't you—just for a moment—think that *anything* is possible?

Now why can't every day be like this? Why can't we be that calm and self-assured all the time?

This magical feeling *can* exist for us in our own lives. All we have to do is create it. And any of us determined enough, can learn how. The secret that the Young & Successful know is that if you want to make something incredible happen, *first you have to dream it in vivid, colorful detail.* What do I mean? Just as you were able to transport yourself, ever so briefly, to a perfect spa oasis, consider beaming yourself to another destination—your future. Your Ideal Life is the place where everything that you've always dreamed of having and doing is real and yours. It is not a picture of a perfect day, it's a *vision of a perfect life.* And right now, you're about to take the first step toward making your dream of a perfect life come true.

On top of imagining a life where everything seems just right, I also want you to dream on a scale larger than you ever have before. Don't imagine yourself just getting a nice raise or moving into your boss's office. Seriously indulge yourself here—have some wild and wonderful dreams about where you're headed. That's what figuring out your Ideal Life is all about—throwing your day-to-day reality out the window for a bit and getting lost in the fantasy of just how far you can go. I know it may seem difficult or even ridiculous to be thinking this way when the actualities of everyday life are beating down on you, but try it with me. I promise you'll like it.

⚡ Why Dream So Big Right Now?

Your personal journey may be at its most critical juncture right now. You're probably making, or are about to make, some of the most important decisions of your life: how to steer your career, where and what to call home, whether to get married, start a family. All these life-changing choices and more start landing on our plate during our twenties and thirties, whether we're ready for them or not.

This is also the time when we set the stage for what we're going to accomplish. Of course, we can take a passive route—sit back, hope our lives just come together, and delude ourselves into thinking that everything will somehow work out for us. Or we can take charge and do everything within our power to ensure that our lives turn out the way we want them to. As you've probably guessed, the Young & Successful choose the latter. You should, too. Success is all about the choices we make. And choosing which dreams to pursue is one decision you're better off making now while so much is open to you and up for grabs.

You probably think you already have big dreams, but no matter how big they are, I want to show you how you can go further with them and why you should. It's one thing to want to own a business, become the vice president of a company, or start a charitable trust. But those goals, as specific as they are, are still far too vague and limited in scope to lay the foundation for you to create a practical, workable plan for your life. Simply stated, unless you start by creating a very detailed, complete, comprehensive vision of your Ideal Life, your ability to actually make it happen will be seriously hindered.

But maybe you're thinking, "I already know what I want for now," or maybe you've already considered the bigger picture of where you're going with your life and your career. Maybe so, but here are a few questions that may challenge you, regardless:

- Have you considered what the pinnacle of your career will be?

- What's the highest position you will ever seek to hold?

- What is the most impressive, impactful thing you want to accomplish?

- What would you like to be known for?

- What will your days and nights be like?

- Where will you live? and play?

- What symbols of success do you hope to possess? (Think about the substantive and the more materialistic stuff, too.)

Until you can see this vision of your Ideal Life in your mind's eye as clearly as today's lunch, you really haven't given your dreams the chance they deserve.

Your future starts right here, right now. Let your imagination get the best of you, and I'll show you how to translate your dreams into a practical, real-world plan of action that will lead you to everything you've always wanted in record time.

⚡ The Big Question

After having worked with thousands of people over the past decade, one thing has never ceased to amaze me. No matter how ambitious, how passionate, and how motivated to accomplish great things people might be, most have never contemplated what their Ideal Life looks like. You ask them what their endgame is, or what they're ultimately striving for, and their faces go blank.

It's a logical enough question to ask, don't you think? But most of us are so focused on getting that next big promotion or customer, finding a generous investor, or being able to afford a bigger place that we fail to think enough about the really big picture. Often we're not asking ourselves the most important question: Why am I really doing what I'm doing today?

When you ask the average person what his Ideal Life looks like, the initial response is usually the same. He starts by looking at you funny. A smile creeps in and he sheepishly admits, "I'm not quite sure." Then a quizzical expression washes over his face and he sinks into a deep state of contemplation. Silently, he thinks for a minute or so, searching for the answer. In a flash, his eyes get brighter and a smile comes to his face. "Aha! I know! If I could do anything I'd . . ." That's the kind of spark we're looking for here. That's where the vision starts to take shape. All you need to get started are the right questions:

· What would you have if you could have anything?

· What would you be doing if you could do anything?

· What does a perfect day look like to you?

· What kind of work would give you the most pleasure?

· What type of opportunities excite you?

· What could you potentially do better than anyone?

· Who or what do you love and adore so much, you'd want with you always?

· What really matters to you?

· What could you not bear to live without?

The answers to these questions are the foundation of your Ideal Life vision. If you haven't contemplated them yet, this might just be the perfect opportunity. Take some time *right now* to start giving these the thought they deserve, and I promise that having this image of your Ideal Life clearly set in your mind will only make achieving it all the more possible. (We'll get really specific about just how you do this in the next chapter.)

Common Logic?

As we grow older, we tend to put our dreams and idealistic visions away and settle for things that logic tells us "make sense." With maturity comes the ability to navigate through life more responsibly but often, at the expense of our need for personal adventure and conquest. Ultimately, you're not only battling everything the outside throws at you but also your own internal clocks and cautions. Most people throw themselves into their work, thinking that years of toiling away will pay off *at some point* and that someday they'll be able to do the things they truly love to do.

The Young & Successful don't subscribe to that logic. Staking a claim on their Ideal Lives *now* is a big part of what moves the Young & Successful to act so early and so aggressively.

Your Ideal Life vision is a powerful, motivating force that can pump you with so much adrenaline that you feel unstoppable. But the kind of passion that this vision produces can't be generated forever. Sure, we can dream until the day we die, but firing up the tenacious energy and drive that we need to achieve our loftiest goals and dreams is a clear benefit and gift of youth. When we're young, we're ready to get into the game. We want to explore the unknown and we're fascinated by the possibilities.

It's kind of like a bottle of soda, when it's new and you have to pry open that cap to take your first taste. With that first swig, all those frantic little bubbles and that crisp effervescence tingle your insides as the sweet liquid washes through your mouth and rushes down your throat. The sensation takes over your body, a jolt surges through you, and for that instant, you feel alive. You shake your head—because that first taste always seems to take you by surprise—and unconsciously, you smile. This is how we experience the world when we are young. Every new experience, every new taste, is explosive.

Put the cap back on it, tell yourself you'll come back to it later, and what do you find when you return? The fizz is a little weaker. The excitement dies with it. Leave the bottle alone for a while, subject it to the elements, and it starts to get flat. I see this happen to people all the time. When they're fresh and unexposed, they bounce off the walls and feel like they can take on the world. But many bottle up what gets them most excited. For one reason or another, that jolt scares them. When the rush hits them, they can't put the cap back on the bottle fast enough.

Some of them, after they hear about the power of the rush, never open the bottle up in the first place. Soon their motivation and ability to dream big fizzes out, too. Well, I don't care if you slapped the cap back on too early or never opened the bottle at all, I'm going to open a new bottle and arm you with all you need to keep your excitement and passion bubbling over for good.

WHEN YOUR IDEAL LIFE MEETS YOUR REAL LIFE

Remember when you were little and you used to dress up as your favorite superhero? Or maybe you snuck into your parents' room and put on all their clothes or jewelry. Did you ever deck out your younger siblings in makeup or venture to accessorize for your pets? Were you ever so impressed with your creations that you wanted to share them with the world? Wendy Diamond did. In fact, she's still doing it.

Today, though, when Wendy dresses up her pets, thousands upon thousands tune in to TV shows and flip through magazine pages to hear all about it. Think I'm joking? Meet the founder of *Animal Fair,* the magazine for animal lovers (or as it's affectionately referred to, the "magazine for pets and their celebrities"). Yes, Wendy dresses up animals and people for a living. She also photographs them, writes about them, and publishes their pictures and stories in a quarterly magazine. Then she ships it out to newstands nationwide and to more than 200,000 loyal readers who adore their furry friends as much as Wendy does.

Wendy Diamond has always lived her life as dictated by her dreams. She doesn't waste her time with anything that doesn't excite her. A jolt goes through her body, her mind races with a fresh new idea, and she's off and running. It's always been like this, too.

One day when she was about eighteen, Wendy was home watching television when a commercial asking for support for the homeless came on. She was so moved that she called up and volunteered. From then on every week, Wendy went down to a local shelter and helped feed more than one thousand people.

A few months later she was hanging out with a friend who happened to be putting together his own cookbook, just for fun. That's when her next big idea hit. What if she published a cookbook and donated the proceeds to homeless organizations? Ask me if she knew anything about publishing. Or cooking? Nope, but she did have a friend in the music industry and that revelation made her vision complete: She'd create a cookbook with recipes from rock stars. Okay, we've all heard a million and one random ideas like this, but Wendy locked her sights on her vision and set out to make it happen. After a few months, the project began to take shape and this crazy idea turned into something of real substance.

And that was the dream that led to *A Musical Feast*, which Wendy self-published and turned into a 100,000-copy best-seller. In it were recipes from music legends like Mick Jagger and Paul McCartney. You could even get the secret recipe for Madonna's favorite cherry tart.

You probably think Wendy had loads of connections, right? Well, Wendy started from scratch. She called everyone she knew to find out who they knew, and along the way, she talked her way to assistants, limo drivers, stylists, managers, agents, and even the mothers of many of the biggest names in music. Anything to get the project done. And it worked. She followed her first best-seller with *All Star Feast*—a sequel with recipes from professional athletes. Overall, she raised more than $500,000 for charities.

When you meet Wendy, the first thing that strikes you are her wild blue eyes and her electric personality. You're instantly drawn to her and can instantly become enthralled by her latest and greatest dream. That magic of hers has worked on quite a few people, too. *Animal Fair* has become so popular with local television producers that she's now working on a new TV sitcom. I'm sure you could come up with a hundred reasons why this shouldn't work either, but remember who we're talking about here. This is someone who has a "just dream, then do" philosophy guiding her.

So is it possible that Wendy's seeming disregard for the challenges she might face enabled her to successfully pursue her ideal vision? I think it's very likely. In fact, it just might be the challenge that drives her. She hasn't let her fizz run out. She's kept that same childlike imagination alive and continues to use it to create wonderful opportunities for herself and for so many others.

Dream Wildly and Childishly

Wendy, like so many of the Young & Successful, knows that there are times when being a grown-up—being *responsible* and *logical* and *analyzing everything*—is the last thing in the world you need to do. This may sound odd because we spend so much of our lives in such a rush to grow up. We constantly ask ourselves how we can become successful if we don't throw ourselves into the pursuit early. In many ways, becoming Young & Successful involves getting younger, shedding the pessimism we start to adopt with age, and thinking and dreaming just like a kid again.

A friend of mine has an adorable five-year-old who crystallized this very concept for me not too long ago. Dashiell is her name and adventure is her game. Recently, she approached her father with her latest and greatest plan. "Daddy, here's the menu for my new restaurant." (Remember she's *five*!) Bob looked down at her and, like any good father, bought into the dream. "You're going to start a restaurant? That's a great idea!" Then he encouraged her to take it a step further. "Have you developed all the recipes yet? Because you know that any good restaurant has to have very special recipes behind its menu." She contemplated this idea for a minute then confidently nodded. "Uh-huh. I'll be right back." In a flash, she was off to the kitchen with her notepad.

Think about it for a minute and realize that this was simply the most logical next step for her. There was nothing to hold her back. She certainly wasn't going to overanalyze what she was doing.

Funny thing is, Dashiell is probably a lot more likely to execute her plan than most of us would be. Why? Because like most little kids with wild imaginations, she just dreams it up and does it. Now, we all know she's not likely to open a café anytime soon, but don't be surprised if she shows up on the sidewalk with cookies to sell. Don't laugh either, because not only is that a very real possibility but it's also exactly where many successful people start. These childhood adventures and whimsical plans are often converted into the confidence we need to take action throughout our lives, eventually leading into more and more substantive achievements.

Switch gears for a minute and consider much older, much more sophisticated students in business school. They too dream up wild ideas and attempt to put them into action. However, they may be far less likely to actually execute their plans (in some form) than, say, a five-year-old. Sounds outrageous, but it's true.

After he's spent years of training in strategic analysis, data collection, and feasibility studies, there's a lot of prep work that will happen before an MBA, for example, will launch into a new venture. And rightfully so. But as the distance between dreaming and doing grows, the average MBA is more likely to talk himself out of an idea than execute it. It's such a common phenomenon that it even has a name—"analysis paralysis." It's the notion that the more information you gather about something, the more likely you are to be completely paralyzed by the analysis process.

As driven and strategic as the Young & Successful may be, they do know there is such a thing as overdoing it. When it comes to making things happen in the real world, one of the most tragic things that can occur is when the passion that sparks the idea gets drowned out by the relentless consideration of all the things that can go wrong. It's actually quite common for intelligent people to think themselves out of the belief that something actually is possible. And oftentimes, they're right. But then again, most successful inventors, entrepreneurs, and leaders were told that their ideas were impossible, too. And they never would have found success without the courage to act.

Watching Dashiell is a lot like watching Wendy. Despite the twenty-year or so age difference, they are both big dreamers. And most important, their actions follow their dreams. There's not a lot of noise in between. If they have a dream, they'll find a way to make it happen, plain and simple. Whether it's opening a mud pie stand or packaging mud mask spa treatments for dogs, catch a glimpse of either of them when a new idea hits and you, too, can be swept away in the excitement of their imagination.

If you want to join the Young & Successful, dreaming isn't enough. You have to dream *big*. Then, throw logic and reality out the window for a bit. Dreaming and fantasizing is where the Young & Successful get their start. This is where they get their first glimpse of what they can become. (Don't worry, we'll bring reality back into the mix soon enough but not just yet.)

Putting the Dream Together

I was crazy about jigsaw puzzles when I was a kid. I loved the process of dumping all the pieces on the table and beginning to put one, two, ten pieces together until the picture emerged. And if I got stuck, I always knew that I could look at the picture on the box at any time to give me a little guidance. Just a quick look and I immediately had a much better idea of where all this colorful chaos scattered across the table needed to go.

I guess it's not surprising that this fascination has spilled over into my work life. I'm constantly dealing with many different people, projects, organizations, and resources and trying to piece them all together in symbiotic ways. In fact, I've turned into quite a matchmaker over the years, constantly making introductions for people. Anyone who knows me will tell you that when I see new and interesting opportunities, my mind takes off, trying to fit the pieces of any conceptual puzzle together. That's probably why I fell in love with the idea of working with entrepreneurs a few years back. Every person had a different picture, or Ideal Life vision she was working toward, and everyone had a very unique set of pieces, or variables, that she was working with. My challenge then was to help them take all the elements—their personality, resources, goals, opportunities, skills, hang-ups, assets, etc.—and find a better way to utilize them to make their businesses successful.

Think of your Ideal Life as the picture on the cover of the puzzle box. If you open up the box and let the pieces fall onto a table in front of you, where do you begin? You look at the picture on the cover, right? You try to get a sense of what you're trying to achieve, so that the pieces can be put together with some context (or logical order) in mind. Otherwise, you're left randomly trying to make connections, almost as if you were blindfolded.

What if the contents of that box did represent your Ideal Life and all the pieces that would make it complete? Do you really want to waste your time trying to figure out something as important as your future without that picture to guide you? The Young & Successful have learned that having this Ideal Life vision clearly embedded in their mind is the best way to successfully work toward achieving their dreams. Crystallize this Ideal Life picture of your own now, and you'll be far more likely to achieve it. Arm yourself with the *Secrets of the Young & Successful*, and you'll do it a lot sooner, too.

The Three Ideal Life Components

To project out to a point in the future where everything you've always wanted is yours, we need to think about what your life will look like in vivid detail. Now let's add depth to it so that even if your vision is still a little hazy, here's some help to sharpen the view.

There are three major categories to consider if we're going to create an Ideal Life picture that is truly balanced and representative of all the major areas of our lives. They are:

PROFESSIONAL · Since most of our time, once we get out into the real world, is spent at work, this is our first major category to consider. In your Ideal Life, what do you do for a living? What is your profession, your trade, or your career you'll retire from? Where do you go every day? What do you do? What kind of people do you work with? How do you make money and support yourself and your family? What will you have accomplished professionally? What is the most fulfilling thing about this kind of work or focus?

PERSONAL · As we achieve greater levels of success in our professional lives, this is where many of the Young & Successful strive to concentrate more and more of their time—on their personal lives. How do you define yourself outside of your career? Think about your home life.

Where do you live? Who is your family? Describe your friends, pets, neighbors. How do you feel, what do you look like, and what do you do on a regular basis? Do you have any special daily routine? Consider your health, happiness, spirituality, and free time.

PLEASURE · Pleasure accounts for all of the rewards that are yielded as a result of your personal and professional life activities. For the Young & Successful, life is about overall happiness, satisfaction, achievement, and reaping great rewards for hard work and diligent efforts. So what will you enjoy in your Ideal Life that represents 100 percent fun and enjoyment? What are the toys or other symbols of success that you intend to have? Describe the indulgences, the adventures, and the irresistible pleasures that are all yours. What gives you your greatest thrills and enjoyment? Be as materialistic, selfish, or outrageous as you want here. It's okay—you've worked hard for all this!

Your three components must all contain powerful motivators to draw you toward the fulfillment of this picture. Each category will tell a story of its own. Together, though, they blend to form this perfect, complete vision of your Ideal Life.

The Ideal Life picture is the big juicy carrot that dangles just far enough in front of you to knock you in the head every so often and say, "I'm right here, come and get me." It's the picture of everything you've ever dreamed of being, having, and achieving after it has all come true.

As you achieve your goals or decide some may not be the goals you need or want right now, don't be afraid to reset, reinvent, and otherwise adjust your Ideal Life picture. My picture has changed a few times as I have gotten a little older, have been exposed to new possibilities, and achieved success in different parts of my life. You and your life are likely the same— a work in progress. So remember that and treat yourself accordingly.

Getting comfortable with our Ideal Life is the best way to get a little uncomfortable with our real life and send us marching toward what it is we want in the first place. And that's a great thing, when you consider that being Young & Successful doesn't allow much room for settling, because you're constantly on the move to do more—whether that's becoming more physically fit, more active in your community, landing your dream job, or giving your life a serious makeover. Major changes and big achievements begin with crafting your Ideal Life vision.

Your Life Will Never Be the Same

At some point we all dream of hitting it rich somehow. Of suddenly becoming totally free. Of not having a care in the world and eliminating your everyday stresses. It's actually one of the easiest ways to imagine your Ideal Life. Who hasn't gotten a little lost in the fantasy at some point? But your Ideal Life is not about fantasy at all. It's about freeing your mind and your imagination up enough to formulate your own picture of what would truly make you most happy. All too often we become debilitated by reality (work, bills, stress, uncertainty, boredom), so much so that we unconsciously lower the bar for what we hope to accomplish. It's understandable, really; it just helps us cope. But to outperform even our own perception of what's possible for us, we have to raise the bar to an idealistic level.

Let's imagine that you're at work one Friday afternoon. You're just getting back from lunch when a lawyer named Mr. Kurnos calls. He says he's calling about your uncle Albert who's just passed away. You're shocked and sad. Uncle Albert was a great guy and he taught you a lot. But he had a long, happy life and you smile as you remember some of the good times you had together. For a moment, you wish he hadn't lived so far away so you could have had more of those good times.

Mr. Kurnos goes on to tell you that he's sorry to be the bearer of bad news, but that Albert had asked that you go to his office immediately after his death for a meeting. You're a bit confused, but you grab your things and quickly head out to meet the attorney.

Just a few miles away, in an impressive towering building, you usher yourself through the doors, hit the up button on the elevator, and soon you're at the reception desk in a magnificent suite of offices. You can't help but wonder how Uncle Al could afford a firm like this. The receptionist informs Mr. Kurnos of your arrival and he soon emerges with a warm friendly smile. In his office, you're invited to sit, and as soon as you do, your questions are immediately laid to rest by the attorney's first few words. "You might not have known this, but your uncle was a very rich man. He has left you a fortune, one hundred million dollars."

You don't really respond at first, because he's got to be kidding. But the look on his face quickly tells you he's not kidding at all. You start to explain to Mr. Kurnos how crazy this is by telling him about how Uncle Al used to buy all his books at garage sales. "Look," he'd say, "just a quarter apiece." Mr. Kurnos smiles and says nothing.

Finally, Kurnos starts to talk again. "Your uncle set out a few conditions that I need to go over with you right now before I can finalize the paperwork." You knew it! This really *is* too good to be true. You look around to spot the hidden camera but see none.

Part One: Your Ideal Professional Life

Mr. Kurnos tells you that with wealth of this magnitude comes great responsibility and virtually limitless choices. As such, the money will be made available to you over a period of ten years, in two different parts.

"You may not have known the extent of your uncle Albert's work, as he was pretty low-key about it, but he always worked hard—and loved what he did. He told me many times that doing what he loved was the secret to his success.

"That's why he set your inheritance up the way that he did. He didn't want you to be tempted to stop working, because he believed that if you did, you'd lose your passion for pursuing the things that you truly love in life.

"Although he may not have expressed it to you as often as he would have liked, he was quite proud of how far you've come at such an early age. And he didn't want to see that stop, so he designed your inheritance to ensure that you had whatever you need to pursue whatever made you most passionate in life.

"That's why to get the first half of your inheritance—the first fifty million dollars—you have to continue to work, at least fifty hours a week, at something you love. You can do whatever you like, so long as you sincerely believe that your efforts will be productive and worthwhile to both you and others. As long as you continue to work, you will receive five million dollars a year, in the form of a check each month for four hundred and seventeen thousand dollars for the first year to get you started, and one five-million-dollar check at the end of each year thereafter."

So, what will you do? Will you return to work just as you did this morning? Will you stay in the same field? Or will you try something completely new, something you've always deep down wanted to do? Now that what you earn or what you do is no longer of concern, the sky is the limit. This is your chance to work on just about anything you ever dreamed of.

To finalize the paperwork for your uncle's estate, you will soon need to inform Mr. Kurnos of what you decide to do.

Take some time right now, think it through, and jot down a brief description of what you're going to tell Mr. Kurnos.

Part Two: Your Ideal Personal Life

To get the second half of your inheritance, Kurnos tells you that you have to commit to living a life of significance and substance. According to Mr. Kurnos, your uncle defined that simply: He wanted you to be a kind, caring person who has a positive impact on the lives of others. You knew how he always talked about and lived a life centered on strong family values, community and charitable contribution, and sound education, all while living a healthy, active lifestyle. So, Mr. Kurnos tells you that you must create a list of a minimum of twenty great accomplishments you will strive to achieve over the next ten years. Then Uncle Al insisted that you go out and make a real effort to reach your goals.

You are allowed a few days to come up with your list. You marvel at how this is an excellent chance for you to do something spectacular with your life and some of your newfound wealth. If you can cross off at least one new accomplishment on your list annually, you'll receive an additional five-million-dollar check at the end of the year. Sounds fair! He says that each year, you'll also have the ability to add up to five new grand accomplishments to the list to adjust for new areas of interest that you discover as you live this new life.

So, what will you decide to do? What great accomplishments would you like to tackle that you believe will have a positive impact on others? What causes interest you most? And what form would you like your giving to take? What could you set out to do that few others in your new powerful position could do? Take some time and put this list together below or on a separate piece of paper, in no particular order:

1. _____   11. _____
2. _____   12. _____
3. _____   13. _____
4. _____   14. _____
5. _____   15. _____
6. _____   16. _____
7. _____   17. _____
8. _____   18. _____
9. _____   19. _____
10. _____   20. _____

Part Three: The Pleasures You'll Experience from Living Your Ideal Life

Mr. Kurnos lets you know that you have a week to decide what you'll be doing professionally and to submit the list of twenty accomplishments you'll set out to achieve. Still in a daze over how the day's events have unfolded, you graciously reach out to accept Mr. Kurnos's card, and he hands you a set of keys as well. What are these? As if life could possibly get any crazier today, he says, "Now I'm sure you're well aware that your uncle knew how to have a good time. That's why he always encouraged you to spend your free time exploring a wide variety of activities. He had many friends and many responsibilities, too. With all the demands on his time, he realized the importance of making adequate time for himself to regroup and rejuvenate. He believed strongly that it kept his head clear, his momentum strong, and his ability to be effective in all areas of his life at their peak.

"To get away, your uncle had a wonderful cabin up in the mountains only a few hours from here that he escaped to several times a year when he came into town. He claimed it helped him to center his mind, body, and soul. That house is also now yours. Here's a train ticket, along with the directions to the station and cabin. Your uncle requested that I send you there soon after we spoke, as he knew this would all be quite overwhelming for you. He was adamant about your having the right environment to consider everything we discussed today. You do have some very important decisions to make."

With that, Mr. Kurnos escorts you to the elevators, and within minutes you are back on the street, through the same doors, but in a completely different place.

Early the next morning you find yourself stepping into an old train station and onto a large platform to wait for your ride. You feel as if you're in a daze, as if this is all a part of some wonderful dream.

"Hey you," a scruffy voice calls from behind. You turn to find an elderly man in an apron and old golf hat, standing in front of an enormous newsstand. How you could have missed it before you have no idea, but, "Hey," he says again, "you there. You wouldn't happen to be Uncle Albert's nephew, would you?"

Startled, you nod in reply. "Why, yes, that's me. How did you know?"

"He told me I'd be meeting you soon enough. Come in, put your bag down. Take a look around." You accept the offer and inch forward. "You know your uncle was quite an avid reader. There's not one time in thirty years that I saw him that he didn't buy a stack of magazines from me to read on his trip. He was such a generous man and so fascinating. Always took the time to stop and chat and shared with me the most wonderful stories about his work, his hobbies, his family. And of course you. He talked about you quite a bit. Said he expected great things of you. You were his pride and joy, you know.

"Here, be my guest. Take some magazines for your long journey as my gift. Your uncle used to say that it was through my magazines that he'd indulge in all of the wonderful things he loved, right here on this very train. He'd always pick out the most eclectic mix of publications, too. Said it was his escape within an escape. It helped him remember some of the things that got lost in the day-to-day shuffle. Go ahead, grab as many as you can carry. Your train will be arriving soon."

You walk around and scan the categories on little wooden signs above the racks:

Animals/Pets	Art	Auto
Aviation & Boats	Business/Finance	Collectibles
Computers/Tech	Cooking	Crafts
Education	Electronics	Entertainment/TV
Environmental	Fashion	Gaming
Health & Fitness	History	Home & Garden
Hunting & Fishing	Medical	Music
News	Parenting	Photography
Political	Real Estate &	Religion
Sci Fi & Mystery	Home Building	Science & Nature
Sports	Technology	Travel/Vacations

Go ahead, list ten magazines (or categories) that you'd choose:

_____   _____

_____   _____

_____   _____

_____   _____

_____   _____

You thank the old man for his generosity and for being such a good friend to your uncle. Then you say your good-byes and board the waiting train. Settling into a big comfortable seat, you flip through your new stash of magazines. As you begin to let your mind wander through the glossy pages, you start tearing out images that you find intriguing, compelling, attractive, and inspiring. After a while, you begin to fill the seat next to you with a pretty serious pile of clippings.

Make this story yours. Pile up those images in your head, just like you did on that seat beside you. See the things you love, the things you need, the things you want, desire, covet, adore, feel great passion for, one after another after another. Imagine that pile of clippings and what they'd look like if you pinned them all up on a wall at home. What story would they start to tell? What image of your Ideal Life would they convey? Now hold on to that image, that collage, for a minute, because it's time to really make one of your own.

It's time to immortalize these dreams of yours and put them into a format that can serve as a constant reminder of all the things you're striving for. We call this your Ideal Life Monument.

Your Ideal Life Monument™

Before we begin formulating a plan to make your Ideal Life happen, we want to ensure that your vision stays as clear to you as it is right now.

It's easy for us to lose sight of our dreams and what's most important to us if we don't give ourselves the right signposts and keep symbols of our greatest motivations close by us at all times. To do this, the Young & Successful create all sorts of *monuments* to represent their Ideal Life—tangible symbols that represent or illustrate all that they're striving for, and act as powerful daily reminders of why they must work as hard as they do.

Knowing that an Ideal Life Monument can take on many different forms, *what would yours look like?* Curtis, whom we mentioned earlier, has an entire wall in his office covered with pictures of his dream life—travel, antiques, big family gatherings. My friend Lisa carries a journal with her everywhere that's filled with pictures, quotes, goals, and notes all focused on the body, the relationships, the perspective, and the lifestyle she's devoted to having. Scott has a picture of a Maui sunset on his wall, and an illustration on his computer desktop of the beach compound he wants to buy someday. He even keeps some unused tile and crown moldings on his desk from a nearby house he fell in love with (and used to sneak into on Sundays while they were building it!). In his personal library, a room spilling over with books, he diligently maintains a section of travel guides of the many exotic destinations he wishes to visit someday. He also has a detailed sketch of his Ideal Life with a scribbled little wish list from both of his parents framed on his office wall so that one day he can be sure to make his parents' dreams come true, too.

Many Young & Successful people do the same thing in one form or another. Whether their monument lives within the pages of a private journal, on a napkin taped on a patch of spare wall, or resides in a photo montage mounted on a bulletin board—they create a powerful message to themselves that's always right there in front of them. It could be a miniature model, some sort of altar, a shrine, a picture, journal, sign, poster, calendar, wall chart, symbolic object, sentimental relic . . . anything that lights a fire and propels them to move forward and keep going. When you ask yourself "Where am I going?" it boldly answers back with a strong, yet silent call to action and a message of inspiration and hope.

Make Your Own Ideal Life Monument

You've drawn imaginary pictures of your Ideal Life in your head, created dozens of images that show you what you want to do, have, and be. Now is the time to get them out of your head and put them up where you can see them. Whenever you need help focusing or a little boost in your confidence, your Ideal Life Monument will be a constant reminder of where you're headed and what you need to do to get there.

Just Say the Word

We all have different strengths and weaknesses. Some people think in images, some in phrases. One of the simplest Ideal Life Monuments can be made of words. Create a bulleted list of desires or an elaborate description of what you want. Tell yourself about what a day in your life will be like ten years from now, then twenty years from now. Write down what the room you wake up in is like. Spell out how you feel and what you wear. Tell yourself the story of this day all those years from now, focusing in on the people you meet and the work you do, the things that surround you and the way that you interact with them all. Include as many details as you can.

A Picture's Worth a Thousand Words

Grab a stack of magazines, a glue stick, and a pair of scissors and go to town. Cut out five, ten, a hundred images of the world you want to live in and build your own picture of the life you want to have. This doesn't need to be art, just a visual snapshot of where you're going that conjures up thoughts of what you're striving for each time you see it.

One Solitary Symbol

Warren Buffett, arguably one of the greatest investors of all time, recently invested in a company that leases private jets to corporations and the very well-to-do. According to him, the ultimate luxury is being able to go where he wants to go, when he wants to go. Bob, a friend of mine, agrees with him wholeheartedly and keeps a picture of a Learjet on his desk to remind him of how he wants to be traveling in a few years. For him, this picture says everything there is to say about how far (and how fast) he wants to go.

Is there one thing that does it for you? A car, a house, a place that says it all for you? Figure out what that symbol is, then put a picture of it, a model, a sketch, or even a set of plans somewhere close enough to you, so that you're always reminded of where you want to be, what you want to do, and what you want to have.

Remember, in whatever form of expression you choose to document the vision of your Ideal Life, it must speak volumes to you. You don't have to share it with anyone if you don't want to; however, I will tell you that many Young & Successful have found that doing so with at least a few trusted supporters helps to strengthen their commitment to their dreams.

The Young & Successful know that money and the freedom it can buy aren't really the point. Few of us will ever be handed a blank check that will allow us to do everything we always wanted to do, but we don't need money to give us the power to choose. That is a gift we give ourselves, once we come to realize just how much we're really capable of.

It is our own personal visions of an Ideal Life that motivates us, gives us the drive we need to transcend the barriers that real life keeps putting in our way. Our Ideal Life is what helps us keep moving toward what it is we really love—that shows us that these barriers are merely challenges, and not something that we should allow to stop us.

The First Step in Your Journey

Common sense tells us to be practical when it comes to planning our futures. But incredible success rarely comes to those who take the safest routes. The most revered business leaders, artists, teachers, and even scientists all started out with a grand vision of what might be possible. Now, it's your turn. Take a few minutes to reflect on the realizations you've had and the decisions you've made thus far. How has your perspective changed? Can you see where you want to go a little more clearly? By now you should be able to picture many of the elements of your Ideal Life in vivid detail. This vision represents your greatest motivation.

Now let's go make it happen.

The Grand Plan™

THE AMAZING LIFE YOU'VE ALWAYS DREAMED OF may start with a dream, but it happens with a plan. For the Young & Successful, it doesn't matter whether their ideas seem "feasible" because once they make a decision, they do what it takes to make even their wildest dreams a reality.

Consider for a minute someone everyone knows, but a little story you may not. Tiger Woods, one of the greatest Young & Successful athletes of our time, was just nine years old when he decided he might stop playing golf. After some serious discussions with his parents, he reconsidered, then dove into training harder than ever. In his room, on the wall right above his bed, Tiger went to work on his own Grand Plan. Through a series of pictures and statistics, Tiger created a time line that laid out the then twenty-year career of Jack Nicklaus, his idol. On it he listed Nicklaus's every major milestone, benchmark, award, and tournament championship, then tracked his own career below. Even at nine, Tiger had already beaten some of Nicklaus's early records, but with the steps to his dream of ultimate success clearly mapped out, he had the Grand Plan that he needed to become the best, and do it earlier than Nicklaus did.

One of the most amazing *Secrets of the Young & Successful* is that their "dream, then do" instinct eventually becomes second nature. That is why once they get started achieving, they become unstoppable. This seemingly innate ability comes from an understanding of how to convert their visions into reality with a plan.

For the Young & Successful, their plans are a way of seeing the "big picture" of their career, their work, their successful future. We call it a Grand Plan. It's the filter you use to sort your dreams and aspirations for success into workable, realistic steps. Your Grand Plan maps out the major benchmarks that can get you from where you are today to the point where you can realize your Ideal Life vision. And it doesn't matter what the dream is, either. If something is possible, the Young & Successful will find a way to make it happen. (They've also been known to change people's perspectives on what was once thought to be "impossible," too.) So, when you dream your wildest dreams of success, rest assured that your Grand Plan will fill in the "how-to" and the "what next" pieces of the puzzle. But without going through this next step, fantasies of success will remain just that. Execution is indeed the tough part, but with a carefully crafted Grand Plan, you're sure to have the tool you need to start making your dreams materialize.

Getting Started

The Grand Plan is like a business plan for your life. This doesn't require you to quit your day job, work for nothing, wallpaper your bathroom with stock certificates, or travel around the country begging people for money. This is about you. And one thing is for sure; we're going to base your plan on plenty of substance by the time we're through. But be forewarned: At first your Grand Plan may look a lot like *Mission Impossible*—to you and the rest of the world. I won't lie to you, this is going to take some serious commitment to make it work. But it can, and will, if you want it badly enough.

Developing your Grand Plan involves looking at where you are now and where you want to go, then connecting a few dots in between.

So what we're going to do here is simplify that process and help you create your own Grand Plan in a few logical and easy steps. With this as a filter for your initial ideas, we'll begin to put everything into a real-world context so you can be off and running in no time.

The first draft of your Grand Plan can be sketched out on a napkin, an envelope, or anything you have handy when the inspiration hits. Just getting the ideas out of our heads and on paper is a huge step forward for most of us. What do you need to write on that napkin? The top five or so major milestones, accomplishments, or benchmark events that you need to achieve to get to that Ideal Life of yours. These events are mostly professional in nature and form the basis of the Grand Plan. And, as you'll see in the coming pages, once you figure out what your milestones are, finding the steps between them is often pretty easy. Don't believe me? Well, let me show you what I mean.

Say, for instance, you're ambitious and you want to succeed . . .

WITHIN A BIG CORPORATION · Your goals are to get in the door, find a mentor, earn your first promotions, get your hands on some real responsibility, gain control of larger projects.

IN YOUR OWN BUSINESS · You need to write your business plan, create your pro forma financials, work on your start-up budget, secure your financing, set up your office, build your team, sign up your first clients, achieve profitability.

OUT ON YOUR OWN FOR THE FIRST TIME · Your primary concerns are probably graduating from college, figuring out what you want to do, creating a great résumé (or bio) and game plan, giving yourself a professional makeover, leaving a great impression on your first interviews, and getting a job.

See, I told you it was easy. Once you have your Ideal Life vision, plotting out a few easy steps to lead you there is a matter of common sense.

ARTISTIC VISION ON A GRAND SCALE

Jackson Pollock, a world-renowned painter, was famous for building picture plans in his head, then transferring them to canvas. When he was thirty-one, gallery owner Peggy Guggenheim commissioned a twenty-foot painting to put in the foyer of her town house. For weeks, Pollock stared at the canvas, not even picking up a brush. Then in one night, he completed the entire mural. When he was confronted with that massive canvas, Pollock had a dream of creating great art, but for this piece and place, greatness required a plan. Like Pollock, sometimes we have to chew on our ideas for a while before they make sense to us and the process becomes clear.

The Grand Plan allows us to see the whole story from where we are to where we want to be all at once, kind of like what Pollock did in his head. The execution of Pollock's plan was on canvas, though, and permanent. Ours can change at any time, and it will.

Our Grand Plan is an ongoing process, a detailed account of how we're going to execute our vision of success, starting with the general concept overview and walking through all the different stages of development. It's a step-by-step, job-by-job, role-by-role list of what you must accomplish to arrive at your Ideal Life. And as such, it's sure to evolve as you learn more and do more.

Strategic Thinking

Strategic thinking is the key to creating a successful Grand Plan that will pave a manageable, realistic path between your life now and your

Ideal Life. Strategic thinking means looking at the big picture and thinking through or calculating your moves before you make them. If we try to play the game in the traditional way, relying solely on hard work to get us what we want, we might never get there in time to enjoy it all. It's up to us to find clues, opportunities, assistance, and shortcuts along the way. There may be a lot that separates us now from what we want, but in order to bridge that gap and find our shortcuts, we have to be smart about the moves we make.

Why is it important to be strategic? Because it

- gives us more confidence knowing that we've considered all the contingencies and have a good idea of what we can expect

- allows us to pursue our dreams more aggressively because by thinking strategically, we develop more sophisticated plans

- eliminates much of the fear that holds so many back because our path becomes more familiar and predictable

- helps us enlist the help and support of others because we can tell them with assurance what we need, what we have, and how they can help

- makes us aware of potential consequences of our decisions

- takes some of the riskiness out of our risks by helping us craft exit strategies

- helps us determine just how far we're willing to go for what we want

- facilitates our explanations of the "big picture" to others so they can understand what we're setting out to do.

For those of us who seem to spend a lot of time explaining ourselves to others (and I know I'm not alone here), strategic thinking helps when we're confronted with critics and skeptics. How? Because we learn to speak more intelligently about what we're up to, even if it may sound crazy on the surface. Just remember nine-year-old Tiger Woods committing to becoming the best golfer who ever lived. Even as good as he was, it must have sounded crazy, until he disclosed his Grand Plan and laid out just how *possible* it actually might be.

GETTING EVEN SMARTER CAN BE A PLAN

Julie Joncas had some big plans of her own, but she quickly realized that she needed to turn those dreams into practical steps and aggressive actions, or dreaming was about as far as she'd get. Growing up in Grafton, Massachusetts, a small town about an hour outside Boston, Julie could barely utter a word to strangers. She was paralyzed by shyness. But Julie was a good kid who did her homework, helped her mom at home, took care of her younger siblings, and got along fine in the little community she had known her whole life. As she got older, though, she noticed that most of the people around her—including her large, extended, French-Canadian family—had never left the town they were born in.

Now, Grafton is not a bad place to spend your life by any means, but Julie began to dream of the much bigger world outside her little town as big ideas swarmed in her head. Living in the city, going to great restaurants, shopping for shoes (a must for Julie), meeting exciting new people, getting some impressive degrees, working for a big consulting firm, and even becoming the dean of a business school one day were all objectives that topped her list. But if she was going to get anywhere with all of this, she had to stop dreaming and start doing.

Unlike so many countless small-town girls and boys who dream of getting away, Julie devised her own Grand Plan and made a commitment to make it happen. Her initial plan took the form of a list that included the following:

- coming out of her shell: she'd never get far being introverted

- focusing on getting into a big school in the city and doing well there

- earning the first degree in her family

- going to work at a prestigious company to gain some hands-on experience

- getting into the best business-school MBA program she could

- becoming a high-paid consultant for a prestigious company

These steps made up Julie's initial Grand Plan. And while it started out as just a bunch of big ideas, she realized that dreaming and plotting was what she needed to begin the process. She also knew that once she started to work her way down the list and through her benchmarks her options would be virtually unlimited.

It hadn't been easy, but overcoming her biggest hang-up—fear—was essential if her plan was to work. After all, it's hard to be a great leader and an introvert. So in class, Julie started raising her hand more often, she volunteered to make oral presentations, she actively pursued new friendships, and she started hanging out with more outgoing people. Getting over that first hurdle was just about taking a bunch of baby steps until she felt comfortable in making larger strides. What she found was that the more she talked, the more people listened. And when she reached out her hand in friendship to a few, many more returned the sentiment. Over the next few years, Julie was accepted to and excelled in Boston University, where she made terrific friends—and lots of them. Julie had clearly come out of her shell. The change in her life was gradual, but over time, she went from being one of the shyest people she knew to one of the most confident. She even got elected president of the School of Management.

After graduating with honors, she became an assistant buyer at a major department store chain for about a year, left to become vice president of a small marketing company (mine, actually), and just two years later applied to Harvard Business School . . . and got in. She continuously had worked her way through all the different steps of her plan, one by one, deliberately making moves she knew would help her realize one big goal after another. All this, she was sure, would eventually lead to her Ideal Life.

But despite all her hard work and having finally achieved some of her loftiest goals, Julie, like millions of others, fell on hard times when the economy took a dive and the big management consulting company she joined right out of grad school drastically downsized its offices around the country. Luckily, Julie's employment contract enabled her to get a modest severance package that kept her afloat while she looked for another job. When she was offered a job with a fast-growing foreign telecom company, it came not only with a VP title but with a nice salary and great perks, like frequent trips to Europe. But within months, that company shut its doors as well and Julie was out of work again.

This time, there was no severance and no new opportunities to be found anywhere.

Soon the crunch was on.

With a brand-new degree from Harvard Business School, more than $100,000 in student loans to repay, a great brownstone apartment on Commonwealth Avenue to pay rent for, and even the most basic bills and personal expenses piling up, Julie was suddenly in a position she never dreamed of confronting. Was her decision to go back to school all wrong? Could her timing have been worse? Was it really possible that one of the most prestigious of degrees, not to mention alumni networks, couldn't land her even a mediocre job? Julie was dejected and depressed. This was not part of her plan at all—especially the part about being unemployed for more than eight months. Her luck had to change at some point, she kept telling herself. And while it took some time, new opportunities started to surface after the economic dust settled a bit.

Well, in the end, Julie's plan might have gotten thrown off track, but she stayed committed to finding a nice stable company and eventually found a dream job in an industry she'd always wanted to work in—health care. Best of all, the job was in Boston, right in the heart of the city she loved most.

Today Julie makes six figures as a consultant for one of the most prestigious health-care companies in the world. She has since updated her Grand Plan and is already on the fast track to realizing even greater dreams and goals. Her ultimate goal now, more realistic than ever, is to one day become the dean of a business school. And it's all because she made that initial plan as just another high school kid in a small town, and put all her energy into fulfilling her own Grand Plan.

Where Do I Start?

The simplest answer is: *Start from where you are.*

It's tempting to think that success would come easily if we just had more time, money, better contacts, greater support, and more favorable circumstances. But dwelling on what we don't have wastes valuable time. All we really need to do is know what we have to work with, come up with a plan, lay out our benchmarks, and spend the time to fill in the details. The earlier we start, the more room we have to take chances and make mistakes at this point. But the longer we wait to get the ball rolling, the harder it will become.

Don't be tempted to put off planning or making your big move until you're more comfortable or more successful. You should always be moving forward and getting better. Baby steps certainly work, too. Don't feel like creating change has to happen through major life-altering leaps. Go with what's comfortable for you, then push yourself a little further. It's just like working out. What's most important is consistent movement and your commitment to progress and improvement.

The Young & Successful know that wherever they may be when starting out, they have to keep moving forward and maintaining their momentum. Even if they fall down or veer offtrack a few times along the way, they know that they have to start from wherever they are. Slow, small, and steady steps forward are totally fine, if need be (but if you want to take giant leaps and catapult yourself over a handful of steps, I certainly won't discourage you). The reality is that the faster you figure out where you want to be, the faster you'll get there, guaranteed.

If you think you have legitimate excuses for why you haven't gotten started cultivating and working your plan yet, forgive me, but I must show you just how naïve that concept is. There are no good reasons for settling, for not striving to do better and be happier. And I certainly don't want to let you get away with reading this whole book and not making some serious changes in your life for the better. After all, that is why we're here, *isn't it?* Let's face it, we all can do more.

How? Well, your options are pretty much unlimited. But if you're at a real loss for ideas, just think about what you can do with even thirty *relocated* minutes a day. We all can spare that. How could you put that time to the best use to make yourself and your circumstances better? Remember, these are just baby steps, but you can scale them or kick them up a notch however you see fit:

- Take a half hour run in the morning to get a great start to your day.

- Read the newspaper to keep on top of what's going on in the world.

- Pick up a trade journal and learn something new about your field.

- Tell someone you meet about what you do and practice telling your story.

· Get to an important meeting early so you can review your notes and make the best possible impression.

· Spend a little extra time at a party or event and make a few new contacts.

· Call someone you know who's doing something you're interested in and ask him or her to tell you more.

· Drop in on a friend who's having a tough time and see if there's anything you can do to help.

· Close your eyes amid a chaotic day and refocus yourself, think about your Ideal Life, and remind yourself why you're working so hard.

Now that wasn't so hard, was it? We all can do more, and simply have to if we hope to accomplish great things (not to mention amazing personal satisfaction) very early in life. If you're game for this, plot out your own benchmarks and I promise, simple opportunities for you to do more will become increasingly clear.

LIVING A MORE GLAMOROUS LIFE

When people talk about having it rough, they often talk about a lack of money in their lives. So, let me tell you how Marsha Bialo went from making $1000 a month, working two jobs and being miserable, to making $6,000, working part-time at one and absolutely loving her life . . . *and* spending her days and nights with some of the most glamorous people in the world!

Now I know this story is going to sound pretty incredible, but what's really incredible is that my friend Marsha had no special advantages when starting out. It was all in her attitude, her determination, and the constant reexamination of her Grand Plan . . . once she finally figured out how important that was (even she'll admit, it took a little while for her to catch on, though).

See, Marsha started life on what you could call the wrong foot. Like many others, she spent most of her teens struggling to find herself. But not just because of the usual challenges. She had lost her father at thirteen, had a mother who was totally dependent on her (both emotionally and physically because she had never driven), and, to make matters worse, school was a miserable experience thanks to a serious learning disability.

Her early twenties weren't a lot better. Always in search of work, Marsha focused on how to pay the bills, but never on what might make her happy. There was no such thing as an Ideal Life vision for her, and certainly no Grand Plan to speak of. Marsha seemed destined for nothing special, and there certainly was nothing much she could look forward to. But watch closely and I'll show you how she went from serving frozen yogurt to pampering celebrities. It took a little time to get the ball rolling, though. She didn't have a Grand Plan, so she found herself accepting anything that was thrown her way. At twenty she was working three very random jobs:

- serving customers at a yogurt shop ($3.35 per hr.)

- working as a cashier at a health food store ($5.50 per hr.)

- teaching at a preschool ($8.50 per hr.).

Was she happy? Try exhausted. But one day, Marsha made another random decision that eventually would change her life entirely. Growing up, she'd always been fascinated with acrylic nails. They looked so beautiful on the women who wore them, she thought, and she wanted them too. Problem was, they cost almost a full day's salary to get, and Marsha just couldn't afford to blow that kind of money. So she learned how to do them for herself. She dropped two of her three jobs and enrolled in a night class at a local community college for summer school. When the semester ended, she completed the three hundred hours of field training over the next few months using her friends and family as guinea pigs. But Marsha never took the State Board Exam to get state certified, because even after all these years, tests still scared her.

So the stream of odd jobs continued. She worked for a while as a nanny, as a restaurant hostess, and even as a file clerk on the graveyard shift for the Bosley Medical Clinic, famous for hair transplants and their 3 A.M. infomercials. There was no direction and no connection in any of her decisions. A friend finally informed her that her fieldwork hours would expire if she didn't take the licensing test within five years. So she bit the bullet, returned to a classroom for one day, and ended up passing with flying colors. With her license in hand, Marsha began to see opportunities all around her.

Within a few weeks, Marsha had talked her way into a spot at a Beverly Hills salon. That first week she made $500. She was floored. She was also on to something. Marsha spent about a year at that salon learning the business and, for the first time, contemplating her future. This is when her Grand Plan began to unfold before her.

Now watch how her plan started to take shape and her focus sharpened as success began to happen for her.

One day she walked through the Ritz Carlton hotel with her boyfriend when she noticed a manicurist sitting with a client in a beautiful little private room set off from the main lobby. Marsha examined the prices for the service and tried to calculate how much money this woman was making. Within seconds, she was headed for the front desk with her boyfriend calling her crazy behind her. But she still asked the question. "I was wondering what might be involved in coming to work here."

"It's funny you should ask," the lady replied, "because we just put an ad in the *L.A. Times*." Marsha beamed. Her timing couldn't have been more perfect.

After her first week working at the Ritz Carlton, Marsha got a check for $800. Now she was making in one week what, a year before, she was making in a month. And she was only working part-time, three days a week! Soon she was spending her days chatting away with major executives, wealthy socialites, and even celebrities—and making $1,000 a week.

But Marsha was working her plan now, and she was only getting started. Her confidence was bolstering, her skills becoming refined, and her customers were now raving about how talented she was. The next career move took her to the Peninsula Hotel, one of the most luxurious hotels in the City of Angels. There she worked for three years with the top celebrities in Hollywood: Allison Janney of *The West Wing*, supermodel Cindy Crawford, the Dixie Chicks, country music stars, and actress Andie McDowell. In fact, it was actually Andie who told Marsha about an agency that hooked up the best stylists in the industry with top fashion magazines for photo shoots. It took her a month to call, but within a week she was doing Gillian Anderson's hands for the cover of *Movie Line* magazine. Soon Marsha's Grand Plan was taking on a grand form. Her reputation as a celebrity manicurist was spreading through the city; she was working at the hippest and hottest hotels in L.A., like the Standard, the Mondrian, the Argyle, W, and the Bel Air Hotel, to name just a few. Best of all, every day was a new adventure for her, meeting the most photographed people in the world and visiting movie, TV, and photo shoots. All while making more money than she'd ever dreamed of.

Today, Marsha makes a great living working (mostly part-time) on the pretty little paws of stars like Angelina Jolie, Brandy, Jamie Lee Curtis, Patti LaBelle, Pink, Jennifer Love Hewitt, and Tyra Banks. At any given time, Marsha's responsible for celebrity manicures that appear on the covers of at least two or three fashion magazines each month (like *Cosmopolitan*, *Vogue*, *Elle*, *Glamour*, and *Tattler*). And now she's also a commercial spokesperson for OPI, a top producer of women's nail polish. By using their products on all the celebrities, their name and hers appear in the credit lines of the magazines, giving OPI exposure to hundreds of thousands of readers at a time. Marsha now gets written up in these magazines sometimes, too, as a celebrity manicurist and top expert on nail care.

So what's next for Marsha? Why, her own product line—called Bialo Basix—of course! With her Grand Plan now clear as day and consistently getting more and more ambitious, Marsha knows that the best way to move up from here is to do what only a handful of other stylists have done to make millions while living out their own dreams. And she's well on her way.

We won't always see the whole big picture (from summer job to CEO) in the beginning. But we should see the biggest picture we can and run with that. Again, when the horizon changes, we can always adjust and redirect our trajectory. After all, with every new experience and nugget of inside information, our perspective and expectations will become more refined and more focused. Just be sure you're pointed in the right direction, and you can't help but make great strides, if you keep moving.

How do you know if you're heading in the right direction? Well, think of it as if you're in your car working your way through traffic. Do you see pockets of free space opening up? Or are you staring at a wall of cars? Do you have room to keep moving, to make progress, or is it all too clear that you're going to be continually stopped? If so, you probably want to start looking for an exit or thinking about a few alternative routes. What do you see waiting ahead of you in your life? How are you going to negotiate that road?

Creating the Plan

Simply stated, creating a Grand Plan is a process of draft and detail. We start with a few sketches and gradually grow more detailed. At this point it's no longer enough for us to talk about our mission conceptually or categorize our goals as merely "personal" or "professional." Now we have to go deeper, and get more specific. While your Grand Plan can be as basic as a page, Scott and I are hoping you're compelled enough to want to build a solid plan that covers *all* the critical areas of your life.

To start, all you need is one piece of paper on which you are going to analyze one specific component at a time:

- career (work, education, degrees, special training)
- health (physical, mental, emotional)

· financial (salary, investments, additional streams of income)

· contributions (family, community, political)

· spirituality/religion (activities, involvement, initiatives, faith)

· relationships (friends, family, professional)

· personal (hobbies, social events, rest, renewal)

Keep it simple at first. Start to think about the goals you have in each of these different areas and what kinds of changes you'd like to see. Make some rough notes. Start to see a process taking shape in each area, with a beginning (now) and an end (your ultimate goal—your ideal life).

Then you need to create five or so benchmarks (milestones or major achievements) that are most necessary to propel you from where you are to your specific goal. Just remember the story of young Tiger Woods and how he created a simple plan of his own with milestones based on the career of his idol. These benchmarks can include anything from getting a degree to becoming a top executive, writing a screenplay to watching your movie on the big screen, or writing a business plan to capturing your first or one thousandth customer. The three elements— your starting point, your ultimate goal, and the benchmarks in between—are the "draft" piece of the equation.

In the intermediary steps, spell out what you need to learn, do, schedule, and overcome to achieve the goals that you've established for yourself. Your intermediary steps are what get you to your benchmarks.

So, Ya Wanna Be a Rock Star?

To show you how this process of drafting and creating a plan can help you figure out how to achieve even the craziest of dreams, let's take a look at an example that at first might seem totally over the top. Who hasn't thought—if only for a minute—of being a rock star? We could just as easily use the example of a doctor, a lawyer, an engineer, a teacher—or any career goal for that matter. But as we've discussed, we want you to dream big and bold. So we'll just indulge here for a bit.

First, I'll just ask the obvious question: Do rock stars really plan out their success? To get a real expert opinion, I decided to ask Allie Brown, a young, very cool and very successful producer for VH1's *Behind the Music* series. Allie is one of a handful of people VH1 sends all around the world to places like Bosnia, Jerusalem, and England, to interview top rock stars like Keith Richards, Cat Stevens, and Snoop Dogg. Then she turns all those interviews into documentaries on how they found their own fame and fortune. (How great a job is that?)

According to Allie, rock stars have Ideal Life visions, too. "It seems like across the board, most successful musicians do have a big-picture plan of where they want to go." In her experience, most seem to have always known that they wanted to be successful, and pieced together some sort of logical steps to get there. "You do need to realize that every little thing you do matters. For one thing, every person you meet along the way has the potential to take your career in a new direction. It could be a girlfriend, a drummer, a producer, a booking agent, or a stylist. Fame finds people in all different ways and sometimes at very random times, so it's important to keep your eye out for any opportunities to take your art to the next level."

There's an old saying, "The harder you work, the luckier you get." Well, it seems that the Young & Successful have a similar view of their own—the more you plan, the more strategically you think, and the harder you work your plan, the more you will accomplish. Unquestionably.

So what does the road to becoming a rock star look like? Let's find out. Pull out that CD collection of yours, that giant poster on the back of your closet door, or those old rock and roll magazines you've kept all these years. Turn on MTV, VH1, or BET and imagine yourself performing in front of a live screaming audience of thousands of fans. Hear your name being chanted. See the flicker of all those little lighters in the stands. Feel the beads of sweat rolling down your face and the blinding lights above that highlight your every move. Open your mouth with that first lyric and hear the crowd roar. Ready?

A Clean Sheet

If you were to start a draft of this—yes, a Grand Plan that can lead you to becoming a big rock star—you could map out the process just as we talked about before. On the top of a blank page you'd write, "My Life Now: I'm the lead singer in my own small band." At the bottom of the page you'd jot down, "My Ideal Career: Rock Star." Then, to make that goal really clear, you'd add a brief description about the crowning achievement that would symbolize to you that you've made it. As a successful rock star this could include the number of sold-out tour dates, the number of gold and platinum albums, or the number of hit music videos produced and aired on MTV.

Now that we know where you want to go, it's time to establish your benchmarks to figure out how to make this happen for you. To be a rock star, you might consider these as your major benchmarks:

1 Produce my own CD.

2 Get discovered by the press or a big agent.

3 Sign a major recording contract.

4 Sell a million copies of my smash hit.

5 Land on the *Billboard* music chart.

Look at your five major benchmarks and consider whether there are any *major* steps you've left out. (Remember, your benchmarks are milestones, and there's likely to be many steps in between.) You're never going to get all the steps and the ideal path down on paper the first time. That's why we like to think of this as a sketch, something that you'll re-draft pieces of and morph as you get more information and experience.

You don't have to stick to five benchmarks; it's just a guide. If you need to, add a few more, but keep them focused on major achievements or milestones. Fill those in with a dark marker or make them bold.

You're just going to keep building the plan from here, making adjustments as you go along.

Intermediate Steps

Now that we have the benchmarks, let's go ahead and fill in the blanks.

Okay, big rock star, try to imagine what the intermediate steps or specific actions between these benchmarks might be. Take the first set for example. Let's connect the dots between you today and the first major benchmark. How would you go about producing your first CD if you just have a little band of your own? Think about the intermediate steps or actions you'd probably need to do to accomplish this. Again, this is a rough idea of the path you could follow:

You Today: LEAD SINGER IN MY OWN SMALL BAND

1 Choose and perfect our ten best songs to record.

2 Work out the concept, name, and design of the album.

3 Figure out what the costs are and how to pay for the project.

4 Find a recording studio where we can lay down the tracks.

5 Identify the best place to copy and print the CDs and jewel cases.

6 Determine the best distribution and sales strategy.

7 Assess the risks and rewards.

8 Execute the plan to create the CD.

Benchmark 1: PRODUCE MY OWN CD

Banging through these intermediate steps would surely lead you to the creation of your own CD. Now I'm sure that there still might be some things we're overlooking, but you can't say that with all this information laid out so clearly, you couldn't figure out what you're missing along the way. So keep going. Work through all the different benchmarks by identifying and knocking out their corresponding intermediate steps.

Now let's step away from our rock star example for a minute and assume you wanted to make a move in the more familiar "real" world. Say you've just earned a special degree and want to get a great new job. Try to determine, off the top of your head again, the intermediate action steps between your benchmarks.

Benchmark 1: GET A SPECIALIZED DEGREE

1 Visit a career counselor or recruiter.

2 Put a new résumé together.

3 Research the industry.

4 Surf the career sites online.

5   Talk to a bunch of friends in the business.

6   Get referrals to companies that are hiring.

7   Meet with some potential employers.

8   Go on several interviews.

9   Make a final decision on the best opportunity for you.

Benchmark 2: LAND A GREAT NEW JOB IN MY FIELD

Now doesn't it make sense that if you can put together a logical set of benchmarks to get you where you want to go and connect the dots with solid action steps, you make just about anything look possible? It's all about how well and how fast you can connect a few dots.

If you want to really rip through this new to-do list of yours, take another look at your Grand Plan with a different question in mind— how to eliminate or skip various steps. That's part of the beauty of having this all charted out, too. Once you can see the process as a whole, as a series of multiple benchmarks, you can start to look a few steps ahead and find more creative ways to get where you're headed faster.

So where can you find shortcuts? Be creative. See if you can be working double duty on some of these. Knock out two, three, or four birds with one stone whenever you can. (Like in our example above, you could go see my favorite career counselor in the world, Bob Cohen, work on your résumé with him, get great leads from him on who's hiring, and check the on-site library of reference materials he keeps stocked, all in one visit.)

Also keep in mind that while we've set this Grand Plan up with some chronology in mind, feel free to jump around or mix up the order if you can check off items faster by taking a different route. This process is merely meant to provide some structure and clear goals to focus on. But by all means, adjust your plans so that they work for you. These are just guidelines to get you started.

Setting Up Time Lines

Okay, so let's go back to dreaming about becoming a rock star so we can take one more step to help spring you into action. Let's think about time for a minute. After all, one of the most popular excuses people use to justify why they don't have what they want is the one about not having enough time. So let's try to dispel that myth and look at what's really involved in taking these actions. Consider how long it might take to get to the first major benchmark—creating your own CD. Some time estimates would be helpful here, don't you think? Again, this is just an estimate. Keep in mind that a lot of this work can be done concurrently, too:

INTERMEDIATE STEPS	ESTIMATED TIME NEEDED
Choosing and perfecting ten best songs	1 month
Concept and design	2 months
Cost projections	2 weeks
Financing	TBD
Recording studio selection	1 week
Finding best printing and copying vendor	1 week
Distribution and sales strategy	2 months
Assessing risks and rewards	2 weeks
Executing the plan	45 days

In putting together estimated time lines it helps to consider the following:

- What really has to be done?

- What are all the components?

- What are my different options?

- Who do I know who can do this or help?

- Where will I get the resources?

- How am I going to pay (or barter) for what I need?

- What are potential challenges?

- What specific questions do I have?

- What information am I missing?

Once you've answered these questions for yourself, you should be able to see your own path taking shape. Then there's just one more question you need to ask: "What can I do *now*?" That's actually the crucial question that puts your plan in motion.

Start Now

Remember how we've seen that the Young & Successful just dream, and then do? Seemed so simple then, but if you were actually to start following some of the intermediate steps here to work on your first CD, you'd be doing just what they do already. Now that's not so hard, is it? If you make a big deal out of taking that first step, you probably never will.

The reason we look at our Grand Plan in such simple form is that we don't want it to be too complex in the beginning. Expecting to sit down and get every step of your future down the first time you try to plot it out—every job, every kind of work you'll do, every significant achievement you'll manage—is unrealistic and actually, totally unnecessary. No one expects us to articulate perfectly our plan right as we're formulating it. That's like your casually telling a friend that you're thinking about starting a business, and her asking for your business plan three minutes later. At this stage? Yeah, right. You're not going to put together a forty-page document just to kick around an idea. But you do want to have a good story to tell about what you're up to in the meantime.

In our Grand Plan we want to make a few sweeping generalizations and assumptions off the top of our heads. Turning that general inspiration into specific initial action steps right off the bat gets us working on our plan right away, instead of waiting for the "right time" that will likely never come. Creating this rough sketch reduces inertia. It allows us to get things done. How far you take it from here is your call. But I certainly hope you don't stop now. If you don't already have one, commit to writing down your Ideal Life, and how you plan to achieve it, through a Grand Plan of your own.

The Detail Is Up to You

When you look at this list of benchmarks, then at the intermediate steps, consider the fact that you have another choice to make: How detailed you get from here. Some people are more "big-picture oriented" or macro thinkers, while others are more "detail oriented," micro thinkers. But I can't tell you how far to go with your Grand Plan, because that's a choice you have to make on your own. There are some who will argue that too much planning leads to lack of doing. And there are just as many others who'll disagree and claim that too much doing and not enough planning is irresponsible and reckless. You have to be the judge for yourself. How you approach planning and goal setting is going to be largely dependent on your personality and your style—being "big picture" or "detail focused."

My job is to show you both ends of the spectrum and have you play the whole field, rather than getting too comfortable or stuck in one particular style of doing things. You will naturally gravitate in one direction or another and that's fine. I just want you to be as prepared as possible. What do I mean? Well, here's a quick example. Take me and Scott. Within our organization, we have two styles of doing things, but because we share the same goals, we have to work together to balance. Along the way, we're forced to consider both sides of any equation. This is where you can walk the fine line of being compatible, complementary, and on the verge of killing each other. Welcome to the world of partnerships!

As far as Scott and I go, naturally, I have my way and he has his. Scott thinks strategically and is big picture in his thinking, but he is still more detail oriented than I've ever been. Before he does something, he researches it exhaustively, calculates every contingency, and contemplates dozens of options. I, on the other hand, am action oriented, preferring to spend my time plotting, promoting, marketing, and selling rather than dealing with logistic and minute details. Scott argues to take more time and contemplate. My inclination is to start now and see what happens.

Either approach, if relied on to the extreme, would be risky for business.

What makes our partnership work so well is that we each drag the other to our side to convey our perspective, before agreeing on a common ground. As a result, we first get the benefit of looking at the whole spectrum of options and approaches.

That's what I want you to do when creating and executing your Grand Plan. You don't need a partner to consider all the options and play both sides of the field. I didn't have a formal partner to lean on for most of my career, either. But I did always have a few outstanding people—whether they were employees, consultants, advisors, or friends—close by to keep me grounded in my planning and objective in my decision making.

Whether you're working on your own or with others, never forget that there are a variety of ways to handle any given challenge, situation, or opportunity. And as I like to say, you can't run out of options, just creativity. Think as many options through as you can imagine and I promise this approach will pay off in spades for you. Yes, it's more exhausting, but the benefits to being both macro- and micro-level focused are significant:

- You will have a more complete understanding of what you're dealing with.

- You'll make smarter, better informed decisions.

- You'll waste a lot less time and energy.

- You'll have answers to the questions and criticisms of your chosen approach.

- You can better evaluate the probable consequences to any decisions before you make them and choose accordingly.

- You will limit the likelihood of unwelcome surprises.

Considering all the benefits, how could you not at least give a Grand Plan of your own some serious thought?

Our job right now is to help you develop a Grand Plan that works for you. You do have to be ready to make some decisions and choices, though—not only about what you do, but *how* you do it.

Now, we want *you* to do it, not your friend or teacher. Below you'll find a simple worksheet for starting your own Grand Plan, in case you haven't begun to sketch it out already. Just like we showed you above, all you have to do is pick a specific goal in one of your Ideal Life areas, plot your points, and connect the dots. When applied to each of the different components of your Ideal Life, this simple tool will help jump-start the creation of *your* Grand Plan draft and details. Most important, it's a flexible tool that can be easily adopted or adapted to guide you in achieving even your loftiest goals and dreams. So pick a major area of your life that you want to start with and give it a shot.

Advanced Grand Planning

If you've had enough of this planning for now, don't worry about it. You can always come back and finish this section later. However, don't forget that this chapter is all about how you create a workable plan of action to make even your most ambitious goals come true. We won't be insulted if you decide to skip ahead to the next chapter for some quick gratification. But if you're really serious about expediting yourself on your path to success and getting started immediately, this next section should be exactly what you're looking for. Here, we'll walk you through, step by step, the creation of your own Grand Plan.

Give it a shot. You could be only a few minutes away from seeing your options in a completely different perspective.

GRAND PLAN DEVELOPMENT SYSTEM™

On the following work sheet or on a separate sheet of paper, follow the simple steps below to create the beginnings of your own Grand Plan.

1. **Ideal Life Component/Category**
   Chose an area of your Ideal Life that you want to focus on. Remember to use a new work sheet for each new area or major goal (career, finances, personal development, health, relationships, etc.).

2. **Status Today**

   Include a brief description of your current situation or where you're starting from at this exact moment in time, in this particular category.

3. **Major Benchmarks**

   Write out the major benchmarks or achievements (in chronological order) that would form a logical path to lead you to achieving your Ideal Situation.

4. **Intermediate Action Steps**

   Work out your first set of intermediate steps that, when taken, will lead you to connect one benchmark to the next. You might want to write the intermediate steps between each of the benchmarks on a separate piece of paper.

5. **Estimated Time**

   Take a guess at how long it should take you to complete each action step and record your estimates at the left. Commit to a fair time line that you will target to complete each of these steps.

6. **Top Assets & Liabilities**

   Refer to your Personal Balance Sheet (described on pages 39–44) and list any assets or liabilities that may help or hinder you as you pursue each of the action steps. Use this list to think about how you can either strengthen, build upon, or acquire any assets that may help you in your quest for success. Likewise, consider how you can minimize the effects of or eliminate altogether any liabilities that could hamper your progress.

7. **Ideal Life Realization**

   Last, finish off the exercise with a little reminder of what you're working toward in the first place. What will signify for you that you've achieved your Ideal Situation or goal?

GRAND PLAN WORKSHEET

Ideal Life Component/Category:

_____

Status Today:

_____
_____
_____
_____

Major Benchmark 1:

_____

Intermediate Action Steps:	Est. Time:	Top Assets & Liabilities
_____	_____	_____
_____	_____	_____
_____	_____	_____
_____	_____	_____

Major Benchmark 2:

_____

Major Benchmark 3:

_____

Major Benchmark 4:

_____

Major Benchmark 5:

_____

My Ideal Life will be realized in this category when:

_____

_____

_____

⚡ Productive Dreaming

When it comes to considering, creating, and working their Grand Plan, one of the *Secrets of the Young & Successful* involves learning to make great use of their downtime. The trick is in identifying little pockets of time throughout your day when you could actually be dreaming about and planning your future. Think about it for a minute. How confident are you in your ability to achieve all the benchmarks you've laid out for yourself? If there are any looming questions in your mind, the answer might just be to work a little harder or, even better, think a little smarter.

The Young & Successful are always contemplating their situations, their strategies, and their opportunities. Whether they're standing in line at a movie theater or a store, driving, walking to a meeting, or waiting for someone, the Young & Successful are planning their work and working their plan. The more time you spend consciously thinking about how your plan will all come together, the more active your subconscious becomes in uncovering the solutions you've been searching for. Consider this for a minute: if you spent just twenty minute a day—instead of mindlessly *standing* in line, *waiting* for friends, or *sitting* in a car—over the course of one month, you'd have spent ten hours contemplating your Grand Plan and execution strategy. Half an hour a day, of otherwise wasted time, would give you fifteen hours, and stealing an hour a day (even in little chunks) would give you thirty hours a month! Now compare that to the time you're currently investing in crafting your strategy to get everything you want.

The Young & Successful are constantly asking themselves: "What will it feel like?" "What will I need to do?" "How will my lifestyle change?" "How can I achieve these objectives faster?" You should too. This is still a form of dreaming, just a more proactive and productive way of doing it that makes the dreams of the Young & Successful concrete and complete. By doing this, they already have considered what the various pieces look like, feel like, smell like, and to them, their plans, their dreams become that much more real and exciting . . . not to mention achievable.

People used to tell me that I exhausted them. I always had a new idea or a new project to talk about. (Okay, I admit, maybe I still do.) My brainstorms and epiphanies were a constant source of excitement and motivation for me—but they could be overwhelming to anyone listening to me talk about them.

That's why I love Dashiell's and Wendy's stories, because I'm the same way, too. When I'm at the movies, I get ideas. When I watch television, I see new opportunities. When I go for a walk on the beach I remember things that have gotten lost in the shuffle. When I'm sitting on a plane, I chat up the people around or plunge into a pile of articles I've been meaning to read. When I sit at a café or go for coffee, I'm thinking about how I could be doing things better, or about what I'm missing in my current approach to something I'm working on. This isn't to say that I'm not enjoying what I'm doing. I thrive on multitasking. Some people watch television and read the Sunday paper at the same time. It's no different.

I don't want to come across as if I'm saying you should work constantly, because that's not my point. It's certainly critical to let our brains rest and our bodies go down for the count. Downtime is definitely a must. But what I'm concerned about is the time we waste in the course of day-to-day life when we're not working and not resting but meandering in between.

For example, I used to laugh at Scott and my mom for always having articles and books with them wherever they went. Whether it was to a car wash, a movie, the market, the bank, even to a Broadway play, I could never understand how they could be so concerned with having something to read within arm's length. Did they really feel compelled to read every spare minute? Why wouldn't they just enjoy what they were out to do in the first place? Then I started hanging out with them more, and started to notice that there were a lot of times that we were just sitting around waiting—at the bank, car wash, dentist office, in a twenty-minute line for a movie, or even a forty-five-minute wait at a restaurant. And during all that time, they had interesting things to do. I didn't.

Soon, I was carrying stuff around with me too (a few letters, some note cards, bills, a magazine, pictures, etc.). It meant that I had a choice when I got stuck at a big intersection: I could open a bill and at least know where I stood with Citibank, or I could just sit there and stare at all the cars around me.

The point is, few of us ever seem to have enough time to do all the things we want to do. And we run out of time far too often. The Young & Successful solution: Beg, borrow, or steal time wherever you can to make more room for what's really important to you. That's the beauty of multitasking. Acting strategically by dreaming productively makes a difference in practically everything we do.

RULING THE AIRWAVES

Paul O'Malley was a student at Ithaca College when he got his first taste of how a little strategic thinking could help him pursue his dream of being a broadcaster. He didn't waste any time either. As soon as he discovered that the college had its own TV and radio stations, Paul signed on, one after the other, as an on-air personality. A little experience and a lot of strategic thinking later, Paul found that the Grand Plan he was slowly forming did not necessarily involve having his voice and face on the air. Like many Young & Successful people, Paul found his Grand Plan revealing an even better path and a more perfectly suited career. Within a few years, an old softball coach of Paul's who worked at a local radio station encouraged him to come work in the sales department. Actually, when Paul arrived, his friend just threw a big city phone book at him and instructed him to go sell advertising time to whoever would buy it. I guess that's what you call "baptism by fire."

So Paul spent six months on the phone hearing, "no, no, no, no," until one day someone said "yes" and his lucky streak began. Turns out, he claims to have been so naïve that he just kept calling these businesses over and over until they couldn't resist (or get rid of him!). Soon Paul, the youngest employee at the radio station by fifteen years, was selling more ad time than anyone, and his friends were shocked at the money he was making. By twenty-two he had given up his dream of being an on-air personality and set his sights on being the president of a radio station.

After working in his hometown of Rochester for a while, Paul was given an opportunity to move to New York City to join Katz Media, the biggest national radio ad sales firm in the country. By twenty-eight, Paul became the youngest vice president (of only four) and watched his salary jump from thirty-five thousand dollars to seventy-five thousand almost overnight. Katz then promoted and moved Paul to Atlanta to manage sales for a leading station there, then to Washington and St. Louis.

Apparently his employers weren't the only ones hearing about his stellar reputation. One day the general manager of a Los Angeles station, KYSR, Star 98.7—the sixteenth largest in the nation—called to invite him on board as the director of sales.

Four years later Paul's boss left, and guess who became general manager and head of the station? While GMs of top stations in major media markets like Los Angeles are typically in their mid forties, Paul again is about ten years ahead of the game at just thirty-six. And as yet another rewarding perk, his job also involves grooming another young star who's years ahead of *his* time. At just twenty-six, Ryan Seacrest is Star's afternoon drive-time host and is fast becoming one of the highest rated personalities in America. You might have even seen Ryan (one of the hottest Young & Successful people out there) hosting *American Idol, Extra!* or as one of *People* magazine's Top 30 People Under 30.

Oh, and as for Paul, to date he's credited with driving his station up to seventh in the nation . . . and he's just getting warmed up. Nice to have achieved your most outrageous dreams by your mid thirties, eh?

Ready to get serious with your Grand Plan now? Well let me show you one last example. Prepare to witness some strategic thinking that's perhaps more intense than anything you've ever seen. For this, you have to meet Phil Tirone.

TOO WIRED TO SIT

Philip Tirone is by far the most detailed, comprehensive, and intensive Grand Planner I've ever met. In fact, he's kind of fanatical. But I figured you might learn a thing or two from him and his dedication to constantly improving himself. I sure have.

At any given time he might have fifteen pages of goals printed out that he reads through every day and updates at least every three months. Think he's crazy? Well so do his coworkers, but his record of success speaks for itself. And besides, Phil stopped listening to people who didn't motivate or support him years ago.

Phil has had big dreams since his first day on the job. He's also realized that if he wanted to make them come true, he needed a plan. What was the dream? Well Phil always wanted to be in the real-estate business. That's what his father had always done, and that's what Phil began doing right out of college. In those days, Phil was selling homes of a retirement community in Arizona. Not a bad job, just not the most exciting career for a young guy like Phil.

He knew he wanted a change, and he created the most comprehensive, thoroughly scrutinized long-term plan that I've ever seen. Since then, he's calculated just about everything in his personal and professional life, and he's created forecasts that carry him well into the next twenty-five years. He's constantly reworking and readjusting his Grand Plan. But he wasn't always this anal. It was actually back in high school when he found himself graduating with a 1.8 GPA and an 800

SAT score that he started to plan. You may think it unnecessary for you to chart *everything* the way Phil does. But the fact
that he looks at every part of his life and business in depth, at
regular intervals, and believes that this is a key to his success,
should make you think twice.

The following page is an actual copy of Phil's summary sheet. He
was sweet enough to share it here with the world for two reasons: First,
Grand Planning changed his life, and he's always up for the chance to
encourage others to try it for themselves. Second, Phil is big on creating
accountability, which means he likes to share his goals with people he
trusts so that they hold him to his pursuits. (Speaking of accountability,
this is another little secret of the Young & Successful—they share their
aspirations with people who stimulate and motivate them so that they
have that extra level of accountability.)

Looking at Phil's goals (just a year's worth, mind you), you can just
imagine what the other fifty pages look like.

For some people, goal setting is all about business, but for Young &
Successful people like Phil, Grand Planning is something they use to
sculpt their entire life.

Take a look at how Phil lays out his goals and illustrates his plans.
As you'll soon see, Phil's Grand Plan has been known to motivate quite
a few people to try to achieve more in their lives.

Phil Tirone's Three Most Important Improvements
in Each Area of Life: 2002

1. **Health**
   A. Coffee only on occasions
   B. 80 percent live foods
   C. 8 percent body fat and 160 lbs.

2. **Relationships**
   A. Being there for those important moments in my friends' lives
   B. Better relatedness when I'm in a conversation—NO DRIFTING
   C. Meet my future wife

3. **Money—Make and Handle**
   A. 1.0 mil net worth by 9/1/02
   B. Meet with CPA and financial advisor—1x/quarter
   C. Passive income to be $7,500 by 12/02 (alternative income from other investment requiring little or no ongoing effort)

4. **Time**
   A. Not completely controlled by my business, however, maintaining same growth
   B. More detailed schedule, which will make me more effective with my time

5. **Capabilities**
   A. Being able to control my body—through dance, martial arts, and piano
   B. Being able to sell and motivate unlike any other
   C. Being able to pray in silence without falling asleep

6. **Reputation**
   A. Warrior/confidence—*"He's very sure of himself, and at the same time, a very real person . . ."*
   B. Relentless conviction—*"When he makes up his mind to pursue something, he does so with relentless conviction . . ."*
   C. Symbol of integrity—*"When people want to talk to someone grounded in integrity and morality, they go to Philip X. Tirone . . ."*

7. **Clients**
   A. Receiving hourly referrals from my past clients and spheres of influence
   B. Giving each client the impression of providing a service that's *"over the top"*

8. **Delegation and Teamwork**
   A. Inspiring people to act
   B. Knowing what to delegate—delegate, not abandon

9. **Contribution to Community**
   A. My energy—by eating healthier, I will have more energy and be able to do more
   B. My money—tithe 11 percent of income

10. **Personal and Spiritual Growth**
   A. Renaissance man—able to enjoy the arts
   B. 30 minutes of silent prayer/day
   C. Attend mass every day in 2002

11. **Professional Growth**
   A. #3 at First Capital in 2002 earned income

How well has this system worked for Phil? Well, at the age of twenty-nine, with less than *four years'* experience, Phil's one of the top residential mortgage brokers in the country, earning a substantial six-figure income, totally on commissions. Now how's that for results?

Phil's business is all about numbers—numbers of calls, numbers of relationships, numbers of deals. His professional plan calculates the numbers for everything, including tracking his historical and projected closing ratios. From day one, his goal was to post numbers like no one had ever seen before. In his second year in the business, his professional plan called for him to make 45,000 calls. (The industry average is around 25,000.) And he did it, right after he threw out his old office desk and replaced it with a special architect's desk that forced him to stand as he worked. Why would he do that? Because he said it keeps him on his toes while he makes his calls. It also inspired him to install a second phone line and phone so while he is leaving a message on one, he can be dialing a new person on the other. And believe it or not, he has now managed to maximize practically every minute of his time at work.

What's different about Phil is that he's a disciplined dreamer and planner. He dreams of what he wants, plans his actions, works his plan, and reaches or exceeds his goals consistently and religiously. Then he moves on to the next goal, raising the bar with each success under his belt.

As ironic as it may sound, this is really simple, folks. Every business, every idea, can—at least in part—be reduced to a set of achievable, strategic goals. You just need a few of the initial steps laid out. Then it's all about connecting the dots.

GRAND PLAN ACTION OVERVIEW

In each of your Ideal Life components, let's start to add some accountability into the mix and get you committed to working your Grand Plan today. The most challenging part of strategic planning is taking those first few steps: writing out your goals and starting to check them off the list. They can be improvements, actions, or specific achievements—whatever ambitions continue to linger at the top of your to-do list. Use this simple work sheet to put your own list together and commit yourself to knocking off your top three goals or priorities as soon as possible. The power and momentum it will give you are certain to propel you forward and likely to get you closer to your Ideal Life than ever before.

My Ideal Life Category: _____

Top Action Items: _____

Target Date: _____

Personal
(physical, mental, health)
1. _____
2. _____

Key Relationships
(family, significant other, friends, advisors, colleagues)
1. _____
2. _____

Career/Professional Life

1. _____

2. _____

Education

1. _____

2. _____

Financial/Money Matters

1. _____

2. _____

Spirituality/Religion

1. _____

2. _____

Giving Back/Contribution

1. _____

2. _____

Other

1. _____

2. _____

Making the Plan Yours

Your Grand Plan may start as a sketch and end up as fifty pages with one hundred different benchmarks. It may also just remain a sheet of paper with a few bullet points. You just want enough detail to see the path that can connect where you are today to where you want to be.

Time spent envisioning your future and making plans to make that vision real is time well spent—as long as you're doing things to keep moving forward and progress in the rest of your life. A plan doesn't come together in a minute or a day. It takes time. Time you have to carve out of your days, time that you have to steal from the rest of your life. Commit the necessary time to start crafting your plans now. Figure out the steps that will make your vision materialize. The Young & Successful know that this is one of the most valuable things they can do with their time.

Focus on You

In order to accomplish all of the things you need to do, you may have to do something your mom warned you not to—be a little selfish, with your time that is. Now don't misunderstand me and take this out of context, because I'm the first person to tell you to do everything you can to help other people whenever you can. However, far too many young people forget that this is perhaps the only time in their life that they're not attached at the hip to other people. And I don't mean girlfriends or boyfriends here. In the first part of our lives, we typically live under the roof of other people who take care of us and raise us. We clearly have serious responsibilities to them while we're there. When we grow up and get married or have kids, again, we share a roof with others. This time, it's our responsibility to be the providers.

What I'm trying to say is treat the precious few years in between these two stages as yours and yours alone. Your life won't always be so flexible. Realize that your youth affords you the ability to be a little selfish now, perhaps for one of the only times in your life. Make as much headway before your life gets crowded with other concerns, and you don't have the luxury of being able to focus as intensely on yourself and your own personal development as you can right now.

This is not the time in your life to waste time and slack off. This is the time for you to get ahead and give yourself every possible advantage. What you do and accomplish now can make all the difference in how the rest of your life plays out.

Part Two

5 Master Your Universe™

FOR HUNDREDS OF YEARS, MAN BELIEVED THAT Earth was the center of the universe. When a young astronomer named Copernicus challenged the theory with one of his own—that *the sun* was in fact the center of the universe—he was condemned for contradicting Scripture. Then more than a hundred years later in 1610, Galileo looked up to the sky with the right tools and began to confirm Copernicus's theory. With a telescope in his hands, Galileo reported that he had seen the moons, the stars, the planets, and that they did not, in fact, circle Earth but rather the sun. He had finally obtained proof.

The Young & Successful know that you can theorize all you want but, eventually, we all have to do the research, find the right tools, and prove our grand aspirations to ourselves and to the world.

The Young & Successful have an uncanny ability to acquire the valuable information they need to get where they want to go. That's why learning to "master your universe" is such a powerful secret to them. It's easy to find people who want to be a part of a world or industry but have no clue how to do it. It's also commonplace to see people within an industry or career who really have no idea how it works, who the players are, how to leverage what they know, and how to become successful within it. These are all mysteries for lots of people. If you're one of them, I promise it won't be a mystery for you much longer. Because once you learn to master a universe, the way that the Young

& Successful do, you'll be able to enter and thrive in any world you choose.

This is a complex issue—I won't sugarcoat that. But because Scott and I really believe that this represents one of the biggest skills (not to mention secrets) that separates the ultrasuccessful from everyone else, it was important for us to analyze it and boil the process down into a system that we could teach. So here it is.

The process of mastering your universe involves five steps:

1 identifying the world you want to play in

2 articulating your critical questions

3 making your own map of the universe

4 doing high-level research

5 leveraging what you learn to master your universe

We Live Among Many Worlds

Our first order of business is to identify the worlds we want to play in. But before we do that, we need to define these different worlds and understand how they affect us, whether we're intimately involved in them or not.

For example, on any given day, you might interact with a few dozen different worlds:

· wake up and take your vitamins (*the pharmaceutical world*)

· turn on the news (*the media world*)

- grab some eggs and bacon for breakfast (*the agricultural world*)

- hop in your car (*the automotive world*)

- go to your office (*the corporate world*)

- lunch at a drive-through (*the fast-food world*)

- spend a few hours at a trade show (*that industry's world*)

- eat a nice dinner with friends (*the fine dining world*)

- go to a movie (*the entertainment world*)

- stop in the bookstore (*the publishing world*)

- catch a recap of the big basketball game on TV (*the sports world*)

Just as vast as the stars are the different industries, communities, cultures, people, and places that we live among right here on Earth. If you look closely, you'll discover that the universe is a big place that's intricately linked. And each of these worlds is explicable. Once you find the ones most important to you, you can open them up, gain an intimate understanding of how they work, and carve out your own special place within them.

If you haven't yet thought about which worlds affect you—both professionally and personally—you should, because your experience within them will become so much richer, and your ability to achieve success within them, significantly greater.

One world that Scott and I are particularly consumed in (especially since we came up with the idea for this book) is the publishing world. To turn the grand idea we started with (publishing this book) into a reality, we first had to craft our own Grand Plan. Then we had to identify the world we needed to play in (publishing, in this case) and arm our-selves with all the information, insight, and knowledge possible to suc-cessfully hit our benchmarks. But there were so many different things to understand and so many little areas that we needed to become compe-tent in. So we dove in and followed the very systematic approach we're explaining here. First we had to break the world open.

How do you break open a world that you're interested in? Just think about this book you're reading, which has taken an enormous amount of people and processes to get to you. In fact, for this dream to materialize, people from all areas of the publishing world had to be brought to-gether. For example:

- We needed to pitch it.

- Our lawyer needed to negotiate a deal.

- Our publisher had to buy it.

- Scott and I had to write it.

- Our editor had to edit it.

- A copyeditor and proofreaders needed to review it.

- A designer had to lay out the final text.

- A cover designer had to illustrate the cover.

- The sales force had to generate orders from bookstores.

- Printers had to print the books.

- Truckers needed to ship boxes around the country.

- Bookstores needed to stock it.

- Other successful authors and industry leaders had to en-dorse it.

- Trade publications had to review it.

- Magazines and newspapers needed to write about it.

- TV and radio shows had to talk about it.

- And you, or someone who cares about you, had to buy it . . .

All that so our idea could be transformed into the book you hold in your hands right now. If we hadn't taken the time to learn this process, and how this world works to put these plans in motion, neither of us would be here right now.

If you're not in the book business, you've probably never given much thought to what goes on behind the scenes in this world. And that's understandable, but take a look at the worlds that are important to you—your industry, your career, your community—and think about how tapped in you are where it does count for you.

Whether you're a movie junkie, sports fanatic, or big industry expert, you're probably more familiar with those worlds than, say, what happens behind the scenes at your favorite night spot. The point is that based on who we are, what we do, and what interests us, we participate in all these worlds—and more—every day in varying degrees.

As you can imagine, when Scott and I go into a bookstore, our experience is probably different from yours. This is a part of the publishing world that has not only become important to us but has also become fascinating, as we've continued to learn more and more about it.

If you go to a bookstore, you'll see a lot of people run in, grab a magazine, and bolt out. When Scott and I go into a bookstore, we take the place apart. We engage fully. On any given trip, we're likely to dive deep into this world, picking up dozens of books and magazines, scanning the aisles, analyzing the displays, talking to the employees, and even watching what people buy. Since we're hoping to make our mark on this world, we strive to extract all of the pertinent information that we can. And if it takes us two hours to get our fix, we're thrilled to have had the opportunity to spend so much time in this world and extract so much while there.

What do we do with all this information? We're searching for ideas to formulate new marketing strategies. We're looking at all the new books so we can assess the competitive environment. We're noticing how different sections of the store are being expanded or scaled down to ensure we're focused on a growing category. We're watching the people coming into the store, what they're picking up, putting down, and what they're eventually buying. When we study the display tables, talk to the associates and observe the traffic patterns, we further understand which books are selling and why. We're looking for emerging trends so we can best address what readers are looking for.

The inside scoop that we get from analyzing a bookstore is important because it arms us with insight useful in formulating our plans. That information, in turn, we can share in big meetings and presentations—not only to earn attention and respect but to help guide us in making strategic decisions that can propel us in the right direction.

Now, granted, this is a pretty intense example, but when I sit down with a bunch of guys who are watching a great sporting event, the conversations and analysis can get just as intense. Often the exchange of knowledge and depth of insight are simply staggering. Some people behave similarly when they go shopping, when they travel, when they tackle a new career path, or engage in any world they have a real passion for. What the Young & Successful know is that it's actually necessary to dive in like this if you want to gain the real-world expertise and experience required to fast-track your route to success, however you may define it.

Scott's Adventure in the Restaurant World

This process of breaking open a world and finding great opportunities within it is a familiar one for Scott, because he's done it before, in the restaurant industry. As he approached graduation from the University of Maryland, Scott had developed a real passion for international business strategic planning and knew that whatever he did, business development and consulting would be a big part of it. He hadn't, however, figured out what industry to focus his energy on. After analyzing several different markets, Scott narrowed his choices down to the real-estate world and the food business. His logic was pretty straightforward—everyone needs a place to live and work, and everyone has to eat—so these industries would always be around and hold a variety of opportunities. After completing a real estate sales course over the summer, he realized that while he might want to invest in real estate in the future, he was not interested in making a career out of it. So he began to explore the restaurant industry.

While taking the real estate classes, Scott had also begun watching various trends in the quick-service (fast food) world unfold, more specifically in the emerging fast-casual and gourmet-frozen-dessert niches. He was pretty familiar with frozen dessert concepts, as his family owned and operated a couple of Baskin-Robbins stores while he was growing up, but he had never really looked at it from this new perspective. Having liked the higher quality concepts he saw emerging within the industry, he made the decision to dive headfirst into the restaurant world. His thought from there was, "If I'm going to go into this, I'm really going to learn this business." And he did.

His journey began by searching for the main trade association. One Internet search later, he found the National Restaurant Association in Washington, D.C. Picking up the phone, he asked about what information he could get on the industry, and they gladly mailed him a big package of literature produced by the organization (a list of facts about the industry, many internally published reports, membership information, etc.). They also recommended a number of books and publications. Like many trade organizations, they maintained a comprehensive library of information on their industry. After reviewing the material they'd sent him, Scott enjoyed what he'd read and decided to take a trip to the headquarters to visit this library.

Within minutes of arriving, Scott was blown away. Not only was there an incredible amount of industry information all in one place (which, incidentally, dated back decades), but there were courteous librarians on staff to help visitors like him weed through the vast collection of books, original trade publications, articles, and reports. (What a warm welcome to a foreign world!) There was information here on every aspect of the industry imaginable.

Scott recalls: "It was like taking a step back in time to the beginning of the industry. I was able to trace the major events, learn about the key people and companies who shaped the industry, and read and photocopy practically every story (whether it was pro or con about the industry) I was interested in that had been written. It was incredible!"

Soon, Scott decided to order subscriptions to all the leading trade publications (several of which were actually free), including the weekly "industry bible" *National Restaurant News,* and magazines like *Restaurant & Institutions, Restaurant Business,* and *Chain Leader.* He also read the biographies or autobiographies of many past and present industry leaders including, Ray Kroc of McDonald's, Dave Thomas of Wendy's, James McLamore of Burger King, and Howard Schultz of Starbucks, to name a few.

By doing his homework, devouring books, talking to people in all areas of the industry, and taking a taste of the industry (both figuratively and literally), Scott collected and analyzed hundreds of menus from around the country. With every bit of new information, Scott became even more convinced that he wanted to work within the restaurant world and perhaps even develop his own concept. He continuously asked himself questions about which areas fascinated him most. Soon it was clear that his primary interests centered around how concepts were developed, refined, and then mass duplicated all around the world, either through franchising or in-house corporate development.

After Scott talked over some of his ideas and discoveries with his mentor, Dr. Rudy Lamone, former dean of the University of Maryland business school, Dr. Lamone introduced him to Kurt Aarsand, a Young & Successful restaurant operator, who owned numerous Taco Bell and KFC restaurants in the mid-Atlantic region. Kurt agreed to meet Scott and walk him through the steps involved in starting and operating a chain of franchised restaurants. He also gave him a firsthand look at how he ran his own company. Sometime later, Kurt even set Scott up to spend a day visiting a handful of stores, right alongside his director of operations, who oversaw his entire operation.

On the strength of what Scott had learned so far, and what he was shown by Kurt, Scott went around the United States exploring and uncovering information about new, emerging concepts. A little after graduation, he moved to Boston, a hotbed of new restaurant concept development. After spending a few weeks getting settled, and a little more research on local fast casual concepts, Scott found an article about a great local Italian concept that was gearing up for major growth. The owner was a guy named Frank DePasquale, a leading restaurateur in Boston's famous North End. (This particular restaurant, turned out to be just one of Frank's seven unique restaurant concepts!)

Scott loved the food and the concept so much that he decided to track down the owner. At one of Frank's other restaurants in the area, Scott told the bartender how much he wanted to meet Frank and why. So the bartender went over to Frank and soon waved him over. They hit it off immediately. Frank said he was impressed by Scott's effort to come and see him and all the research he had done and knowledge he had gained in such a short time. Within a few weeks, they settled on terms for Scott to help him further develop and roll out his new concept.

It wasn't long after he started working for Frank that Scott found himself gaining tremendous hands-on experience—negotiating a slew of new contracts for soda, paper goods, produce, real estate, website development, register systems, bank lines of credit, etc.—with some of the giants in the food-service industry. He was also charged with documenting the complete operational systems of the concept for its first operations and recipe manuals. That gave him the opportunity to attend his first industry trade show. Before long, power meetings and deal brokering with companies like Pepsico, Micros, Grubb & Ellis real-estate brokers, and many others were becoming second nature. It was truly an incredible training ground.

After about a year, personal reasons caused Frank to scale back his original plans for the aggressive rollout of his concept, and before long Scott found himself consulting for a wide range of entrepreneurs and local industry players. With each experience, his goal became more and more clear. He wanted to try to develop and grow his own concept.

With a ton of research, a string of tastes, and a good amount of real-world knowledge and experience under his belt, Scott decided to move to Los Angeles to continue his consulting business and take a crack at developing his own concept. Soon he began to meet many of the local players, and was even elected as the youngest member to the L.A. board of California Restaurant Association—a branch of the National Restaurant Association, which had kicked off his whole exploration of the industry in the first place!

In between consulting projects, he met several new mentors with great experience in the industry. As he proceeded to open and build his first concept—a healthier, higher-quality quick service restaurant—he encountered some tough (and pretty humbling) experiences. Though he had put together some of the most impressive plans, menus, documentation and operational experts his investors claimed to have ever seen, Scott's biggest challenge was securing the necessary development capital to proceed. As the final missing piece, his plans were eventually devastated because his own pockets weren't deep enough.

After a few weeks and some serious depression, Scott managed to pick himself up, reflect on what he had learned, and bounce back to develop his own gourmet frozen dessert concept. This time, he opened a concept store and even got his first feature article (with a giant color photo!) on the cover of a special section of *The Wall Street Journal*.

Throughout his four-year adventure in the restaurant world, Scott gained access to some of the most successful companies, entrepreneurs, experts, and educators in the industry—like the founders of the Cheesecake Factory, Boston Market, and California Pizza Kitchen, the former chairman of Burger King, the president of Baskin-Robbins, the author of *Winning the Chain Restaurant Game*, the publisher of *National Restaurant News*, and many other.

Along the way, Scott discovered just how powerful research and gathering specialized information is to the Young & Successful and how much you can learn by strategically navigating around an industry. Most important, he learned that the restaurant industry is a tight-knit world with its own unique history, norms, successes, failures, power players, and niches. The more knowledge he acquired, and the more people he met, the more connections he was able to establish, resulting in the creation of an intricate web of relationships. Best yet, each and every person he met, whether he or she was the manager of a small store or the CEO or founder of an international chain, added another dimension to his knowledge base. As in any industry, there were many layers and angles to consider, so Scott focused on a niche—the quick service fast-food franchise market—and dove as deep as he could. Because his intention was to gain the most sophisticated level of under-standing possible, and to really become as much a "master of this uni-verse" as he could, he dove headfirst into the most comprehensive research effort he had ever undertaken.

In record time, Scott went from someone who knew almost noth-ing about the quick-service industry to a respected expert who, as a con-sultant, was well paid and respected for his knowledge and unique insight. Today, he strongly believes that anyone can accomplish similar, if not greater results, in any industry she chooses in record time if she takes a systemized approach as he did.

As in all great adventures, Scott had plenty of highs and lows. Soon Scott found himself in a quandary. The once booming restaurant indus-try was maturing to the point where the market for new concepts was growing less and less fertile for the rapid-growth strategy that Scott was intent on pursuing. He knew he had to reassess his options and plans. During a big restaurant finance conference in Dallas, he got the answer to his biggest question. The summary of all the discussions that seemed to be taking place was loud and clear. "If you have a new or young con-cept and you're not already a 250-million-dollar company, or don't have access to plenty of your own money, either find a way to acquire your way to this size, or consider getting out of the business. The money to develop and grow hot new concepts has pretty much dried up in this economy." Hearing this from the top people in the industry (and not having an uncle Albert!), it became all too clear that if Scott was to stay on this path, he'd likely have to struggle through the next ten years to *hopefully* get to where he wanted to go. Or he could take all he had learned and move on to something else.

Armed with a new, intimate understanding of how to do research and uncover the most intricate details and emerging opportunities in any world, Scott knew he'd acquired and refined a powerful new set of skills. It was clear that he could replicate his efforts and gain this kind of insight in virtually any industry. Besides, the idea of tackling an entirely new world now seemed like quite an interesting challenge. Now he only had to decide which one.

So Scott made the tough decision to get out, sell his frozen dessert concept store, and move on to something more attractive, even more personally fulfilling, with shorter time lines, greater available capital for growth, and strong long-term potential for success. Out of the corner of his eye, he had been watching several new niches developing within the media and education worlds for some time. It wasn't long before he realized that these were the industries he wanted to jump into next. Incidentally, that's when we joined forces, and Young & Successful Media Corp. was created. What happened from there is a whole other story. This book is just the first part of that.

So Whadda Ya Wanna Know?

Now let's think about the questions you have to answer. You've probably come up with quite a few at this point already, but I want to build that list so that you have a clear purpose in mind when we show you how to uncover industry research like a pro.

Go back to your benchmarks and construct a laundry list of questions that will fill in any blanks for you. If at any point you wondered "How do I do that?" "Who can help me?" "Where do I find the best resources?" or "Who has done what I want to do successfully?" then you're already on a roll. Keep going. It can't be stressed enough how important it is to learn to formulate your own probing questions, then learn how to answer them on your own. It may sound rather simplistic, but you'd be amazed how difficult this is for so many.

Try to identify every possible piece of information that's standing in the way of your getting what you want professionally. Maybe there's one big lingering question you have about how to make it all possible.

This is where you're going to find your answers. It's also where you'll learn how to answer any question you could ever have, about anything you ever decide to do, from here on out.

Knowing how to research is a success secret that will serve you at every stage of your life and career. If a particular field or industry interests you, learn all you can about it before you make your bigger moves. At first, if you're not sure where to start, stick to the basics. Use your Grand Plan to start formulating your questions. You can always also focus on the three most critical factors in any industry:

1   Who are the customers who buy and the target market that's being pitched?

2   Who are the industry players or most prominent and most pivotal people?

3   What do the economics of the industry look like?

Or as one of my favorite professors in college, Jules Schwartz, used to say, "How do you make a buck in this business?" Start finding answers to those three questions and you're guaranteed to start hitting on some of the most critical information you need in any career, business, industry, or community.

Oh, the Possibilities!

Regardless of what you're looking to do, your chances of succeeding improve immensely when you have a grasp of the players, the whole playing field, and the big picture. There's an enormous amount of information out there to be uncovered . . . if of course you can find it.

Odds are there's no one place and no one set of facts sitting out there waiting for you. When you start finding the information you need, at first it's probably going to look more like a scavenger hunt list than you'd like. But what do you expect? You're going to be looking for information on people, places, things and, oftentimes, numbers. Sometimes the more random the information, the better, because you never really know how the pieces fit together until you have a bunch of them to throw out on the table and compare. Always remember that you should first cast a wide net, then let the information guide you to your goal because

- You never know where or when some piece of information can come in handy, or just what or who having it may lead to.

- You may discover something you never knew existed.

- You may find something that others have dismissed too prematurely.

- You could find evidence of a possible new opportunity or niche for yourself.

- You could stumble upon a missing piece of the puzzle for yourself.

- You may find something that could be helpful or interesting to someone you know.

Bottom line: Be as wild and as free with your research while you're still trying to figure things out as you were creating your Ideal Life and Grand Plan. Take chances. Don't worry about being too specific with what you're looking for. And don't be too quick to dismiss new findings and discoveries—they can often mean more than all the targeted information in the world. Taking a taste doesn't mean making a commitment, and neither should your initial research.

So, speaking of hunting for and sifting through information, here's something else to toy with. In a scavenger hunt, we rely on someone else to lead the game. We expect someone else to create the list of things for us to find. In real life we need to start that list ourselves, then go to others for more. Just like with our Grand Plan, where we first made a rough sketch, here we want to do the same thing *and* start asking advice from other people on what we should be doing to best accomplish our goals at the same time. And as they create their own lists of things for us to do, we should pursue all the angles we can, collecting those to-do lists, just as we start to build our collection of trusted advisors and useful information.

As you begin to gather your research, take a closer look. You may discover that there are inherent things in your career of choice that you never knew. Things like the fact that most teachers get about four months off a year could suddenly seem *very* important to you. (A very nice perk for an aspiring writer or someone who wants to start a family.) Or, if you're thinking about being a florist, learning that you have to be at the flower marts at about four or five A.M. to meet the growers could take that job right off your list—if you haven't been up before ten A.M. since you left high school. The point is that what you find out about your career and life choices will range from the mundane to the amazing, but you have to get the information and begin working with it now.

What you learn through research here is going to give you real power later in the game. If you're going to meet a new boss, client, or prospect, knowing how to do a little fast and dirty research on that person and/or their company will often uncover the sort of information that can give you a competitive edge. Let's assume for example that you're going out to interview for a big new job and really want to wow the interviewer. Try answering the following questions before you go into the meeting. It could give the extra advantage of knowing a heck of a lot more than you're expected to.

· What's their background, their history?

· What does their company do?

· Who are their clients?

· Have they received any special recognitions or awards?

· Are they particularly well known or highly regarded for something?

Imagine how impressive you'd be in a meeting if you could very casually slide in a mention or two about some of your findings during your conversations. Most of this information can usually be found just by visiting a company's website, and quite honestly, it is the very least you should do before important meetings, as a sign of respect and professional courtesy. Just think about the last time someone new spent time gathering this much information about you. (Okay, maybe it was a blind date your mother insisted on setting you up with or a guidance counselor you were forced to meet with back in school.) Put it into a professional context, though, and I promise you, this is some pretty powerful stuff. Again, arming yourself with information like this before any big meeting is sure to leave new prospects with a lasting impression.

Julie Anderson, director of documentary programming for Home Box Office (HBO), receives more pitches from aspiring filmmakers than she can count. But she makes it a point to mentor others whenever possible, thanks largely to the inspiration she received when, as a young filmmaker of color, she attended free Saturday workshops at Long Island University that Spike Lee conducted. However, Anderson, who has since gone on to commission Academy Award–winning films for HBO and earn four Emmys herself for her work on documentary films, cannot afford to waste time.

In her world, a well-researched pitch can make the difference between Julie scheduling or passing on a meeting with a new filmmaker. "It is essential that someone has done due diligence on HBO, before they approach me," she explains, "including research on past programming, awards the network has won, filmmakers with whom HBO has worked, the network's style, etc. I look for someone who understands our language." Making a successful pitch requires more than mapping out an idea; it requires a solid story, conceptualizing the film, and understanding the appropriate format. Add passion and commitment to the mix, and you may just get a sit-down with this high-powered executive.

As you can see, half the job is in knowing the right questions to ask. Finding the information you need is the second half of the challenge. Here we'll get the answers. In fact, we'll teach you how you can find answers to almost any questions you might have. With the following tools you can start to master any business, opportunity, or challenge by quickly tapping into the most current and pertinent information available.

Mapping Out Your World

Every profession and industry has its own little world. If you want to do anything big or become anyone special in it, you *must* know what it looks like, how it operates, and who runs it. That goes without saying. One of the best ways to start is by getting an understanding of what the playing field looks like. To make your dreams come true, *where do you have to be?* I say, go right to the center.

For example, if you thought you might want to be a sportscaster, then your new world would be found within the confines of the sports and entertainment industries. To make a map of this, so you can start to learn your way around that new world, you're going to want to know things like:

- Who are the most successful sportscasters?

- How did they get their jobs? And what did they do before that?

- Which are the top broadcasting stations?

- Who runs the top sports franchises?

- Who are the players and what are their stories?

- What kind of training or experience do you need?

- How big is the industry itself?

- How does it work and run, and what are the career options available within it?

- From a geographic perspective, where is the real action?

- Where can you get the most reliable news?

- What are the industry politics, trends, prospects, etc.?

You can ask similar questions about any job, business, or industry that you want to research. Look at every bit of information you can get your hands on. Consider every angle you can: the people, media, organizations, companies, vendors, hangouts, headquarters, events, legends, history, young up-and-comers, resources, literature, articles, educational resources, books, websites, chat groups, user groups, magazines, geography, hubs, examples, all-stars, trends, gossip, buzz, and so on.

So, what do you do with all this information? Let me show you how one Young & Successful sportscaster built a career out of knowledge like this.

HOW TO PLAY BALL

Lee Zurik started to make his own map of the sports world as a ten-year-old frequently glued to the local New Orleans newscasts with his father and brother. Little did he know that the plan he was beginning to formulate back then would land him on that very station as an evening sportscaster just a few years later. Now, exactly where he always wanted to be, twenty-eight-year-old Lee is confident that anyone can get his foot in the door.

As crazy as it may seem, Lee got his first internship at his hometown station, WWI-TV in New Orleans, when he was fourteen. When the general manager agreed to meet with Lee in person, Lee bowled him over with his knowledge of sports and, better yet, with his familiarity with the station's sports coverage. Answering every question the general manager had about the New Orleans Saints was a great start, but thanks to his research, Lee had a lot more to say. He continued by pointing out several new ideas for the station—such as increasing their coverage of local high school sports, which would help attract many more younger viewers, he was sure. Right there, the insightful, professional, highly knowledgeable little kid, who had gotten all dressed up in a suit for the interview, was offered an opportunity on the spot. "Why don't you come in over the summer, intern for the sports department, and we'll see what we can do with you."

That summer Lee became friends with everyone at the station—all of whom were amazed that a kid so young could understand the business and industry so well. Before long, he was reviewing highlight reels and even being assigned interviews. When the summer ended, Lee let everyone know that he wanted to stick around, and he was invited to keep working on the weekends. So on Friday nights he'd play high school football and on Saturday mornings, stumble into the station to help produce the weekend sportscasts.

After researching colleges and talking to everyone in the sportscasting business he could meet, it quickly became clear that Syracuse University was where he needed to go. Their radio station alone was known to be a proven breeding ground for some of the best broadcasting talent in the nation. Following in the footsteps of some of the greatest sportscasters like Marv Albert (Madison Square Garden Network), Bob Costas (NBC Sports), and Mike Tirico (ESPN), Lee took that next step and continued his education in the most perfect place he could. During his time at Syracuse, Lee worked at the radio station, interned at the local TV station, and spent two summers at a station in Houston. This is when he began to make his move from behind the camera to in front of it. This is also when his map and understanding of the larger sports world started to really take shape.

Lee read every book on breaking into TV news, talked to anyone in the business he could get to, and even cold-called a bunch of sportscasters whom he wanted to meet. He was now starting to hunt for a full-time job, sending out his résumé, following up with every station right after, and keeping in touch with every contact he'd made along the way. Within two weeks of graduation and just five hours after the general manager of a station in Greenville, Mississippi, got his tape and follow-up call, Lee landed his first full-time, paid job as a TV sportscaster. Looking back he says, "If I had never made that phone call, I never would have gotten that job . . . And when I finally got on the air I wasn't even nervous. All that earlier experience, time in the sports world, practice on TV, and studying the business prepared me so well that it was just so comfortable and so right."

Lee spent a year in Mississippi at that station and two years at a top-rated NBC station in Alabama, before a buddy who he had interned with in New Orleans years before called with a heads-up on a new opening in Baton Rouge. Again, Lee was persistent with his follow-through and even stopped in the middle of a trip to cover the College World Series in Nebraska to check in with the station. He ended up getting the Baton Rouge job on the spot because as the general manager explained it, "Anyone who would call me from Omaha, Nebraska, from a pay phone in a tunnel, in the middle of the pouring rain, has got to be a great worker." Soon Lee was on a plane back to his home state. A few months after being there, an old friend he'd worked for when he was a teenager and still kept in touch with offered him a job. His career had come full circle and landed him right back home at the station that started it all for him. And the people he had worked with ten years before were thrilled to welcome him back.

Lee says it's interesting to see that, after all those years away, what people remembered about him most was that he was a hard working, dedicated, knowledgeable kid who'd made a great impression when he was a teen. Lee's advice to anyone is: Make sure you make a great impression on everyone every step of the way. Stay in touch with all the great people you meet. And never stop making friends, growing, learning, pushing, persisting and getting your name out there. It will all pay off sooner or later.

Create Your Own Map

Once you've gathered your information, imagine there are six circles, representing the major areas of influence in your industry or world. Look at the list below and consider how you might fill in the circles with the names of specific people, places, and groups.

Step 1: Draw Your Outline

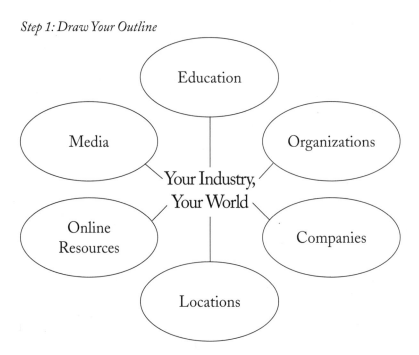

Here are your six circles:

Media: Magazines, books, articles, newsletters, journalists, critics, TV shows, radio programs, audio tapes, videos

Organizations: Associations, groups, clubs, unions, guilds, charities

Education: Schools, workshops, camps, training facilities, coaches, tutors

Companies: Major players, industry leaders, service providers, sponsors, partners, advertisers

Locations: Headquarters, hubs, hot spots, hangouts

Online Resources: Websites, chat rooms, bulletin boards, user groups, directories, search engines

For example, **media** became particularly valuable to Lee, and his search included trade publications like *Electronic Media* and *Broadcasting & Cable.* From these he learned about trends, players, coaches, scores, ratings, and industry news.

One of his favorite books was *How to Launch Your Career in TV News.* (There's still a worn-out copy on his desk today.) The **people** he started to watch included Mike Hoss, a small-market broadcaster in New Orleans, and Dave Ryan, a guy who interned at his home station and went on to work at ESPN. Lee followed their careers closely, kept an eye on them in the trades, asked mutual friends for updates on their successes, called them for advice, pulled them aside at games to say hello, and so on.

In college Lee joined two important **organizations,** the American Sportscasters Association and the Radio-TV News Directors Association, which incidentally got him hired in Alabama because the news director happened to be the head of the organization and was impressed that he'd taken the initiative to join.

On the **companies** side, Lee knew he wanted to be back in New Orleans, so he kept his eye on WWI-TV and its competitors. **Loca**tionwise, he was already local, and that's where he wanted to stay.

Lastly, searching **online** wasn't all that helpful in Lee's case, because the Internet's sports coverage wasn't what it is today. (Today he'd pull up so many comprehensive information sites in one simple search, it could take days to read through it all!) All in all, the pieces of his Grand Plan and the map of his world came together beautifully.

Step 2: Identify and Model the Key Players

In the sportscaster world, some of the key players and media companies are:

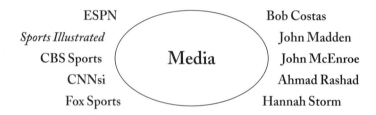

ESPN		Bob Costas
Sports Illustrated		John Madden
CBS Sports	**Media**	John McEnroe
CNNsi		Ahmad Rashad
Fox Sports		Hannah Storm

Start to fill in this kind of information yourself with each of the six circles we outlined above. Look for the experts, founders, leaders, lobbyists, entrepreneurs, gurus, champions, and celebrities. From now on, you're going to focus your ongoing research efforts on these people, places, and you are going to start to reconstruct the paths they took to get where they are today. Some other questions you might ask yourself are:

· What were their biggest lessons, mistakes, or missteps?

· What made them different?

· What special skills or talents did they have?

· What kind of expertise did they have?

· Who helped launch their careers or helped them get where they are today?

- What do they read religiously? How do they stay on top of their industry's news?

- Where do they hang out?

- Who are their closest friends and most trusted advisors?

Once you can piece together the career paths of the people you aspire to emulate or even work with, you're sure to have a solid base of steps to emulate. Your role models will reveal clues about how you can best succeed, whether you follow their lead to a T, use their experience as a guide for your own benchmarks, or just get inspired by their triumphs.

Step 3: Find the Connections

As you start to find the connections, particularly the less obvious ones, between different leaders in your field, you'll get an intimate look at what their world looks like from the inside and how you can start playing in it yourself.

Industries are all one big web of connections. The more you research, the more you'll see. Sticking with our sportscaster example, if you remember, Lee had worked as an intern in New Orleans with a guy who went on to work for ESPN. There were also some current ESPN sportscasters around the country, who, like Lee, were graduates of Syracuse and the campus radio station. He could simply call these people based on their common histories. And odds are, they'd be receptive. (In fact, tapping into alumni networks from any school or organization you've gone to is an outstanding pre-qualifier for meeting virtually any successful person.)

If you were to try to find the connections in this basic chart of the media world above, you're likely to uncover one major set of links through ESPN. Want a great example? Try to follow my web here for a minute. ESPN is a sizable sports-focused media company with their own TV network, radio network, and magazine. But ESPN is part of a larger corporate family that also includes ABC Sports. The ABC network, a television syndicate of stations around the country, is the home to some of the biggest sporting events out there: hockey's Stanley Cup, the Indianapolis 500, the World Figure Skating Championship, and good old college football. But there's more. Both ESPN and ABC Sports are owned by Disney. And it just so happens that Disney, whose headquarters is in Anaheim, California, also owns two major sports franchises: Major League Baseball's Anaheim Angels and the National Hockey League's Mighty Ducks. Of course, Disney is also the proud owner of Anaheim Pond, the state-of-the-art 650,000-square-foot stadium where you can catch the Harlem Globetrotters, the World Wrestling Federation, and Ringling Bros. and Barnum & Bailey Circus. Of course, you can watch the Ducks play there, too. How's that for a web of connections? For a sportscaster, there are literally dozens of points of access and entry in this web alone.

Now create a web from your own map. How are all the people, places, companies, organizations, and media connected in your industry? The more connections you can figure out, the more connections you can make, the more "in the know" you'll be, and the more points of entry you can find in this web.

Find the Center

Look for the circles that have the most connections. It shouldn't take long to realize that certain people, companies, organizations, and places are more connected to one another and more visible or prominent throughout the industry in general than others are. This is the center, and this is where you should be focusing your efforts. Our next task is to get you there.

Who has their hands into everything? Who or what authorities are relied on above all others? Who are the experts who are called on and quoted most often? Where is all the action taking place? Identify the centers of this world, and start to focus your research on them. Finding the center is all about getting yourself to where the action is. Where are you going to learn the most, see the most, experience the most? Find that place and get there. How? We'll answer that juicy little question in the next chapter. But you should have plenty of ideas by now.

Mining for Priceless Gems

De Beers, the world's largest diamond producer, mines nearly 50 percent of the diamonds produced each year. It's a crop worth billions because of the relative scarcity of the stones and the exhaustive mining process needed to extract them. In fact, in order to produce a one-carat gem-quality stone, the miners have to process nearly 46,000 pounds of rock. Then they have to haul it all to a processing plant, crush it into smaller pieces, and have it washed, sorted, x-rayed, analyzed, and classified before they can extract that tiny precious gem.

Just like diamond miners, the Young & Successful are constantly on the hunt for precious gems of information and priceless wisdom. They can come in many forms, too, for instance:

- learning about a new job or business opportunity from an inside source

- finding someone who can put you in touch with someone you've always wanted to meet

- reading an article and learning about a new competitor you never knew about

- discovering a conference where all the top people in your industry will be attending and accessible.

It may take a lot of work to figure out which are the precious gems, but with them come great opportunities, access, leverage, credibility, and respect.

Be wild and free with your research while you're still trying to figure out how everything fits together in your universe. Just like when you created your Ideal Life and Grand Plan, don't be afraid to take chances. Don't be too specific with what you're looking for, and don't be too quick to dismiss new findings and discoveries—they can often mean more than all the targeted information in the world. Remember, even the most precious gems look like dirty little rocks until you take a closer look. And just like great nuggets of insight, facts, statistics, trends, and information, the more gems of precious knowledge you amass, the greater the wealth of wisdom and opportunities you'll achieve.

To tap into the worlds that we want to know more about (and maybe even one day lead), we need to constantly establish new, more focused, and more filtered flows of information coming to us by way of many of the research tools we're about to show you. If you're not doing this already, you need to start getting news on your industry, the leading companies, the hottest people, the most respected organizations, and the biggest trends sent to you via email, snail mail, or other methods.

What stands between you and even greater success is likely a little thumping and a lot of listening and analysis. So let's talk about a few places you're sure to strike it rich in your research efforts.

Top 10 Research Tools of the Young & Successful

The Young & Successful have an uncanny ability and willingness to get to the heart of things in a hurry. They do the research necessary to uncover the information, contacts, resources, and opportunities that they need to make educated decisions about what they should do. This detective work sometimes involves digging into little nooks and crevices where no one else bothers to explore. Integrate this information into conversations, plans, forecasting, presentations, pitches, or any other opportunities where you have to sell yourself or your ideas.

Here is how you can find the bulk of your answers to some of your biggest questions, or at very least, point you in the right direction. The following are a few great tips on how to find that top-level research you're going to need in a cost-effective, timely manner. You may be aware of some of these sources, but there may be some here you've never considered. Use these as a starting point and remember to always try to add tools and sources as you engage in your searches. You'll quickly begin to develop your own personal preferences and researching style.

1. Google. In our opinion, the first step to any research is the easiest, most obvious one. Run a Google search. If you don't know what that is already, allow us to enlighten you. Go online and type in www. google.com. A simple white page will pop up with a blank box. There, just type in the key words of whatever you're looking for (if you want to be very specific, put quotes around it), and with the click of a button, you're on your way to finding a laundry list of whatever is online about your subject. In fact, Google searches through billions of indexed web pages to find what you need. www.yahoo.com, www.altavista.com, www.ask.com, and www.msn.com are also great search engines. Now don't expect to always get exactly what you want right away, because you're bound to get a lot of different things. But take advantage of the more random stuff, too, because you might find some interesting things you never would think to investigate otherwise. Browse through the list, click on a bunch of different links, and try to get a sense of the scope of what you're dealing with. Then just narrow your search down from there. And you don't have to discount foreign language sites anymore, as some search engines will now translate them for you instantly (it's pretty cool).

2. Family, Friends, Teachers, Mentors, and Peers. Whether you're on the hunt for the perfect new job, a mentor who "gets you," a great restaurant to take clients, or a printer who can also handle your design work, often you need not look any further than the people you interact with every day. Ask around to see if anyone knows anything about what you're looking for. Typically all you need is a good lead or two to get you started. I personally attack each challenge (for instance a new web technology that I want to implement) by singling out a half dozen or so people who I know have some sort of experience or expertise in the subject. I'll call one person who runs a site I like, a web designer or two, someone who once wrote an article on the subject, a technology consultant, another business owner, etc. Often I even call up people who I know don't know anything about what I'm looking for themselves, but could surely refer me to people who do. Don't rule out anyone.

If you're looking to hook up with or get the lowdown on a specific person or company, remember that they're bound to be surrounded by many everyday people, any of whom might have great insight to share. Remember our story about Wendy Diamond and her rock and roll cookbook? She followed up on every lead she could find that might get her to the people she was targeting—family, friends, teachers, drivers, stylists, neighbors—and she filled an entire book with seemingly unreachable people.

So stop just asking *what* they know, and start asking them *who* they know, too. Be bold (yet always gracious and polite) and inquire whether they know anyone else who might help you find more info. Chances are very good that the question will pull a multitude of answers out of the woodwork.

3. Bookstores (on and offline). Now this might seem a bit obvious, but we don't want you to skip over anything so easy when you're in hot pursuit of information. Browse through the shelves at the nearest super-size bookstore or log on to amazon.com or barnesandnoble. com and run a search by topics to discover just about any book in print. (Both actually have a service to help you track down titles that are out of print too!) Be sure to check out the little section on each book page that says: "Other people who bought this book also bought . . ." for other good leads.

Also, scan bibliographies and acknowledgments. Most nonfiction books that are packed with research, trends, statistics, and other juicy information about a topic will have a bibliography section at the back referencing sources they used in compiling the book or a good index. (You can assume that if someone went through the trouble to write such a detailed book, she probably did some good research herself.) The acknowledgments, especially in books about high-profile people whose careers you want to follow, can be helpful, too. Look at who they thank. That's typically a little known, but incredible way to find some of the key players in any organization.

4. Magazine and Newspaper Archives. Most major periodicals today now have online archives of past articles, features, stories, and even background on their top reporters. Keep an eye out for major gold mines of info from publications like *Business Week* (www.businessweek. com), where you can access more than ten years of business stories, and *The Wall Street Journal* (www.wsj.com). For U.S.-based publications, other periodical archives like *The New York Times* (www.nytimes.com) and *USA Today* (www.usatoday.com) are also great bets. The search engines you'll find on these sites are usually excellent sources for finding information on prominent people, companies, organizations, politics, social causes, controversial issues, etc. But if you really want to hit the mother lode and tap into one source covering all online English-language media, check out www.newsdirectory.com for a complete directory (with 14,500 links) of newspapers, magazines, TV stations, colleges, visitor bureaus, government agencies, and more. Just think what you could do with the 3,600 newspapers and 4,800 magazines alone!

If you're looking for more regional business information, you're almost always sure to score with local city business journals. Find the one that's perfect for you at www.bizjournals.com. This is a link to American City Business Journals, the largest publisher of metropolitan business newspapers, covering more than forty of the top business markets. And if you're more of a jet-setter, or need your information to cover the international scene, try www.globaledge.msu.edu. We highly recommend their Country Insights and Global Resources sections.

Business journals are an excellent source of information on local city business trends, politics, people, companies, and the overall climate. Best of all, these journals are known for publishing great weekly lists rating everything from the highest paid executives to the biggest real estate holding companies. Often you can even buy a year's collection of these lists in book form, directly through their publication offices. So if you have a client in a different city, are contemplating a move yourself, or want to learn more about different city business environments, this will get your search off to a great start.

5. Trade Associations & Publications. There is a trade organization for nearly every occupation, activity, service, or business you can imagine. Professions, hobbies, products, industries, philosophies, races, religions, political groups, special interests, social causes: you name it and there's some group or publisher somewhere that is at the center of it. These groups exist to spread information about their chosen subject and serve networks of people who are as focused on their cause as they are. So you can be sure that when you find them, you're tapping serious hubs of information, research, and people.

Many of these organizations publish major trade publications (also known as "industry rags") and sometimes a range of other resources that may include newsletters, online updates, topic-specific sites, critical reviews, biographies, and even special industry events. Accessing these groups and trade publications is the best way to tap into a great wealth of information instantly, right from the very center of the universe you're trying to penetrate. Typically, associations will have some free information that you can use to get you started. But then they'll charge a fee for their publications and more comprehensive resources. The best way to approach new organizations is to run a search to find a few that look like they might be a great fit for you; then check out the websites to learn more. If you still feel like you're on to something, call them up and talk to someone live about what they do, who they serve, and what they have to offer.

If you're interested in events, go right to the leading industry organizations first, but then take your search a little broader. Here's another little secret—it's not always the most obvious groups that put on the best seminars, workshops, expos, and conferences, so you're going to need a more all-encompassing resource. Check out www.tsnn.com to tap into the most widely consulted database on the Internet for the trade show industry. On it you'll find information on more than fifteen thousand trade shows and conferences and thirty thousand seminars.

6. Online Newsletter and E-Zines. One of the best things about the Internet today is the sheer amount of free newsletters that you can get electronically, many of which provide a wealth of very niche-focused information. Because experts, small groups, and independent publishers no longer have to incur all the costs of designing, printing, and mailing their weekly, monthly, or quarterly updates, many more on-line newsletters are now available than ever before. And, again, you can find just about anything if you do some dedicated digging. One thing always leads to another, so keep tasting. Don't stop until you're confident you have the latest and greatest industry news coming to you from the biggest, most trusted experts in your world. After all, one of the best ways to master your universe is to learn from someone who already has. (To stay on top of the lives and adventures of Young & Successful people from around the world, and to learn about the latest tips, tricks, tools, insights and resources to help you achieve rapid success, sign up for our FREE Weekly Newsletter today at **newsletter.ysn.com**).

You already know that you need to stay on top of certain areas of information. Newsletters (both online and off) are one of the absolute best ways to do that. A source is E-zine Universe (www.ezine-universe.com), which claims to be the most comprehensive directory of email publications on the Internet, with more than seven thousand listings. You can also check out the E-zine Directory (www.ezine-dir.com) and E-zine Central (www.ezinecentral.com) for even more directories.

7. Fee-Based Research Services. If you have a few bucks to spend, or have access to a school library or lawyer's office, go directly to Lexis-Nexis at www.lexisnexis.com for the best access you can find on anything that's been written anywhere about anyone or anything. Some people say they don't go anywhere without their credit cards; we say don't leave without running a Lexis-Nexis search on where you're going or who you're going to meet . . . if it's important, of course. Their fees aren't cheap, because most of their clients are big companies and law firms, but you can get single-person access for about $200 a month. But call them, because you never know what kind of deal you can get.

8. Case Studies. If you haven't gone to business school, you probably haven't discovered this little underworld of legitimate corporate exposés, but here's the inside scoop. One of the things that makes many of the top learning institutions so well respected is that they teach using real-world examples through case studies. Case studies typically focus on high-profile people, companies, or industries, and illustrate a problem or series of challenges that they had to deal with. Through these two- to twenty-five-page profiles, you can get an amazing inside look at how businesses, systems, and people work behind the scenes. This means you can learn things about key executives, company operations, financials, industry trends, and big deals that are often impossible to find otherwise.

When Scott decided to leave the restaurant industry and dive into the media world, he hunted down every great resource he could find to learn about the business. But despite all of the books, videos, audio tapes, websites, and newsletters he devoured, the most insightful information came from the $30 he spent on five or six incredible case studies discovered at the Harvard Business School Press website. In a few minutes of surfing through their library he was able to find cases on the biggest media companies in the world: Viacom, AOL Time Warner, News Corp., and a few of the other most successful industry players. Through these he was able to learn nuances about internal strategies that aren't talked about in the mass media or industry trades. He learned what industry players thought about their businesses and heard from a range of executives how they approached and dealt with some of their biggest strategic decisions. All this for a few dollars a pop. Since cases are primarily used for academia, the cooperation level of companies typically prompts them to share more sensitive, behind-the-scenes info. But since they're available to the public, you can get the benefit of them too.

The biggest and best publisher of high-level case studies is Harvard Business School Press (http://harvardbusinessonline.hbsp.harvard. edu), but McGraw Hill also has quite a library of its own (www. mcgrawhill.com). Most cases cost only $3 to $8 each for print versions, but if you want videos, research studies, and more comprehensive teaching kits, you can expect to shell out up to a few hundred bucks each.

9. Annual Reports. Every publicly traded company and nonprofit organization in the United States is required by law to publish an annual report and make it available to the public. These annual reports are written to inform stockholders and donors about the operations, the financial health, and the progress that the organization has made throughout the year. How can this help you? Well, if you want a job, a consulting gig, or to get involved in any way with an organization that publishes an annual report, it's a real first-class move to at least take a peek before you meet with them. Annual reports have tough legal disclosures and protocols that public companies must follow and, in turn, point out a company's strengths, weaknesses, holdings, key executives, board members, financial performance, strategic partners, and more. This is always good information to have before you set out to do business with a public company, whether your aim is to be an employee, consultant, vendor, or shareholder. For any annual report, you can call up the organization itself or the Shareholder's Relations department of any public company and tell them you're considering an investment. You can also log on to www.barrons.com for a complete listing of reports that you can order directly for free.

10. Consultants. Now you may not think you're big enough or rich enough to hire consultants, but don't be too quick to dismiss this option. As with everything else we've talked about here, there's a specialist for everything and if you can find them, you can often tap into some of the most knowledgeable people around. Experts make a living by knowing everything there is to know about their given field. And the way they maintain their credibility and reputation is by publishing, speaking, and consulting on their body of knowledge. So find out who these people are in your area (industry trade groups will almost always know the top people) and read up on them or go hear them speak. If you're really into what they have to say and you're serious about getting to the bottom of a given subject, inquire about paying for an hour of their time, either in person or over the phone. Then just prepare your laundry list of killer questions, schedule that appointment, and fire away. Also be sure to ask these people about other great resources or referrals specific to what you're looking for, since they're bound to know quite a few.

For the latest information on these and other useful research sources and tools to help you discover just about anything you're looking for, visit **research.ysn.com** today.

Become a Master of Your Universe

To master *your* universe—whichever industry, career, or hobby you choose to explore—remember the five steps we talked about:

1 Identify the world you want to play in.

2 Articulate and ask your critical questions.

3 Make a map of the world you want to be a part of.

4 Dive in with high-level research.

5 Always find ways to put what you know to work, and leverage what you know to continuously propel you toward greater opportunities and successes.

We've covered a lot of ground so far, and want you to know that truly mastering any universe takes a serious commitment of your time and energy over months and years. It's simply unrealistic to expect someone to absorb everything about a new world overnight; however, the Young & Successful have come to realize that starting down the path, and keeping at it, uncovers tremendous opportunities.

6 Take a Taste™

I HOPE YOU DIDN'T THINK THAT WE were just going to leave you hanging with all those incredible dreams and plans dancing in your head. No, no, no, no, no. Now we're going to learn about the tools and techniques that the Young & Successful utilize to take their Ideal Life "out for a spin." After all, you don't buy a car without a test drive. Even Baskin-Robbins believes you shouldn't have to buy ice cream without a sample or two of what intrigues you. So let me ask you this: When was the last time you sampled some of the things you aspire to have or got a real taste of who you want to be?

Whatever you want to do with your life, we'll show you how learning to take a taste of the action will help you ensure you're making the right decision.

If you think about it, you've actually been taking tastes of new and interesting things your whole life. In the beginning, that's all we really do. We learn about the world by exploring. That's how we learn to speak, understand, read, learn, and meet people, and it's how we become the people we are.

When your parents took you to the zoo, when you worked a summer job or internship, or you ventured out on a date with someone from a totally different world, you were doing it. You were sampling what life had to offer you. College is where you probably first started taking tastes of new opportunities more seriously. If you studied abroad, joined organizations, or dove into a specialized field of study, you were taking a taste of different worlds. Maybe you got a taste of what corporate life would be like, or maybe you've taken some time to work in an industry that intrigued you. If these experiences aren't what you want to spend your life doing then they're just an appetizer—a taste.

Sampling is a critical part of finding out what we truly want for many reasons. First of all, like success, it's addictive. The habit of trying new and unusual things will keep the everyday grind from becoming a bore. Padding your life with little incentives or previews of what's to come can be really inspiring, too. What fun is dreaming big if you don't get to enjoy a little bit of these wild aspirations along the way?

How the Young & Successful Take Their Tastes

The Young & Successful learn early how important it is to first taste what they're striving for. See for yourself how one Young & Successful guy had his tastes morph into life-altering experiences.

ROYCE: MAKING THE CALL

When things go right, one or two great tastes can tell you that you're definitely headed in the right direction. Royce Bergman was a twenty-three-year-old guy who gave up his dream of going to law school after his father died. He wanted to go where the action was and believed his destiny was to become a Hollywood agent. But when he reached out for a job that would get his foot in the door, the big agencies didn't quite share his vision. In fact, they didn't even return his calls.

After a few months of persistence, relentless follow-up,

and checking in with the human resources offices twice a week, the new HR director at Endeavor, one of the leading talent agencies, called him back. As luck would have it, Royce was one of the first calls she made on *her* first day and, incidentally, he turned out to be her first hire. The two became fast friends and it was clear that Royce had made an important ally and an awesome advocate. In the mailroom, the standard entry position, Royce made sure to become particularly helpful to the assistants in the big executive offices, and he was always right there when they needed anything. Royce worked intensely, remained supremely focused, and moved right up to assisting Ari Greenburg, who at twenty-two was the youngest agent the company had ever hired. Then Royce moved on to assisting Ariel Emanuel, the founding partner.

In just a year and a half, Royce found himself in the prime position to be promoted to the agent track. But while he loved his job, his taste of the business made him wonder if there might be a better place for him. Working at the agency, he was able to interact with dozens of high-profile people a day and had his hands in numerous projects at once. But Royce yearned to be closer to the creative side of the business. He wanted to be more intimately involved in the projects he was encountering. And at the end of the day, he wanted to play a more substantive role where his efforts were critical to the overall success of the projects he worked on.

So, once again his appetite for bigger opportunities and desire for new tastes of what was really possible struck him like a hunger pang, and prompted him to make his most fateful move yet. He picked up the phone and called one of the agency's clients, John Melfi, an Emmy- and Golden Globe–winning producer who had been with HBO for ten years. Not sure how Melfi would react, Royce dropped his boss's name, told him he wanted to find out what a nonwriting producer did, and asked him if he'd meet for coffee. John said absolutely, and the two met the next day.

For two and a half hours, John *drilled* Royce with questions about what he was looking to do, and finally Royce said, "Why are you asking me all this? You know it's kind of making me depressed, thinking of all the things I want but don't have." John, the big executive producer, then smiled and asked Royce if he'd move to New York to be his assistant on *Sex and the City,* the number-one rated television show on HBO. Two weeks later, Royce was on a plane to the Big Apple, and he has since spent two of the best years of his life working with the hottest people in the business, learning the trade, and again, moving himself into a beautiful position to take bigger and better tastes of his Ideal Life.

MTV: A Dose of Reality

In some cases, a negative is the best way to prove a positive. In an unusual, yet incredibly effective TV special, MTV's smash hit *Scared Straight* gave a taste of life behind bars to a group of kids who were flirting with danger—drugs, crime, sex, and worse. The experiment introduced them to the prison life that they'd likely end up experiencing if they proceeded on their current path. For one brutal day, MTV took the kids into custody, carted them off to a hard-core high-security prison, and left them to be taunted and lectured by some of the worst inmates, who encouraged them to make smarter choices. Once these teens got a taste of what life was like behind bars, their perspectives changed forever and so did their lifestyles. And even as a TV show, I'd venture a guess this little taste of the big house hit home with countless viewers as well.

While the *Scared Straight* program was of course an extreme example, this is an important point to consider for any of us. In the spirit of turning negatives into positives, we all need to keep in mind that encountering situations that we don't like can be extraordinarily helpful because they help us better hone in on and focus on what we do want. This is every bit as true for a bad internship, job, boss, new city, involvement in a group, or even new relationships.

So sometimes the taste you take will teach you that what you're tasting is *not* something you want any more of.

Step up and take a taste of a larger life. The Young & Successful do. You should do the same, and can. Want to see how? It's really very simple if you think about it. If you ever wanted to . . .

Speak another language . . .	Hire a tutor for a few hours and learn some basic introductions, conversation starters, and key phrases. Then buy a book or tape and practice at home or in your car.
Drive a luxury automobile . . .	Try renting one for an hour or, better yet, get dressed up in your fanciest outfit to test-drive the car of your dreams at the nearest local dealer.
Work in a science lab . . .	Tour a hospital or research facility. Ask the admissions or human resources department if there is anyone you could talk to to learn more about their program, work, or career choice. Go right to the people in charge of recruiting people just like you! Do your homework so that you can ask some tough questions. Or invite a research fellow, or

someone interesting that you can get on the phone, out to lunch to learn about their life and career.

Fly your own plane . . . Visit a small nearby airport and take a test flight at the flight school. Hang around for a while and watch the planes take off and land. Ask about pilot certification classes.

Live in a foreign country . . . Buy a few guidebooks and some posters for your walls. Find people online who live there or have visited and ask them about their experiences. If you can, scan the travel sites for a super deal and take a quick trip, or better yet, go backpacking around. Investigate whether you can live with a family there for a little while. Or consider swapping apartments with someone from another part of the world who wants to experience your city for a few weeks.

Own your own business . . . Swing by a chamber of commerce or a Small Business Administration event. Or get the Sunday classifieds from your local paper and call some of the businesses-for-sale ads. Then make an appointment with the broker or owner to "explore" buying it. ou can also surf until your heart's content at www.entrepreneur.com as you access up-to-date subject matter on virtually any topic related to starting, running or growing a successful business.

Figuring Out How to Do What You Love

Stop for a minute and put together a list of all the things you would love to be doing if you could do anything. I don't know if you've tried something like this in a while, but it's fascinating to see what such a simple exercise can uncover. Even more amazing is discovering how much we tend to neglect what turns us on the most.

I used to do an exercise like this when I taught business start-up workshops to aspiring entrepreneurs. In order to find a concept that was perfectly suited for them, I'd have them use a sheet of paper to brainstorm lists of their favorite hobbies, pastimes, activities, interests, and most rewarding special skills. With this list of raw and random passions in hand, we'd then start to brainstorm another list of possible connections and applications. You wouldn't believe some of the crazy things that we'd come up with. For example, if someone's initial notes looked like this . . .

basketball
sports
fashion
music
graphic design
travel
science fiction
action movies
sales
international trade

. . . we'd start a group brainstorming session and try to come up with a laundry list of possible connections to formulate a new business opportunity, such as . . .

developing a hip new sportswear line
establishing a sports company to ship basketball jerseys abroad
internship with sports or music agent

graphic design services to new musicians
merchandising company
ticket brokerage
basketball camp for kids
travel agency specializing in action adventures
movie lovers club
online video sales and reviews
lecture series featuring top young designers
importing foreign and eclectic music from abroad
producing concerts with up-and-coming artists

. . . and so on. After a few minutes, the person making the list would start to gravitate toward a few of the rough ideas. We'd circle what was interesting, cross out what didn't work, and proceed to dissect what we were left with to come up with a new, more refined list. In essence, we were mining for great ideas. And although we were just using paper, we were taking a tiny taste of what could be possible.

You can create a business or even invent a new job description out of just about anything you love. To this day, I'll never forget the greeting cards for teens or the Boston shoe directory for shoppers that the students produced. And that idea shouldn't die just because you've moved, or are about to move, into corporate life. I'm a firm believer that if you look hard enough and are sufficiently strategic, you can find ways to do what you love even in the most structured and corporate of careers.

These days, doing what you love is just as possible in most corporate environments. The theory of doing something entrepreneurial, or launching a new division or enterprise within another company, is often referred to as "intra-preneurial." This is because lately corporations have to do more with less, so in some ways there are opportunities to do so much more from within.

Take this list of yours and, as I showed you above, search for possible connections. Spend some productive dreaming time and contemplate how you could incorporate your passions into your life now, through little tastes, and possibly even sculpt a career out of it all. This is where taking a taste can be the most powerful. This is how you discover untapped opportunities to do (and make money at) things you never imagined possible.

AN APPETITE FOR LIFE

Sometimes you have to take a *number* of tastes to find the one you want to stick with. Jennifer Iannolo discovered her passion early in life, but had to work her way through at least a half-dozen jobs to discover how her passion could translate into a career that could fulfill and sustain her. Jen was just eight years old when she discovered her true passion in life—food. While most of her friends were watching cartoons and picking out outfits for Barbie, Jen was watching Julia Child and the Frugal Gourmet, and starting to learn the cooking secrets her mother had been taught by her Italian grandmother.

In college Jen chose to study business at New York University, figuring that if she didn't end up cooking, she could always have a business career. (Little did she know both—years later—would come together in a most unexpected way.) At NYU, Jen helped to organize a big conference on social responsibility and entrepreneurship, and found a golden opportunity to meet someone who would become one of her greatest early mentors—Bill Shore. He was the founder of

Share Our Strength, a non-profit that brings great chefs from all over the world together to feed the hungry, and educates low-income families about their food choices. Jen tried to absorb everything she could.

At graduation, her next big opportunity hit. A friend of hers was starting a gourmet food company and brought Jen aboard as the director of marketing. This was her first job out of college, but since everyone already knew what she could do as an entrepreneur (she started two companies while going to school full-time), no one batted an eye over her hire. That was her first big taste of the industry as a whole, and she couldn't have been more thrilled.

When the small company went under, she moved onward and upward, and joined Pierre Deux, the sister company to the world famous Le Cordon Bleu cooking schools. Pierre Deux sold French country furniture, and Jen found a way to make cross-merchandising of LCB's food products part of her job description. That's how she found heaven on earth at her first gala—the *Bon Appétit* Wine and Spirits Focus event at Lincoln Center in New York City. "There I was, in an evening gown, drinking Champagne and eating caviar, surrounded by some of the biggest people in the business. I helped Le Cordon Bleu's chef perform his live cooking demonstrations, and that was it for me—the clincher. At that moment I knew where I wanted to be." Jen was just 23, a year out of college, and on that day, she knew. She wanted to do food events.

*Let's just stop and think about this: just **two** years out of college, Jen had taken a taste of so many different areas of the food business* *that she had already discovered a tremendous amount, both about herself and the industry.*

When a close friend moved to Boston and needed a roommate, Jen jumped at the opportunity to get in on the city's emerging culinary scene. But moving to a new city meant finding new work, and hopefully getting closer to that Ideal Life of hers. Once in Boston, there was much to explore; after she contacted the local Share Our Strength office, the new city began to open up to her. Taste of the Nation, their biggest annual event, was being organized at the time and once again, Jen jumped into help as a volunteer. She immediately got exactly the job she wanted: She was put in charge of the celebrity chef demonstrations. The problem was, there wasn't much money in it or any of the things that Jen wanted to do as a freelancer, but she was determined to start her own business. Because her goal now was to build her own event company, traditional jobs were not an option—they wouldn't allow her time to work on her own projects. But this decision had harsh repercussions—Jen struggled quite a bit while trying to find a way to pursue her dreams and make money.

Jen (like many of us) was put on a strict budget. She maxed out all her credit cards, drove her credit rating "to hell," and had to humbly ask her family for help. "I sacrificed everything for a major project, and when the deal started to crumble, I had a feeling it was time to go back to New York," she recalls wistfully. Suffering from a severe case of burnout, Jen returned home, picked up her old contacts and was able to work on some of the industry's most prestigious events, including the biggest event in the food world: the James Beard Awards — known as the "Food Oscars." While Jen was having the time of her life, she soon realized that to be successful in the business she would need far more stability.

Jen finally decided that she had to go corporate. "I thought I'd build my nest egg back up, pay off debts, and get a sense of what hard-core marketing was really like." So she went to work for the promotions agency that handled Pepsi's marketing campaigns. There she did what she had been trained to do: events. Grass roots marketing, event tours, hip-hop and Spring Break events mostly. "It expanded my horizons a lot. But I was miserable."

Then one day, her Ideal Life called her up on her cell phone. Jen was stuck in an airport on a business trip. The call was from her old client at Relais & Chateaux, a French company she had briefly worked with a few years before. The voice on the other line said, "Jennifer, Relais & Chateaux has just bought a company called L'Ecole des Chefs ("chef school" in English) that organizes cooking internships for passionate amateur cooks in some of the greatest restaurants in the world. We want to offer this program throughout many of our top properties, and we'd like to know if you'd be interested in running it." Tears came to her eyes. "It was everything I had ever wanted—all in one perfect package."

That turned out to be just the beginning. After successfully launching L'Ecole des Chefs for Relais, Jen once again returned to the world of entrepreneurship. She created an on-line food magazine, The Gilded Fork (www.gildedfork.com), that is now on its way to becoming a portal for all things culinary. Just six months after launch, the site was nominated for a World Food Media Award along with the BBC, chef Jacques Pépin, and international food magazines. Then Go-Daddy.com called—would she be willing to star in a national television commercial since she used Go Daddy for all of her web projects?

As Jen said to me recently, "It has been a long, sometimes painful road, but now it's *all coming together*. I have never been this excited or happy each and every day." With media properties in podcasting, online publishing, and a new line of home and food products, all of Jen's worlds are now converging into that thing we call the Ideal Life.

As you can see, in order to find that ideal opportunity Jen had to do a ton of personal, hands-on exploration—and simple, old-fashioned pounding the pavement. Young & Successful detective work sometimes involves digging into little nooks and crevices where no one else bothers to explore.

So, How Big a Taste Do You Want?

Now don't let any of these bigger tastes and more ambitious adventures scare you off. As I said before, a taste can be a small bite or a major feast. It's up to you to decide how much you want to bite off and what will actually satisfy your cravings and curiosity. If we were to look at the different degrees of tastes that you can take in terms of commitment required, we could come up with a list of options that range from a few hours to a year or so. Here are a few to consider:

New tastes: one day to a few weeks

· Spend an afternoon in the bookstore reading up on something new.

· Attend some meetings at a local chapter or industry organization.

· Go to a workshop.

· Volunteer.

KEEPING A MEMORY ALIVE

Speaking of tiny little commitments that can pack a punch, check out Justine Staman's story. *The New York Times* reported, "Friends call Stamen an irrepressible advocate for the poor." She was just a teen when she got her first small taste of volunteer work, and after two days of feeding hungry people at a local soup kitchen she was hooked. By seventeen she herself had helped set up a soup kitchen that today still runs and feeds about four hundred people a day. After tasting a few other opportunities to help others—one of which earned her the nickname "can girl" in high school after she collected 35,000 cans of food for the needy—Justine realized her mission and passion in life could be best fulfilled if she started her own organization.

Today her nonprofit, the TEAK Fellowship in New York City, helps low-income, high-achieving junior high school students get into top high schools. TEAK was started from the belief that too many gifted students attend overcrowded schools that can't offer the proper support these students need. TEAK therefore supports them during high school and through their college application process, helps them land summer internships and jobs, and exposes them to the arts. It is TEAK's belief that helping talented but economically disadvantaged students get exposure to strong peers, advisors, and mentors provides them with more equal footing from which to compete and succeed.

Watching her best friend and her most talented student murdered as teens pushed her commitment even further. "I believe that young people need to hear that very terrible experiences can help us do very positive things in order to heal. Doing this work in memory of these two good people . . . and helping kids have opportunities that my friends Teak Dyer and DeWitt White did not have, is very fulfilling to me."

Justine has even made it a requirement that every student who goes through her program—which is actually named for her close friend, Teak—does the same and finds a charity that he or she can embrace. Her organization has since placed one hundred kids in their first and second choice schools, all with full financial aid awards.

New tastes: few months

· Field trips.

· Join political campaign.

· Take some classes.

· Summer program.

· Join a theater troupe.

· Volunteer.

· Find an internship.

In 2000 Keith Wagner led Northwestern Mutual's 8,000 insurance agents as the #1 producer in the country. But Keith was probably never nominated "Most Likely to Succeed" in school, because as he put it, he probably never would even have gone to college it if weren't for the movie *Animal House*.

Even five years of college didn't change Keith that much. When Keith told his four college roommates that he'd been talking to a recruiter from Northwestern and was thinking of selling life insurance, they couldn't quite speak, because they were all too busy laughing. It turns out Keith's biggest inspiration was getting the three credits that Northwestern's summer internship had to offer. Knowing that he wasn't going to pursue anything with his psychology degree either, he needed to find something he could do with his life, and soon. With no professional experience whatsoever, Keith figured this might be a good chance to learn about business and sales. And his taste of the business that summer proved to be one of the best decisions he ever made. Within a few weeks, Keith was finally able to pay his rent, and his roommates were stunned. "Wagner's making money?" was their response this time, and within two years Keith's success would prompt them all to join Northwestern too.

Sales turned out to be so perfectly suited to him that he not only excelled, but became the #1 college intern in the company that year. Working part-time throughout his senior year, Keith made $35,000, more than most of his friends who had graduated and were working full-time. Before class, he'd set up meetings to call on new clients, and after class, he'd go meet with people until late in the night. The work ethic that his father, an engineer for Hughes Aircraft, had instilled in him was starting to kick in and pay off.

His friends definitely gave him a hard time for not going out more, but, as he put it, the mortgage company didn't care if he had a great time the night before or not. They just cared that he made his monthly payments on the new condo he'd bought. The BMW dealership where he bought his new car surely felt the same way too. But Keith wasn't overwhelmed by taking on all these expenses, because he knew that what he made was up to him and how hard he was willing to work. In the insurance business he could work whenever he wanted, as much as he wanted, and he was his only boss. Not surprisingly, he worked like he had never worked before, and he loved the rewards.

After college, Keith went to work selling insurance full-time. On an average day, he'd get into the office at 6:30 A.M.

and wouldn't finish his day until 10:30 or 11 P.M. He described his reasoning: "In sales, nine to five are the golden hours. If you're not seeing someone, talking to someone about buying, or closing deals, you're in a slow death spiral. If you're in front of a computer doing paperwork during that window of time, you're not making money. That's why I was always the first one in and the last one out. That was the only way to maximize my time selling. I couldn't go meet with someone at 6 in the morning, but I could get all my administrative work done before most people even got started." Then it was all about reading every great book on sales he could find, taking lots of successful people out to dinner and coffee to pick their brains, and networking like crazy. And that dedication continued to pay off.

Keith's career has since been a history of records being set. His first year in the company he was rated #2 of the first year agents. In his second year, he was rated #1, and in his third year, #2. Within five years of starting, Keith landed in the top 20, and at 31 years old, in his eighth year, he led the company in sales, and became the youngest person ever to do so in 145 years.

If you had told him that he could be making this kind of money when he was 21, he would have called you insane. But now he knows it's possible. Keith's advice: "Take a taste and don't forget that hard work is called hard work for a reason. Most people want to be great at what they do without working hard at being great. If you can understand that and start focusing your efforts, the opportunities can be amazing for anyone, even for someone like me."

New tastes: one year plus

· Join the military.

· Study or work abroad.

· Join the Peace Corps.

· Get an advanced degree.

· Participate in Teach for America.

· Monitor someone.

· Move to a new city or country.

A TASTE OF PARADISE

Ever consider moving somewhere far away, totally out of your comfort zone? Who hasn't dreamed about leaving everything behind and venturing off to an exotic island to live more simply and peacefully? Well that's exactly what Jay Gleason did. Yes, he wrapped up all his loose ends, packed everything he owned, and moved from Maryland to a little condo on the beach in Hawaii on the island of Maui.

Jay wanted to find a place where he'd be surrounded by a different culture, with local people who lived a life at a bit more relaxed pace. He wondered what it would be like to live in a new place where he really didn't know exactly what to expect. Since moving to Maryland for college, he had pretty much lived and worked in the same area for more than a decade. He had started and run a string of successful businesses in the area over the years and, as his latest business venture was winding down, he didn't want to do the same thing all over again. He knew exactly what to expect from a life where he was, and he yearned for a new experience, both personally and professionally.

Before settling on a place to move, he decided to taste several different cities throughout the United States. On one trip, he went to check out Maui and immediately fell in love. Less than a year later he boarded a plane en route to his new home in paradise. Soon after his arrival, he set out to take a major taste of the culture and island lifestyle by talking with lots of locals. Some of these people had also moved to Maui from the mainland. They all told him that there was tremendous opportunity for new businesses on the island due to a thriving tourism industry. But they did warn that the pace was significantly slower and that the business climate was seasonal. One person in particular was a local art dealer in Lahaina. He told Jay, "Art and jewelry dealers here can do really well because visitors want to take a piece of island life home with them. Anyone who can capture memories for people is doing something clever in my opinion." He also talked to some investors in several local shops. They said that there were a lot of wealthy people who had started businesses to keep themselves busy, but didn't necessarily have much experience with running a business. "As a result there were certainly some shop owners looking for people to buy, take over, or help them as consultants in their ventures. You, my friend, seem to be well suited for opportunities such as that."

Since Jay had spent many years in Maryland working with small retail shops, entrepreneurs, and larger retailers, he had a great base of information to share with people. Maui offered him the opportunity to quickly parlay those experiences into consulting opportunities and even new potential ownership opportunities.

One consulting job with an art gallery quickly turned into a partnership. There he applied the marketing and promotion skills that he had learned back home to boost the gallery's sales of art, wood, and glass to both tourists and more than a few of the locals. For a while he enjoyed living and working on one of the most beautiful islands in the world, spending his days in the gallery serving the locals and vacationing tourists and his nights sleeping on his lanai overlooking the magnificent, tranquil ocean.

After about eight months there, Jay came to the conclusion that his little taste of paradise wasn't quite the Ideal Life he envisioned. Sure, he loved the perfect weather, the new casual dress code, the happy, friendly people, the relaxed pace, the peace and quiet, the music, and the to-die-for sunsets. Yet, Jay started to miss a lot of the things his past mainland city life offered that remote island life did not. Or as he says, "On the mainland you can get what you wanted, wherever you wanted it, as fast as you wanted it, at reasonable prices. While on Maui, you are forced to take what they have, wherever and whenever they wanted to give it to you, at whatever price they want to charge you."

This intense change was manageable for him at first, but eventually it drove Jay to make the decision to leave the island after about a year to pursue a new home somewhere back on the mainland.

As all tastes do for the Young & Successful, stepping out of his comfort zone to take a taste of the unknown revealed some important insights that Jay can and will use to shape the direction of the rest of his life. Through his experience on Maui, he realized several things.

- He wants to live in an area where people are genuinely happy and laid-back, as they were in Maui. He liked the fact that hitting your car horn there was considered rude, and road rage was nonexistent.

- He wants to surround himself with more people who are able to keep the bigger picture in mind on a regular basis. People in Maui had a life that was about more than just work. They relished art, nature (the ocean, animals, and plant life), and truly valued their culture and history.

- He took for granted and missed many of the luxuries that he grew accustomed to in Maryland. Same or next-day service, for example, he now realized, was a standard that most of the rest of the world does not live by. The "I'll get to it just as soon as I can" philosophy of life and customer service was not something he was fond of or could ever get, used to.

- You can't really visit an area you are considering making a real move to for just a week or two. You need to be there a good month or so to get past the tourist lifestyle and begin to really experience life there as a true local.

· You can't be afraid to talk to anyone and everyone in a new place, as the collective perspective you'll gain will shed light on a more complete, balanced picture.

· He truly enjoys the change and challenges that living in a new place brings. Moving to and doing business in new and different environments and cultures is something he wishes he'd done much sooner.

Today, in his late thirties, Jay says, based on this taste of living and working in Maui, he realized that he needs to make this type of change a more regular part of his life from now on. Jay no longer wonders "what if" about a life somewhere else. While he doesn't want to live on Maui full-time anymore, he does want to take long vacations there a few times a year. He is currently working toward doing that, while the sweet taste of fresh pineapples and coconuts still lingers, and the fresh mountain air awaits him for his next adventure.

The Comforts of Home

Sometimes the best tastes come from what's right in front of you. Have you ever wondered, for instance, why so many people go into the same business that their families are in? It's because we've spent a lifetime seeing how their world works. For years we watch our parents go to work, listen to stories about their days and experiences when they come home, and maybe even get to tag along with them to work for a few hours here and there. So it's no wonder that by the time most younger people are faced with the stress of having to figure out what they want to do with their lives, the familiar family business or career path suddenly makes so much sense. At the same time, though, you probably have a better idea of whether what your family does *doesn't* work for you than just about anything else too. And knowing what you definitely don't want to do is never a bad thing. It gets you that much closer to narrowing down your options and finding what you do want.

FROM FAMILY BUSINESS TO PERSONAL PASSION

Steve Robbins is a third generation jeweler who grew up working summers and holidays in his father's jewelry store. He remembers listening to wonderful stories from his grandfather about the business that *he* had started and run since the 1920s. All his life, Steve knew that that was what he wanted to do, too. Right out of college, he joined the family business, and soon Steve and his brother Skip took over for their father. From one store, they built fourteen, and from there, they decided to spin off a new concept. They changed the name of the company to Robbins Bros. and set out to build the "world's biggest engagement ring store."

Since then, business has been booming and the company's revenues have increased 600 percent from when they first took over the business. In their eighth year of being in business as Robbins Bros., sales are rapidly approaching the $100-million mark, and now each year more than 100,000 couples come through their stores looking to buy their rings from Steve and Skip. Most exciting of all to them is the fact that several of the great-grandchildren of their grandfather's original customers are their cherished customers today.

Yanik Silver had little interest in his father's medical equipment sales business while he was growing up, but as he got older and wanted to earn some spending money, he conceded and went to work for his dad for a while. At fourteen he was put on the phones selling latex gloves. When he got his driver's license, Yanik was told to go make some cold calls. "So there I was, a sixteen-year-old kid going off to try and talk to some doctors about buying medical equipment." Yanik started to do really well at it, too, and was able to close many new deals for his father's business while reaching out to a whole new base of customers. But it was grueling work. Every day he had to get in his car and drive all over town to meet physicians, qualify numerous leads, all while juggling customer service, customer follow-through, and endless paperwork. Between all of that, and school, it was a lot for a sixteen-year-old to manage. Part of his job also entailed being in charge of all the marketing and advertising for the business. That part Yanik really liked. In addition to cold calling, he also had to write sales letters and marketing pieces to prospective clients. Though it would take a little while to realize it, Yanik had stumbled onto his niche. The letters he wrote were so successful, each mailing was drawing three or four times as many qualified leads as compared to previous mailings. Soon business started booming for his dad, and business owners who were being marketed to were asking who the genius was who had crafted the compelling messages. They wanted the same powerful prose to sell their goods and services, too.

Then one day, a doctor he was calling on handed him a sales audiotape from one of the big marketing gurus, Jay Abraham, and his life changed overnight. Yanik discovered an opportunity to provide sales materials, tools, and templates to doctors. His first product, a $900 kit that shared secrets on how medical practices could become more profitable, made him as much money in two sales as he made pounding the pavement selling equipment all month. So at twenty-three, while already making a not so shabby $60,000 a year, he took a risk on the information sales business and spun off his own venture.

Soon Yanik was selling templates for his most popular sales letters and began offering his sales kits online at surefiremarketing.com to people in all different industries. It's now been just about three years, and he is making an average of $20,000 a month (from just the first site), working part-time from home, selling a range of "powerful tools and resources for entrepreneurs to enhance their businesses." These days, he refers to himself as a direct response copywriter and marketing consultant, specializing in "salesmanship in print." As a result of his success, and so many people asking how he'd done it, he and his wife, Missy, now get to travel to marketing and sales conferences around the world to lead workshops, give speeches and teach Internet marketing to audiences eager to learn the secrets of *his* success. And did I mention that Yanik is only twenty-nine?

Remember, the Young & Successful realize that by taking new tastes, you're not only going to reinforce your feelings about some things, but perhaps more important, you're going to whittle down your list, and eventually find exactly what you're looking for.

Become Your Best Critic

By now, hopefully, you've gotten your first taste of something you've always dreamed about or are about to do so. The Young & Successful realize that like any good critic, they must take away from each experience a better understanding of what they liked and didn't quite care for. You can't expect to like every taste you take. But without trying out several different options, you're never going to experience enough to accurately focus in on and narrow down your best opportunities.

After each taste, sit down and ask yourself some questions about the experience you just had. If you took a taste of a workplace, were you comfortable there? Did the other workers seem like people with whom you could get along? Was the pace one that you could maintain? What surprised you about the people, the place, the business—or was it more or less what you expected?

If you were trying a taste of some of the lifestyle you're hoping to have, did the experience feel like it was worth the price? Do you still feel willing to sacrifice now in hopes of enjoying this later?

These are only a few of the possible questions you need to ask yourself. That's what this process is all about: Do your homework, take a taste, ask some questions, and repeat until you know for sure that you're on the right path. In many ways, you're working to find out about yourself—your needs, your drivers, and your ambitions—as much as you are about the companies, businesses, or lifestyles that you're checking out.

Our editor on this project told us that she realized that she'd hit on the right business when, during a publishing internship, she was filing author correspondence. "Reading the letters back and forth between the authors and their editors, I was fascinated. The day flew by. I knew then that this was where I wanted to be." That's one example of what taking a taste can do for you—show you the place and the work that truly satisfies you, the perfect match for your attitude, skills, and dreams.

File Your Review

Take notes, keep a journal, record your experiences on tape. Whatever you do, realize that you're never going to remember all the details, nor will you discover what you're perfectly suited for unless you have the right nuggets of information to make your assessment. Sure, you'll probably figure it all out at some point, but the big question is, how long will that take and will it be too late for you to do anything about it?

Consider filing your notes. By now I wouldn't be surprised if you need a file or portfolio to hold all the information on where you need to go and what you have to do to make those dreams of yours happen. If so, take that next simple step and give it all a home worthy of such important records! After all, a few years from now when people are clamoring to know your story and the secrets behind your success, these records will come in handy.

Don't Be Afraid to Walk Away

While taking a taste is merely an indulgent experiment to get your juices flowing and your mind wandering and wondering again, the great thing about it is that it isn't a commitment. It's just a taste. And if you don't like the taste, no problem, just walk away and taste something else. Move on to sample something else that may spark your interest.

This isn't to say that we should walk away from commitments we make. The whole idea behind taking a taste is sampling something (well, actually lots of things) with experimentation as the objective. If, in taking a taste, you decide to take a bigger step, such as accepting an internship, volunteer position, or anything that will render people dependent on you, be sure to respect that relationship. If someone offers you an opportunity to do something you've always wanted to try, be very up front about your intentions and, if you do walk away, do it with class.

The Young & Successful understand how important a willingness to walk away is. As leaders who grow into bigger and more substantial positions of power and influence, they learn to spin on a dime and change course when need be, while following through with their commitments. Take initiative and responsibility for your courses of action. Thrive on the freedom, the power of having choices. Take a taste when you crave something new, and learn to move on and walk away if it's not working for you.

Always Be Tasting

Taking a taste works best when it results in constant exploration throughout various areas of your Ideal Life. Eventually, you start to hone in on sweet spots. Take a taste and repeat as necessary. Remember ABT—always be tasting. Step into a new store. Pick up a new book or magazine. Say hello to a stranger. Dine in a new restaurant. Taste something new every day. Even if it seems small or insignificant at the time. Developing a habit of taking a taste, at all levels, in all areas of your life, will help you get that much closer to living out the dreams of your Ideal Life. Just think, one new person, piece of knowledge, or resource you may uncover could open up a whole new world of possibilities for you. This makes for a very interesting and exciting life where, as you continue to taste, you are bound to repeatedly uncover what really turns you on.

Real World University™

TO MAKE IT TO THE TOP OF OUR GAME—and stay there—the Young & Successful recognize the need to be better equipped, better trained, more intelligent, and highly strategic in their thinking. To do this, they develop their own style of learning and commit themselves to maintaining the extra edge that a true dedication to education, exploration, and highly focused study can give them. We repeatedly hear the Young & Successful say that they believe they can do just about anything if they want it badly enough. They thrive on challenges because they are confident that they can quickly learn whatever they might need to make big things happen. Being the best, playing at the top of our game, requires a commitment to continuously and aggressively educating ourselves. Real World University is where all this happens.

We all went to school to learn the basics: reading, writing, and arithmetic. These were supposed to give us the foundation of what we'd need to survive in the outside world. But somehow, somewhere, someone decided that we should learn about calculus, not credit; we spent weeks studying ancient civilizations but not a day on modern corporations. We learned about the goals of historic leaders but not how to set our own. We were taught to write but not to really communicate. *So where were the classes on how to become successful in life?*

When we were in school, many of us were jumping out of our skins, wanting to get out and do something. But when we finally graduated, we quickly realized how much we still needed to know. What the Young & Successful figure out early on is that it's where we take our education *from here* that has the greatest impact on how far we'll go. And it's this commitment to continuous learning that gives the Young & Successful that extra edge to catapult them toward their Ideal Lives.

You've already begun to figure out what you love. Now it's time to learn by doing and by focusing on how to fill in those gaping holes that traditional education left behind.

⧖ Welcome to RWU

Real World University (RWU) is not a physical place . . . yet. For now it's wherever we turn to learn what we need to succeed in the real world. Real World U. is where the Young & Successful acquire the knowledge, experience, credibility, and credentials so critical to their long-term success. It's the college of life, where you're the one designing the curriculum. And that means you can learn what you need to in record time in a way that's relevant, interesting, and perfectly suited to you.

Now that's a new spin on education, don't you think?

If Real World University had a recruiting brochure, this is what it might look like:

Do You Want to Learn Absolutely *Everything* You Need to Know to Achieve Incredible, Rewarding, Meaningful Success In YOUR LIFE? . . .

. . . if so, then consider enrolling in **Real World University**™
                                                    TODAY!

At RWU you'll acquire all the "real world" knowledge you'll need to learn precisely how to give yourself the extra edge you truly deserve in record time—

The Gift of Endless Knowledge & Wisdom

Our unique, completely customized program allows *you* to choose

- whom you study from
- what you'll study and learn
- who will teach you
- how much you pay to attend
- what campus you'll attend
- when your semester begins and ends
- what time of day your classes are
- what type of degree you earn
- which technology and resources you'll have available
- who your classmates are, if any
- your meal plan
- the friends and advisors you'll study with
- when, where, why, and how you'll take tests and how they'll be graded
- and so much more . . .

The right way is your way at **Real World University**! Your fully customized curriculum to learn just what you need, just the way you always wanted it, with no questions asked.

We have programs to meet any and every budget under the sun . . . to fit any schedule you need and want . . . to cover any topic you want—in any style, environment, and format—to maximize your learning the way that best suits **your specific, individual needs**!

Enroll TODAY and we guarantee you'll learn everything you need to know to get everything you want in life *without waiting a lifetime*. New semesters begin every day everywhere.

www.RealWorldUniversity.com

What's In Store at RWU?

It is here that learning and educational experiences become more focused, more gratifying, and more relevant to our lives, our careers, and
our aspirations than ever before. This is where the things we've already
learned are put into a new context and our ability to put what we know
to work is ultimately tested. Best of all, everything you ever wanted or
needed to learn and didn't, you can now learn.

From this point, how well educated you are is up to you. And surely
you have some blank spots to address. We all do. It's our job to round
out our educational experiences on our own to ensure we're well
equipped for what lies ahead. Whether your plans are to set yourself up
in a quaint little town or to dive into a global marketplace, the choices
you make here and now can make anything possible.

In RWU you're in charge of what you learn—when, where, from
whom, and even the style in which you're taught. The question should
no longer be *if* you're going to keep learning but rather *how* you'd most
enjoy and benefit from it. At RWU you can

- focus on studying only the subjects most important and interesting to you

- work at your own pace, whether that's a fraction of or twice
  the usual time

- choose to learn from the people you most admire and respect

- determine who would make the most stimulating classmates

- decide the perfect setting, location, and schedule

- work out a plan for any budget

In your Grand Plan you laid out a series of benchmarks and detailed the necessary steps to move you toward your goals. Now we want to take it further and deal with what you need to know and learn and the credentials you need to get you there.

In this chapter we'll look at *your learning style,* your preferences, your focus, and we'll use that information to *find the ideal campus* or learning environment for you. Then we'll help you *pick your classes,* or the areas you need to work on. We'll help you *buy your books,* surrounding you with the best possible resources for what you're setting out to learn. And we'll *meet your professors,* those industry leaders and gurus who will put everything into context. *Your tutors* will be your day-to-day support team—these are your mentors, advisors, counselors, and guides. Imagine having the answers to some of your toughest questions just a phone call or email away. We'll show you how to load up on these people so you're never by yourself again. Then we'll teach you how to assess all this initial information and use it *to declare your major.* This is where you begin to make some big commitments.

From here, *getting your degree* is just a matter of time. But we're not necessarily after a fancy piece of paper here. Your degree in RWU is really analogous to your credentials in business and your career. And there are so many opportunities to get these, too. You just need to know a few secrets.

Orientation

Here are a few things to consider as you get settled and comfortable in this new world of learning.

1 **The rules:** RWU has none. These are up to you and your industry to determine.

2 **Your learning style:** RWU understands that we all process information in different ways. Your first job is to figure out how you learn best and what's going to make your new learning experiences the most interesting and fulfilling for you.

3 **Your classes:** You can add and drop classes at will, but give yourself enough time to make informed decisions and get what you need out of every experience.

4 **Your time:** If you haven't already, time management is one area you're going to want to tackle. This is, of course, assuming that you have other things going on in your life, like maybe a day job to work around. Try to balance between getting the most out of your time and not completely overloading yourself. It can be a delicate balance, and it will get more important every day of your life.

5 **Fun and enjoyment:** Still, the most important thing is to have fun. If you begin to feel like you might be on the wrong track, stop, regroup, and look at your plan again. It's important to maintain even the most basic level of confidence in the choices you make so you have the motivation and energy you need to do what's required. The last thing we want is for you to be stuck on a track you don't want to be on. There are no required classes here. Do what makes you most fulfilled and most satisfied. And above all, try to enjoy the process.

Getting to the Root of How You Learn Best

Now, let's talk about how you learn best. There's a fascinating field of study out there that has, in recent years, started to uncover how we learn. It looks at how we're wired, how we process information, and most important, how we can overcome any shortcomings, disabilities, or challenges. Mel Levine is the director of the Clinical Center for the Study of Development and Learning and the founder of the All Kinds of Minds Institute in North Carolina. He is perhaps the most recognized and respected expert on this subject. As Dr. Levine explains it, "Our educational shortsightedness can result in a loss of human potential on a grand scale."

That means that our Grand Plans can be severely disrupted if we don't pay attention to and cater to the way that we learn best. None of us can afford to be ignorant, particularly in our field or career of choice. To the contrary, we have to be, at the very least, competent to survive and show tremendous expertise if we'd prefer to thrive.

How many times have you avoided doing a presentation or giving a speech because you were too nervous? How many times have you shied away from new situations or people because you were afraid you couldn't keep up? And what have you avoided doing or learning because you convinced yourself you just aren't good at certain things? Well, if any of that has ever bothered you, I'm telling you once and for all that you can stop being afraid, unsure, uncomfortable, and insecure right now.

The bottom line is you can learn just about anything, if you just know your style. "It's never too late to understand and strengthen a mind," says Dr. Levine. He is adamant about the fact that everyone is different and none of us can be expected to learn in a "one-size-fits-all education system philosophy." In his book *A Mind at a Time* (Simon & Schuster, 2002) he explains:

> *Each kid unrolls an original mural of mind traits . . . the challenge is to understand his or her special wiring and its implications. . . . There are hundreds of different breakdowns in learning . . . and the demands keep*

changing. Learning differences can and do crop up at all different times in our lives, from kindergarten through college.

The same goes for grown-ups too. All along the way, we have to learn to keep up. Dr. Levine urges us to identify and celebrate our strengths. (Remember the Personal Balance Sheet we created in Chapter Two? Well, this is another reason why that is such an important exercise.)

We All Have Our Own Style

If there's one thing we're all experts on, it's ourselves. Think about your best and worst learning experiences, for example. When was the transfer of knowledge effortless for you? What experiences were the most interesting and engaging? Instead of just leaving your assessment at, "Yeah, he was really a great teacher," dig a little deeper. Why? What turned you on about the style? What made the subject so compelling? How can you extract what you liked most about that particular learning experience? When you can answer that question, you can often recreate that experience for yourself and apply that strategy to new things that you have to learn.

Maybe you had a fabulous tutor who took as much time as needed to answer every question you had. You can still find people like this. Interview someone who's doing incredible things in his or her business. Go to a seminar where someone you really want to learn from is speaking. Or better yet, if you can, hire a consultant, then drill him or her for information by the hour.

Perhaps, like Scott, you're research obsessed. You want to become an expert on anything that's important to learn, and you'll stop at nothing until you've read everything there is to read on the subject. You loved that time you got to go to that big industry library and plowed through hundreds of books, journals, reports, articles, and reference guides that you'd never seen before. So re-create it again. You don't have to fly across the country to get to an epicenter of information, either. Give yourself the freedom to indulge in a three-hour visit to the bookstore. Allocate enough time in your week to surf the web for hours until you find everything you're looking for. Or consider signing up for some of those online research services and go crazy running advanced searches.

Whether you're pulling information out of a tutor, an interview, a library, or off the Net, having the information is only half the battle— you have to *own* it. How do you do this? Put it to use. Integrate what you've learned into your Grand Plan. Figure out what it tells you about the intermediate steps in your plan. Make it show you the connections between where you are and where you want to be. Once you've turned abstract information into valuable knowledge, it's yours for life.

Finding the Perfect Learning Situations

In setting up the perfect environment and circumstances for you to really start loading up on all the areas you still need to learn, here are some initial issues to consider about your learning style. This is only a basic assessment, as the goal here is to get you thinking about what works best for you. As you read, start to put together a clearer picture of how you most enjoy learning and what you need to make it a continuous focus in your life.

Environment: Where are you most receptive to new information? Are you happiest when you're curled up in a lounge chair with a great book, some paperwork, or your laptop? Do you prefer the more formal, intellectual setting and the big solid chairs and tables at the library? Or are you more receptive to big interactive group discussions in a room full of fifty or five hundred impassioned people?

Format: Where do you prefer to get your information? Can you get totally enthralled by poring through hundreds of pages of books and articles that you can feel and touch? Or would you much prefer to see everything online where you don't have to bother with hard copies of anything? If you had the choice, would you give the task of researching to someone else? Or is it something that you would rather do yourself? Thanks to the publishing world, we now have many formats in which to get the information we want. Don't limit yourself to just one or two.

There are a great range of formats to consider: books, newspapers, magazines, special reports, research studies, newsletters, manuals; tapes, CDs, MP3s, telephone chats, interviews, teleconferences; television, movies, VHS tapes, DVDs, CDs, multimedia presentations; speeches, workshops, seminars, conferences, trade shows, classroom lectures, camps, hands-on training, consultations; Internet, multimedia, software programs, online learning. Make a mental note of your formats of choice and go out of your way to seek out these opportunities when the need to learn something new arises.

Detail and Depth: How intense are you when it comes to learning new things? Are you a glutton for volumes of five-hundred-page textbooks and resource directories? To feel satisfied, do you need to have absolutely everything ever printed anywhere on a subject? Or are you just fine with summaries and synopses of the most important stuff.

Repetition: How long does it take for new info to sink in for you? Do you like to have the ability to stop anytime and replay vital info? Do you tend to miss things the first time around, or like to hear things a few times to really remember them? Or are you one of those people with a photographic memory, who can see things once and remember them forever?

Credibility: How much of a stickler are you for having the right sources? If something was reported by a "respectable" tabloid, is that good enough for you? Or do you insist that if Einstein (or someone just as credible) didn't validate it himself, then you simply can't trust it?

Timeliness: How time sensitive are you? Do you tend to gravitate toward the latest and greatest, up-to-the-second info available? Or are you one of those who insist your information has stood the test of time . . . and survived the dinosaurs?

Price: How much are you willing to pay for your information? Are you all about taking advantage of the information age and getting everything for free? Or are you ready to spend every last dime on going to the best source and getting everything that they have regardless of price?

Supervision:	How much hand-holding do you need? If you're told once to learn something, can it be considered done? Or does your life (or job) have to depend on something to have you get up and get to it? Do you need to be reminded ten times to do something once? Will you wait until the very last minute?

◪ Design Your Own University

Imagine you have a secret admirer. Someone who's been watching you for some time now, who sees your true brilliance and has all the confidence in the world that your future is bound to be a bright one. He or she realizes that you still have a lot more to learn but know that you are willing to do whatever it takes. He or she is sure of it—even though things may not have clicked for you so far.

Your secret admirer knows that with the right tools and training, you could accomplish extraordinary things with your life. So he or she has decided to make a major investment in you. The "University of You" has been generously endowed, and now it's up to you to build it out to whatever you want it to be.

Don't worry about your grades, your credits, letters of recommendation, or your entrance exam scores. They don't matter here. There are no more requirements to worry about. You're in—it's a done deal. And you're in charge.

Pick Your Major

So let's focus on what's really important—what you want to learn to make your Ideal Life possible and what the best scenario is to do that. To make this the best experience, what you need to think about now is

What do you most want or need to learn? And why?

Who would be your best possible teachers?

How do you learn most effectively? Where would you be most comfortable studying?

Who do you want to share the experience with?

Is there special equipment, technology, or props you want or need?

How intense do you want the program?

Are there any time lines or deadlines that are important to you?

How much money or other resources can you afford to commit?

Answer these questions and what we'll have is a perfect outline for your program.

NEXT STEP · Now you're ready to design your own ideal experience. Use this handy reference sheet to help you sort out your priorities and keep you focused on what you're really looking for.

Subject: _____
(hobby, skill, specialty, basic competency)

Teachers: _____
(awards, affiliations, training, experience, credentials, accessibility)

Format: _____
(in class, independent study, full- or part-time, workshop, personal training)

Location: _____

(local, remote, online, university-based, abroad)

Classmates: _____

(large group, intimate, friends/colleagues only, none)

Special needs: _____

(high-tech equipment, visual aids, experiential learning style)

Perks: _____

(access to industry experts, networking opportunities, informal environment)

Intensity: _____

(high energy, fast paced, move at your own pace, low pressure, beginner level)

Time lines: _____

(flexible schedule, two-week program, summer commitment, evenings and weekends)

Affordability: _____

(free, within specific budget, no limit, scholarship required)

Choose Your Term

In most cases we can't exactly choose how long it will take to earn certain credentials or experience. But in Real World U, we can set the parameters and work around our schedules.

RWU IN ACTION

Spend a few hours or a full weekend exploring your educational options to learn any of the things that you are missing or have been putting off. Check out weekend seminars, workshops, day trips, distance learning, internships, new jobs, weekend volunteering, books, or even mentors to start. You're sure to find at least some basic information to get you started. Then make a commitment to enroll.

Paul Feller had just become CEO of a big high-tech company when he decided to beef up his financial and senior executive know-how with an MBA. Problem was, he was on the fast track to taking the new company public, while his wife was running a company of her own and was pregnant with their second baby. Talk about logistical constraints! He was confident, though, that if he clearly laid out his priorities and assessed his needs, he'd find a program to fit into his schedule and at least meet his basic expectations. But what he found ended up far exceeding them.

After months of investigating dozens of options, Paul finally found a special educational opportunity at nearby Pepperdine University. Their Graziadio School of Business was ranked among the top twenty executive MBA programs in the world and specifically targeted to top corporate officers and fast-track senior execs with a minimum of seven to twelve years high-level working experience. As such, their focus was right on track with what Paul wanted to learn about most:

· Constructing a complete framework for managing an organization strategically

· Anticipating and assessing critical management opportunities and issues

· Identifying and forecasting trends and changes in industries and markets, both domestically and internationally

· Functionally integrating products, services, and concepts to achieve corporate goals

· Providing appropriate quantitative tools that assist in the implementation of strategic plans and improve net results.

Well, you get the picture (and by the way, that's according to the catalog, not Paul). But it clearly spoke to him, because he signed up, got his company to pay the $65,000 tuition bill, and is now thrilled that he made the decision and commitment. Now, once every three weeks for the next twenty months, he gets to work on the MBA he always wanted in an intimate, high-caliber environment with seminar-like classes. Best of all, he'll learn with his peers and enjoy lectures from top educators and outside experts, all while tapping into a network of more than 20,000 alumni, with 1,100 others like him who are currently leading organizations as presidents and CEOs.

See, ask the right questions and just look at what you can find to meet even your most specific and highest of expectations.

Regardless of whether you have a job to contend with or some time off coming that you want to put to good use, think about what kind of commitment you can make and survey your options. Whatever you have to work with, there are lots of ways you can start to get the more intense education and experience you need. Some options to consider:

Short-Term	Part-Time	Long Haul
Boot camps	Night or weekend	Distance learning
Resort courses	classes	Masters or advanced
Workshops	Extension	degrees
Conferences	programs	Total immersion
Expos	Online courses	programs
Summer programs	Counseling	Leadership training
Camps	Home-study	Management
Tutoring	programs	programs
Books, workbooks,		New job
kits		

Select Your Concentration and Classes

By now you should know what your major is. This is the industry you've explored as part of your Grand Plan. In Master Your Universe (Chapter Five), you focused on your industry and made a map of that world. Take a Taste (Chapter Six) got you to start exploring the many options you have to do what you love. Now we have a new challenge to contend with: acquiring the specific education, training, and knowledge that is important if you're going to excel.

Medical schools have a brilliant way of dealing with the need to get a broad range of experience, while drilling deep into a few select areas to find the perfect specialty. They call it "rotations," and it's a program that all medical residents have to go through to insure they're well exposed to the many different aspects, areas, and specialties in their given area of study.

Imagine you're fresh out of medical school and you know one thing: You want to work with kids. That means your specialty is pediatrics and your options for specialization include the following: neonatal care, pediatric intensive care, adolescent care, behavior and development, trauma, rehabilitative medicine, etc. Over three years you'd cycle through dozens of department rotations spending about six to eight weeks in each area, and every year you would rise to higher levels of learning and interact with hospital patients with increasingly more complex needs. Now that's a way to get some serious education and exposure to your options!

RWU IN ACTION

Any one of us can develop our own rotations program to expose us to a variety of different options in our career. For example, if you wanted to go into the wine business but weren't quite sure whether you wanted to tend the vines, become a viticulturist, work in a lab, act as a distributor, or become a sommelier, then consider spending one summer cycling through each of these specialties, spending time volunteering, visiting with, or shadowing experts in a vineyard, a food lab, a distribution company, a fine restaurant, etc. That would give you an amazing new perspective, don't you agree? Try it yourself. Pick a few areas that interest you most, roll up your sleeves, and get some real experience in the field.

Buy Your Books

This is the point where you're really going to miss the college bookstore. Remember walking the aisles with your course list in hand, knowing that all you had to do was find the books assigned to your class and you were done? In RWU, the signs on the shelf aren't as obvious.

Just like we talked about in Master Your Universe, every industry and course of study has specialty publications, reference materials, and news outlets. And by now you know that virtually every industry has a trade organization that can offer you tons of material and other sources. Find the industry standards, the must-reads, the must-dos and get familiar with them. Read up on the key companies and key players in the industry that interest you. These are your guides. Read the books and find the same tools the pros rely on to get their information.

Once you've begun to master your universe, make your universe bigger by reading and learning about the bigger issues: politics (*The Prince* by Machiavelli); history (Stephen E. Ambrose's *To America: Personal Reflections of an Historian*); strategy (*The Art of War* by Sun Tzu); political science (*Rocking the Ages* by J. Walker Smith); or trends (*Dictionary of the Future* by Faith Popcorn or *Megatrends* by John Naisbitt). Don't ignore what great fiction can teach you either. Anything from *The Odyssey* to *Atlas Shrugged* are great bets, too. And certainly never forget classic business books such as *Think and Grow Rich* by Napoleon Hill, *Seven Habits of Highly Effective People* by Stephen Covey, *Raving Fans* by Ken Blanchard, *What They Don't Teach You at Harvard Business School* by Mark McCormack, *Swim with the Sharks* by Harvey Mackay, *The Richest Man in Babylon* by George Clason, and *First, Break All the Rules* by Marcus Buckhingham.

While the magazines and trade journals may give you quick fixes and short-term solutions, great books will always provide richer detail and new knowledge to guide you along the way.

As Tim Sanders, former director of Yahoo!'s in-house think tank and the man who put together the first Victoria's Secret Internet fashion show, says, "To become a person who succeeds in life, you have to have three things: your knowledge, your connections, and your compassion." According to Tim, the knowledge is the easiest to come by, because it's all right there in the bookstore waiting for you. In his book, *Love Is the Killer App: How to Win Business and Influence Friends,* he says that reading the book isn't enough. You need to break it down by underlining everything that catches your eye and summarizing the book's key points. That way, when you finish a book, you know it cold. And if you ever need a refresher course, all you have to do is glance at the notes and it will all come back. Tim's knowledge has served him well, guiding him from a Dallas Internet start-up to the king of start-ups, Yahoo!, where his office has become an unofficial lending library.

RWU IN ACTION

Load up on valuable resources that can teach you what you still need to know about your industry. If you don't have one already, start to build your own reference library. Take all those piles of research notes that you should be accumulating by now and throw them into files or spiral notebooks, or organize them into categories and get a stationery store, printer, or copying shop to bind it all for you. Then gather up all the magazines and books you already have and choose a few areas of interest you'd like to build up over time.

Meet the Professors

Study the paths that others took to get where you want to be. If there are no role models for what you want to do, don't worry—you're just going to have to be a little creative.

Deputy Inspector Philip Banks commands the 81st precinct in the Bedford-Stuyvesant section of Brooklyn, New York. He credits his rise in the ranks to focus, determination, and the inspiration he gained from African Americans in NYPD supervisory roles. Though few in number, those he did meet demonstrated the highest level of professionalism and accomplishment he could find on the force.

Finding role models was never easy for Philip, who early on sensed that many of his colleagues erroneously believed that African Americans could not do well on NYPD promotional examinations and, therefore, could not lead. But Philip had his eye focused on promotion from the moment he entered law enforcement sixteen years ago. And his commitment to succeed drove him throughout. Proving both of those premises wrong motivated Banks not only to excel on the promotional examinations but also to rapidly rise through the ranks and achieve the success he so desired. While Philip had to forge his own path in many respects, today his story serves as a powerful example to others with dreams and passion just like his.

Many Young & Successful people are focused on goals that have never been achieved before, and they create paths by merging those of several people. Great people in your field is one subject you're going to want to keep up with on an ongoing basis.

When real reporters are working on a story, they focus on "primary source" materials—stuff that comes straight from the horse's mouth. If someone who interests you is giving a speech nearby, you should get there. If transcripts or tapes of their speeches are available, you should try to buy them. Getting to know these men and women—the real movers and shakers in the field that interests you—promises to give you a serious edge. Get started digging for articles they've written and tapes of some of the speeches they've made. And it *is* possible to get even more direct contact, but we'll talk a lot more about that in later chapters.

While it's not possible to get all your info from the top, you can find mentors, advisors, consultants, and other experts who know your business or field and are willing to help you. You don't have to become their best friend, hang out with them regularly, or even be on a first name basis, for that matter. But start to surround yourself with people who know what you're doing, support you in your efforts, and are willing to give you the honest truth when you need it.

RWU IN ACTION

Look at the top advisors you currently have in your life and consider who might be missing. You don't need specific names, but perhaps you need to build a relationship with an attorney, a creative salesman, a public relations consultant, or just a great listener who gets you and what you're all about. Once you figure out who you still need in your life, start asking around. Don't be shy about approaching people you don't know but who might fit the bill. You never know what they'll say, but you can be sure if you don't ask, you'll never get what you want. Try asking them out for a cup of coffee, or see if you can get their advice on a few things for fifteen minutes over the phone. You'll be amazed at how many people agree to at least talk to you. Be sure to ask how much time they can spend with you in the beginning, then stick to it unless they say otherwise.

Get Your Diploma . . . and Keep Going

That "piece of paper," your diploma, comes in all different forms in the real world. Instead of degrees, you can get certifications, accreditations, and credentials. But best of all, you get the experience that leads to pay raises, praise from bosses, solutions to problems, and a career that you can be proud of. If there was one lesson that college (both traditional and RWU) should have taught you by this point, it is that the degree typically matters less than what you've learned and can apply.

If you've figured out that learning doesn't stop when you leave school, then you're already far ahead of most of your peers. Launch your own self-designed, self-guided university out there in the real world and commit to a course of lifelong learning, and you'll receive the ultimate degree—success and satisfaction beyond your wildest expectation.

INDEPENDENT STUDY PAYS OFF

Jon Weisner has a lot of trouble explaining what he does for a living. This is true for a few reasons. Jon is a technology consultant whose projects are constantly changing and evolving, simply because his skills, abilities, and expertise are. As a result, he seems to be continuously leapfrogging from one mind-blowing project to the next. One month he's working with a major nonprofit, and a few months later he's heading a technology start-up. Next he's doing research, then he's building a telecom company, while cowriting a book. Then you hear that he's working on independent projects for Microsoft . . . no, DreamWorks SKG . . . no, CNN . . . actually, all of them. The real problem (if you can call it that) is that his career has to move at a pretty fast pace to keep up with his continuously evolving understanding of how technology works.

The most interesting part about Jon's story is that he's never taken a computer class in his life. He's 100 percent self-taught. That's hard to believe for someone who has to know so much to work with so many, but once he explained it to me, it suddenly made a lot of sense. See, Jon looks at technology as an expensive puzzle. Ever since he was a kid and tried to draw a flag on his first personal computer, he's been enthralled with what they can do. Knowing how to do research, ask questions, make cold calls, analyze data, and extract information gave him the tools to conquer all things technical, but it was his curiosity and the ever-changing world of technology that propelled him into this cycle of study. Here's what I mean.

Right out of school, Jon landed a job at Steven Spielberg's Visual History Foundation, which collects, catalogs, and archives video testimonials of Holocaust survivors worldwide. In the beginning, Jon was a production assistant in the technology department. His job—to clean up, organize papers, fix broken PCs, and show people how to use basic equipment around the office. But that started to change as people saw Jon coming in very early in the morning and leaving late at night. His mission: get time on the multimillion-dollar industrial computer systems that most people in the technology industry don't even have access to themselves. This is when he'd actually teach himself the machines, carefully read the manuals, experiment, play, and even break things sometimes (but never anything that couldn't easily be fixed). He knew his boundaries. That was why the big tech guys trusted him.

Soon Jon had his hands into everything. Eventually he became the technical liaison for people in fifty-six countries and his mornings would start out with the same old routine . . . checking in with all his offices: Argentina, Bolivia, Brazil, the Czech Republic, Denmark, Ecuador, Slovakia . . . he found that he was more efficient when he worked through them alphabetically. Remembering what time zones they were in was a whole other challenge.

From there, Jon was hungry to learn more. He began working on a business plan for a new technology company that eventually became a telecom venture, then died in the dot-com bomb. But there was plenty more to keep him busy. This time, a research project for Microsoft. The goal: to assess the true impact of networking technology in affecting sales and efficiency on small businesses. Now, again, Jon didn't necessarily know all the technology or all the software; perhaps most foreign of all, learning how to work with a company the size of Microsoft caught his attention. This time there was a whole new language to learn, but as with any new project or task, Jon locked himself in a room with the computers, new software, and a bunch of manuals, and got down to business. Once familiar, he'd get on the phone with friends he'd made and ask them for advice and insight on the challenges at hand.

One of his latest projects is perhaps one of his most interesting. Having jumped yet again into a different field with different rules, terminology, needs, technology, software, and a brand-new corporate culture to top it all off, Jon is now the chief technology officer for a medical company that develops diagnostic tools and technologies for detailing acute brain injuries. So what has Jon had to learn this time? Oh, nothing much . . . just a little neuroscience. Yes, to do this job properly, Jon had to read medical journals, software manuals, surgery guides, and lots of other technical literature that typically only people in the medical world read, let alone understand. He's had to interview doctors about their needs, observe nurses using existing medical equipment, make recommendations about how the hospital might streamline their procedures, and in between all this, Jon has spent plenty of time strolling the halls of the emergency room and trauma centers. Now, he too can read an electroencephalogram (an EEG) and recognize seizures, strokes, altered states of consciousness, and monitor overall brain activity. No, he's never been to medical school either, but he *is* known as a technical guru at the hospital these days.

Through it all, Jon has maintained total control of his education and continuously upgraded his opportunities and challenges by raising the bar on what he has to know and learn. As any savvy Young & Successful person will tell you, it's this ability to take control of your own intelligence and education that can make all the difference in the real world.

The Young & Successful are always looking for new areas of interest. Just look at Jon. When he's not at work, he's usually configuring a sound system or building some piece of furniture for his house. No matter the project, there are always tools and a manual close by. Whether professional or personal, continuous education is the way to really explore the "extracurricular" areas of your life in substantive ways that are both fulfilling and rewarding.

Commit yourself to maintaining the knowledge you've worked so hard to gain. Then see how much further you can take it. The Young & Successful are constantly pushing back the boundaries of what they can learn and achieve. Fall out of touch with your market, industry, clients, and their needs, and your indifference will cost you your edge. The Young & Successful are always striving to stay on top of their game, and that means committing to continuous education. Identify the key areas in your life that are critical for you to maintain your expertise and training in, and stay on top of them.

Recommended Classes and Continuous Learning

As you embark on this new experience in RWU, there are a number of recommended classes—favorites of the Young & Successful—that we offer for your consideration:

The Gift of Gab
The Ins & Outs of Money
Health & Fitness Mastery
Entrepreneurship 101

For each, we'll offer a couple of books, websites, and courses that can help you get started. Should any of these subjects look particularly compelling, dive right in. By now, you know the drill.

The Gift of Gab

As Julie Joncas, one of the Young & Successful people we mentioned earlier, once said, "I knew that I could never become successful if I didn't learn to overcome my shyness and lack of confidence."

The gift of gab is truly a gift. It's also something that can be learned and refined. Whether you're buying a car, interviewing for a new job, negotiating contracts, or working your way in to an important conference you can't quite afford, few skills can get you where you want to go faster than your ability to communicate. And if you're talking about something you're intensely passionate about at the same time, then the results can be miraculous.

Need a little work on your sales skills? Check out a Toastmasters or Dale Carnegie group near you. These are tremendously well-respected organizations that have chapters and groups around the world and can help you master the art of speaking and giving presentations. They are probably the two best organizations for teaching you to speak like a pro. Then there's always the old tried-and-true methods—learn from others by watching, practice, and baptisim by fire. (That means just throwing yourself out into the things that scare you most, and figuring out what you need to know along the way. And it's not always a bad idea, either.)

The Ins & Outs of Money

Do you know how to read a P&L statement? Or how to calculate your ROI, or write a budget? Do you understand how compound interest works? Or what the difference between interest and equity investments are? Was Chapter Two the first time you ever understood what a balance sheet was? What if you had to amortize a loan? What would you do then? If these terms are totally foreign to you, you may want to consider a little personal finance 101.

None of us can afford to be ignorant when it comes to money. I don't care how much of it you have, how well you trust someone else to look out for it on your behalf, or whether you think your piddly little life savings in that change jar doesn't add up to enough to bother with. You're never going to get anywhere financially if you don't take money seriously. It's no different than staying on top of your health, your career, your friendships, or even your dirty laundry. Ignore any of the above, and the results are bound to get nasty sooner or later.

No one expects you to be a financial genius overnight, but it doesn't take a lot to at least become competent. Need some quick and dirty solutions? There are tons of great books out there that can give you a good overview of what you need to know. Some of our favorites include *Get a Financial Life* by Beth Kobliner, *Rich Dad, Poor Dad* by Robert Kiyosaki, *The Automatic Millionaire* by David Bach, or any of *The Wall Street Journal* financial guides. The *WSJ* guides are my personal favorites because they are packed with pictures and graphs and funny stories that help explain everything *interestingly*. If you're more stimulated by something you can watch, turn on CNBC or Bloomberg any time of the day or night. Have a little free time? Go take a workshop or a class. Or try calling up a few brokerage houses to see what kinds of literature they have for newbies.

Health & Fitness Mastery

We all know that if we exercise regularly, cut junk food from our diets, and catch at least eight hours of sleep nightly, we'd look, feel, and work better. For most of the Young & Successful, the great demands of their personal and professional lives make it increasingly difficult to maintain the top-notch physique and energy of their youth. It doesn't have to be that way, though.

It is possible to take care of ourselves in the best possible way. For some this may mean taking a break in the middle of a grueling day. *Body for Life* by Bill Phillips is an excellent well-rounded program that Young & Successful people have used to transform their body and overall level of health and fitness. We also recommend that you check out *The South Beach Diet* by Dr. Arthur Agatston, or *The Zone* by Barry Sears. The latter shows you how to use food as "your medicine and your ticket to a state or zone where you can achieve ultimate body balance, strength and great health." Others of you might commit to healthfulness by joining Weight Watchers or taking the television out of your bedroom so that you're not distracted from a good night's sleep.

The Young & Successful realize that by keeping on top of their personal well-being, they put themselves in charge of one of the most important controllable areas of their life. They realize that how they take care of themselves affects not only how they feel both physically and mentally, but also how others see them. Taking the time out of your hectic days to reinvest in your body and soul gives you greater overall vitality and passion.

Entrepreneurship 101

Ever wonder how you could really spend your days doing what you love most? Ever wonder why you're not the one in charge? Or how you would run your company so much differently if you were? Feel like you're in a box sometimes? Like your work or ability isn't being recognized? Ever wish that you had more freedom to do what you're really good at, and the time to explore more?

If you're not confident that you can find or create great opportunities for yourself wherever you go, then what you need is to add an entrepreneurial spark to your life. You don't have to start your own business, but wouldn't it be nice to know the option is there if you ever want it?

If there's one subject that I wish everyone could study at some point in their lives, it would be entrepreneurship. Let's face it, no one ever made a six-figure income without selling lemonade, Girl Scout cookies, Christmas cards, or homemade jewelry or mowing lawns, tutoring, or baby-sitting. As trivial as some of these may sound, they have been known to be the impetus for some very powerful lessons. Entrepreneurship is all about empowerment, taking control, and assuming responsibility. It is a mind-set that can make all of our lives better and more productive if we just learn to weave a little bit of it into everything we do. In my opinion entrepreneurship is, after all, the ultimate Real World University. Whatever you don't know, you learn. Whatever you don't have, you find a way to get or work around. Besides, the ability to create your own opportunities is perhaps the greatest definition of what it takes to be Young & Successful.

Want to know more? Open up your perspective a little. Explore how taking control works in both independent and more traditional corporate environments. Pick up a few small business magazines like *Entrepreneur; Success, Inc.; Fast Company;* or even *Forbes* or *Fortune.* Spend more time reading about the entrepreneurs whom you admire or respect. See how the pioneers of your industry made the strides and innovations that they did. Scrutinize their philosophies, their actions, and their decisions. In fact, almost any book that delves into how any industry or company was started is bound to be full of fabulous examples.

Now that you're on your own and your education from this point on is up to you, remember that Real World University is always open, and, in some way, you should always be attending.

8 Weathering Life's Challenges

INTO EVERY LIFE A LITTLE RAIN MUST FALL. And sometimes it rains so hard it floods. No matter who we are or what we choose to do in this life, we all eventually have to cope with setbacks, hardships, or even outright disasters.

Whether we're getting a new business or career off the ground or keeping an already successful life on track, our journey will undoubtedly be filled with major life challenges and life-changing decisions. These can range from financial stress to rocky relationships, the tragic loss of loved ones, being fired from a job, suffering larger career setbacks to a forced move, or even having started a family too early. The question is, how prepared for them will we be, and how will we cope with these inevitable challenges as they come? With foresight, you can often greatly limit the pain and repercussions if not avoid them altogether.

The Young & Successful cope with life's stormy weather by knowing how to soften the blow and limit the impact by being as prepared as possible for the inevitable and unexpected. The Young & Successful are confident that they can survive these tempests because they've worked hard to build the foundation—emotional, physical, spiritual, and financial—that they need to confront life's challenges head-on.

One thing that I've found that makes the Young & Successful unique is that they actually *expect* and anticipate these storms to hit their lives at some point. As a result, they are better prepared to deal with them when they appear.

⚡ Everyone Has Challenges

One of the things that has always fascinated me most about working with entrepreneurs is their incredible ability to persevere through life's major challenges. They've deliberately chosen an existence where every day is a new adventure, and rarely can anyone predict what's coming around the next corner. Their choice means that there are incredible highs, but also potentially devastating lows. Their sacrifices are constant and can range from losing all of their free time to putting their homes and life savings on the line. Their relationships, credibility, stability, and emotional, and physical health are all put to the test in pursuit of their dreams and ambitions. Often fueled by little more than their passion, determination, and creativity, they take this road, understanding its dangers, because they simply can't imagine doing anything else with their lives.

Now this is clearly not the life for everyone, but entrepreneurs aren't the only ones who make this choice. Over and over again, we've watched the Young & Successful defy the odds in their own ways, fighting their own battles to realize their dreams in record time.

The Young & Successful face many entrepreneurial challenges by choosing to take total control of their lives and their circumstances. Reaching for great heights, they both pay a price of instability and risk and deal with challenges and uncertainty on a daily basis. Why do the Young & Successful do it? Because they want a life that offers the most control and the greatest sense of ownership.

⚡ The Art of Anticipation

So what do we do to survive the storms, floods, fires, and quakes in our lives? As the ancient Russian proverb so wisely advises, we *hope for the best, but prepare for the worst.*

It's funny to think about how *many* different precautions we take when it comes to our physical lives and how *few* we take when it comes to our professional lives. What do I mean? Well, think about it this way. In your house you probably stock extra toilet paper, candles, batteries, and pasta or soup, along with bottled water in case you run out or run into trouble. You have smoke detectors, and maybe even a fire extinguisher. In our cars we stock a spare tire and jumper cables. In our banks (or mattresses) we try to stash away a little extra cash. We even purchase insurance policies to protect us in case . . . well, just in case. So clearly we've been well trained to anticipate what *might* happen, and we each know how to protect ourselves from the notorious "just in case" scenarios . . . but how many of us take this well-developed foresight to work?

Knowing that we're all going to have challenges trying to beat down our door every so often, what have you done to protect your job, your career, your income, your passions, and even your sanity when that day arrives?

In order to figure out just what you've done and what you *need* to do in the simplest way possible, let's think of your life as a house. We all know what to do when we have a hole in our roof, for example. We make sure to fix it because we can be sure it will rain at some point or another, and then we'll get wet.

If you had hired a house inspector before the rain started falling, your foresight would have been rewarded. He'd have made a note of this roof problem, right along with a list of other potential dangers that you might face as a result of the way your house was put together and the condition it is in. When the inspector gave you the report, you'd survey the issues, assess your best options for dealing with them, and probably take action.

Since we can't send the same inspector to check out your life or your place of business, the best disaster insurance we can offer you are a few questions that an inspector might ask if he came to check you out.

Your initial answers will probably be incomplete—like your Personal Balance Sheet was at first. The secret is to keep coming back to the questions as you learn more about your situation and yourself.

. What are the potential challenges I face?

. What can I control, and what is uncontrollable?

. What must I protect above all else? What is sacred to me?

. What can I do to limit unnecessary risks and minimize potential dangers?

These questions are part of a process no different than what we go through when we meet with a career counselor, an insurance broker, a financial advisor, a doctor, or a lawyer. We tell them what we want, what's important to us, and what we're willing to risk. They, in turn, give us an assessment of our options, what risks we might encounter, a prescription for what they think we should do from here, and their advice on how to keep intact the things we hold most sacred. But how often do we look at ourselves as analytically as these people do? How often do we open ourselves up to assess what we're most afraid of losing and how well we're protecting it? My guess is not often enough. And, considering the challenges that are certainly ahead, our negligence could prove quite damaging.

So, the next question has to be where do we start?

PERSONAL FIRE DRILL ™

The first thing you have to do is set your priorities. What is important to you beyond all else? Who are the people, the things, the commitments, and the values that you hold most dear? Who would you call if you had great news and only had five minutes to spare? What would you grab if you had to flee your house or apartment in a moment's notice? Imagine you're at home in front of the television, and all of a sudden someone starts banging on your front door. Startled at the sight of a big, burly firefighter standing in your house, you take in the news. There's a fire blazing down the street from you. Look around you right this minute. What do you do? What do you take? Close your eyes for a minute and imagine how you'd react. Make a list of what you'd grab. Then study that list. Does anything here surprise you?

In the event of an emergency, are you most likely to save your

wallet/money	books
passport	religious or
documents	spiritual items
pets	files
clothes	computer
photo albums	collectibles
cell phone	personal journal
briefcase	jewelry
shoes	old letters
home videos	

Honestly, what did you think of first? Was it your family photo album, which shows you that one of your more powerful drivers and desires is to preserve the memories you have of your family and your history? Or was it that great blue suit of yours? ("The house may be in jeopardy, but I still have that big interview tomorrow.") Or did you have trouble choosing, and decided that you'd grab the dog, the watch your grandparents gave you, and those letters your significant other sent from Europe. ("I may be a little scorched, but I got everything that mattered!") What do you think your choices say about you? Were you practical or romantic? Sentimental or cynical?

The fire drill makes us confront two things: Disasters do happen, and it always helps to sort out our priorities before it's too late.

If you were one of the many who said "my contacts list" or "my laptop" ("My whole life is in there!") or "my business plan," don't think that you've turned into some sort of coldhearted monster. Your work *is* a critical part of your life and the tools that move you along that path *are* crucial to you. They can— and often should—be a priority. But be aware of what you're leaving behind, and make sure that at least your second choice (or your third) is something that brings your life into balance. Please know that there are no "right" answers to this drill, other than yours. We're certainly not going to join you because this is your life and these are your priorities.

One of the things that the Young & Successful are best at is maintaining the balance between logic and sentiment, intellect and enthusiasm. It's all a matter of priorities and knowing when you're making a choice that can change your life.

Building a Shelter from the Storm

We all need shelter from the storms of life. The stronger you make yours, the less likely you are to be disoriented, disabled, or knocked down by outside elements. You can try to make do with what you have when the unexpected hits, but short-term thinking isn't going to give you the long-term strength and ability to defend yourself that you need. Building a stable foundation for your life is your first line of defense.

Think of your foundation as if you were constructing a building. The higher you want to build a skyscraper, for example, the greater the number of floors and structural supports you have to construct below ground. Now consider your life in the same respect. If you're setting out to accomplish great things, a strong foundation offers you a greater assurance of safety and a broader range of options down the road. What are the components of a strong foundation? These are some of the pieces that you might need:

- financial knowledge and resources

- a healthy lifestyle

- strategic advisors to keep you on solid ground

- a backup plan or exit strategy

- strong religious or spiritual center

- someone to walk the dog when you work late

- emotional support, love, and reassurance

To construct your own foundation, you need that structural soundness beneath the surface also. That's your history, your integrity, your family and friends, your roots. If that foundation is shaky, even the best materials and all the skill in the world won't hold that building up for long.

As you build up, you're going to want to take care to put the support beams in the right places. This might translate to establishing your credentials, expertise, and experience. Carefully plan the placement of the windows. These delicate sheets of glass are the parts of you that are transparent, revealed to the outside world. These are the windows to your soul, your intelligence, your perspectives, and your motivations. It's your choice whether you shut the emotional blinds or keep them open to reveal the true you, and invite people closer.

The external plaster, brick, or marble is your outer appearance. It's what people see when they walk by, passing you on the street. This is where your grooming, your attitude, your demeanor, and your confidence make their first impressions.

The signage you place on the building is your mission. It's who you are or how you label yourself. It gives others a sense of what you're setting out to do. It's what everyone knows you as and expects of you. It's your personal brand or signature.

What do all these things say about you? How strong is that foundation of yours? And how high are you planning to build? Can you sustain your ambitions of building up into the clouds? Building a stronger base, even when the plans are initially more modest, leaves the possibility for future growth and expansion, with far less hassle and risk. Setting the foundation for a balanced, stable life in the beginning happens only by setting clear priorities and employing some good, solid strategic planning.

What would happen if a storm were to hit you right now? Could you stand strong in the face of danger, or would you fall apart and crumble? Think about what your foundation consists of right now. Is it solid, a bit shaky, or still a serious work in progress? What *should* it look like? Again, think about your ideal, then get to work on what you can realistically do now. Start to survey the area you're building upon. Where are you in the process? What are your current circumstances and how favorable are they for what you want to do? How long will the foundation you have support you as you build up?

⚡ When a Storm Hits

How do *you* react when things get rough? The Young & Successful are *proactive*. Their vision, insight, research, and planning enable them to prepare for most situations before they get out of control. And when things do go the wrong way for them, they stand up and take action. They cut off the danger at the knees and limit their exposure before too much damage can be done. Now these might sound like extreme cases, but our reaction style affects decisions we make every day.

Let's say you heard through the grapevine that your company may be going out of business and that layoffs were inevitable. How would you react to the revelation that you might lose your job?

Here is how your reactions might affect your course of action:

Passive

If you handle this situation passively, you're probably going to wait for the fatal news or for an interesting new opportunity to present itself and magically fall from the sky into your lap. That's fine, if you don't mind living with the anxiety and putting your fate in the hands of nothing all that reliable. One thing you might do is casually mention to a few people that you're looking for a new job and hope that something somewhere clicks, or someone gets the hint and decides to go out of their way for you.

Maybe you'd even look at a few ads in the paper and see if you could find anything there. Or if you're a really passive-aggressive type you might blindly send out a few résumés and sit on your hands waiting for a response. When none comes, you do nothing but wonder why and complain that things are still up in the air. Believe it or not, this strategy is about as far as many will go to pursue something that's important to them. Would you believe that most don't even go as far as visiting an online job search site? That twenty-minute commitment could, by itself, transform a passive approach into a proactive one and turn up a few hundred initial leads.

Reactive

If your style is reactive, you're likely waiting for something significant to push you over the edge before you make your big move. You're waiting for your boss to give you the final news or for someone to call and say, "You're just the person that we've been looking for." You won't start doing anything until the ax falls. Maybe you're waiting for the perfect solution to your quandary to hit in the middle of the night. Maybe you're ready to spring on the first offer of work.

But why haven't you called everyone you know who might be able to help you find a new position? Why haven't you talked to your boss about your concerns? Have you asked yourself lately, "Do I even love this job anyway?" If you haven't done either of these things, figure out what the roadblock is for you and work around it. Don't wait until you're in the unemployment line.

The Young & Successful know that to be in demand, you first need to build your own leverage and ensure you have something that others need and want. Only then can you afford the luxury of being reactive and just walking away or diving into something blindly when the urge hits you.

Proactive

For now, the style that will surely take you furthest and do the rest of your Young & Successful peers proud is the proactive stance. Wait for nothing! Get out and pound the pavement, talk to friends, interview every mover and shaker in your business that you can. Surf the web for hours to survey your options. Investigate every angle and every possible opportunity. Let people know that you're on the prowl, what you need, and how grateful you'd be for any help. Ask questions constantly. Get the answers you need to make your move. You're going to need to take bold steps. Make your résumé or bio as compelling and irresistible as you can.

If it begins to look like the rumors really are true, perhaps you should consider offering yourself up for sacrifice. Think that's crazy? Sometimes volunteering for the ax can actually get you a better separation (severance) agreement. Do your research. Find out who the decision-makers are in your business and get to them. If you think this means you have to be relentless, you're absolutely right. This is the perfect style to describe how the Young & Successful might deal with such an imminent disaster. But it's not the norm for the average Joe, even though it works. (Go figure.) And thus we have another beautiful example of how the Young & Successful manage to succeed by taking control of their situation and swiftly overcoming life's unexpected challenges.

Same Challenges, Different Approaches

Two people from the same small town get accepted to a big school in a different part of the country. Neither has the money to go, but both are equally smart and anxious about the opportunity. The passive one gets really depressed. Maybe she blows the offer off and convinces herself and others that it's not really what she wanted or what's even best for her in the first place. Perhaps she lashes out at her family for not being able to help her. Not only is that behavior destructive, any one of these actions can trigger a dozen other negative effects.

The other girl accepts the challenge as a test. She considers it a small price to pay to get the education she wants so desperately. She works with her family, financial counselors, and the school, and she looks for part-time work that can help her pay the bills. By exploring all the options and never accepting her fate at face value, she struggles and scrapes by for a while, but she gets where she wants to be. Her options from there became abundant. The other girl never leaves home and clings to this passive style for many years to come, as it enables her to hide and protect herself from the potential of failure. She never thinks of her ideal, never makes a plan, and certainly never gets to take a taste of what her life could have been like.

Hurricane Season

While it is impossible to identify all the different crises that could afflict us at one time or another, everyone encounters at least one or two big ones at some point. Forgive me for turning a little pessimistic (or maybe a bit morbid) here, but I'd rather you think about this stuff before you're in a critical situation as opposed to when you're smack in the middle of one, grappling for answers without the benefit of calm, clear, collected thought.

The following list presents some of the most common major life-challenges that we can face:

accidents, debilitation, disease, sickness
debt, collections, bankruptcy, repossessions
absence of nest egg, savings, insurance; identity theft

job loss, business failure, career disaster
major breakups with friends, partners, lovers, spouse
loss of loved ones
inability to cover basic needs (food, water, shelter, transportation,
   medical care, education)
physical attack, abuse, incarceration, indictment, lawsuits
natural disaster, loss of home or personal property, war

Unfortunately, sometimes very bad things can happen. It doesn't matter who you are or what you have. What does matter is how mature, responsible, responsive, and strong you can be when a real hurricane comes blowing into your life. How are you likely to react? Will you be passive, reactive, or proactive? The Young & Successful might be optimists, but they're also able to cope with cold hard reality when it demands consideration and action. But we won't leave you with that thought and images of "what if" festering in your head. We come with tools!

TAPPS

Need a little help working through some of the possibilities of what may come? Dealing with a current crisis of your own? Try this out. It's something we call TAPPS, and it's guaranteed to help you see any difficult situation a little more clearly and find ways to cope with it more sanely. Trust me, it can come in pretty handy. This is how it works.

TAPPS is a strategic planning process that takes us through five simple steps to uncover what we would do if a major life challenge or decision were to hit by identifying the best possible approach. It also happens to be useful when trying to prevent a particular situation from happening or just lessening the impact from something we've already been confronted with. This is what it stands for:

Truth

Awareness

Preparation

Prevention

Survival

And it works like this:

TRUTH

We begin by being truthful with ourselves about what's going on. What is the issue at hand? Be candid. Be clear. Here's a life and death story: A friend of mine went through every one of these steps while facing up to and beating one of the toughest challenges you could ever encounter. If it can work here, we're confident that TAPPS can help you with any crisis that you're ever confronted with.

While he certainly didn't want to believe what he was hearing at the time, Doug Ulman's doctor was quite clear. Doug had cancer. Chondrosarcoma, to be exact. It was real, it was scary, and it had to be dealt with quickly. In a whirlwind of events, he took the necessary tests, consulted the right doctors, downloaded everything to his family and friends, and owned up to the fact that without swift and aggressive action, he could die.

Accepting the truth helped Doug waste little time second-guessing his prognosis and make a firm commitment to getting treatment, before the cancer could spread further.

AWARENESS

Second, we have to gain a strong awareness of the options we have and what the realistic ramifications of our choices could mean. This is where our Real World University training comes in. To ensure we're as up to speed as we can be on the latest research, data, trends, and information, we have to do some serious research and investigation.

In a particularly life-threatening situation like Doug's, clearly you want to do everything you possibly can. Relying solely on the information and opinions of others is not always the best decision either. Armed with some in-depth and intensive research skills, we can find the top experts and latest information on just about anything.

PREPARATION AND PREVENTION

Often even after a crisis has hit, there is still more than we can do to prevent further damage . . . and we must be strong enough both to recognize that and to do what we can. In this day and age, we have access to so much information and such incredible technology that it is possible to arm ourselves against a wide array of potential problems. Whether we choose to do so or not is up to us. But if you merely follow the first two steps in TAPPS (Truth and Awareness), identifying your best preventive tactics will be easy.

Have you ever heard this saying: If we fail to plan, we plan to fail. It's true. We can't prevent everything out there, but we can deal with what's likely and what afflicts us by confronting the situations proactively. Carefully planning our course of action, at any stage, really, can virtually immunize us to many surprises and situations.

Doug Ulman didn't just face cancer once—he beat it three times. Then he turned his attention outward and found a way to help others who had been afflicted early in life as he had. Today, the Ulman Cancer

Fund for Young Adults (www.ulmanfund.org) is a respected source of support programs, education, and resources that are free of charge to young adults and their families and friends who are affected by cancer. From his own experience, Doug quickly learned the importance of prevention and planning and now has the opportunity to pass the wealth of knowledge that he gained to countless others.

SURVIVAL

It's natural to want to give up or hide in bed for days when something goes very wrong, but ignoring problems never makes them go away. And all too often we underestimate the power of the spirit. We can play the part of victim and wallow in our suffering, or we can switch into survivor mode and tackle our challenges head on. That's the true spirit of the Young & Successful.

We consider Doug Ulman to be a prime Young & Successful example not just because he has done so much for so many, but because he himself is the ultimate survivor. To have had cancer and beaten it three times should be enough proof for any of us that we can battle and conquer even the most fearsome demons. Because of the incredible inspiration that he has been, Doug and his survival story were recently featured on the cover of millions of boxes of Wheaties cereal.

And as if that wasn't exciting enough, Doug recently teamed up with another incredible Young & Successful survivor, Lance Armstrong, who himself battled cancer then went on to win the Tour de France . . . *four times* now . . . becoming one of the most celebrated cyclists in history.

So if Doug's and Lance's stories teach us anything, it's not just that we can survive, but that living on allows us the opportunity to help countless others do the same. And what could be more powerful than that?

So for all the ways that major challenges can rock our lives to the core, TAPPS can help us turn those vibrations into some pretty powerful stuff.

⟩⟨ Applying TAPPS to Your Life

We recommend applying TAPPS to a few of the top scenarios and mishaps that could potentially have the biggest impact on your life. Think about the things that scare or worry you the most, and use this tool to demystify and diffuse your fears. You'll probably end up surprising yourself with how resourceful you are and how many solutions you can come up with to conquer anything that's thrown your way.

The point is that the Young & Successful spend time contemplating potential major life crises before they actually happen. While we hope that they are kept to a minimum in your life, understanding how to use TAPPS will enable you to identify the best approach to take if a crisis happens, often before it can sideswipe you. This will allow you to make clear, well-thought-out decisions and develop prudent plans to react accordingly, all the while tempering any disarming emotions and influences.

It's an amazing thing to watch how people rise to their greatest challenges. Even when our hands appear to be tied, we can almost always find solutions if we're willing to be persistent and recognize the incredible range of options that are within our control. Being strategic about how we handle our challenges, yet flexible and resilient enough when we need to, is a valuable secret that can hamper anything that tries to come between us and our dreams. While it may appear to others that your success appears "effortlessly," as a member of the Young & Successful you will never forget all the extra effort and thought that it really took, and just how much you were prepared to overcome to get there.

⚡ Major Life Decisions

The biggest decisions in our lives can be almost as disruptive—emotionally and physically—as the crises that beset us. The fact that we have to make these choices, often on incomplete or ambiguous information, means that they can cause anxiety, sleeplessness, and confusion. They include things like

- Education. *Where to go? Did I go to the right place?*

- Career. *What to be?*

- Lifestyle. *How to live? Urban, suburban, or rural?*

- Location. *Buy or rent? House, condo, apartment, studio? Where?*

- Spouse. *Get engaged or married? Children: to have or not to have? Timing?*

- Spirituality. *Adopt as serious part of life? Become active in community?*

- Retirement. *When and where? Early or after a long, happy career?*

- Financial situation. *What to spend, what to save? Risky or conservative?*

Now this may not be exactly the same as your list of the top ten decisions you'll need to make in your life. Perhaps it doesn't sync with your priorities or where you are right now, but however your list stacks up, what you need is a process of working through the list in a way that helps you make sense of it and helps you reach a decision in the most clear and logical way possible.

While some might believe that the Young & Successful make impulsive decisions, to the contrary, they actually make *very calculated* decisions in pursuing their dreams. Sure, they do win some *and* lose some, but there's typically nothing casual or impulsive about the way that they work out their major life decisions.

REST on the Four Rs

After talking with hundreds of the Young & Successful, we've boiled their methods down to what we call the four Rs. What we realized was that when looking at a potential decision, most of the Young & Successful looked for a "return" on their investment. It didn't matter to them whether they were investing time, money, or energy—their process was the same.

With the four Rs, you'll never again ask yourself, "What was I thinking?" because they will help you measure the level and kinds of *return* you can expect from your investment of *R*isk, *E*ffort, *S*acrifice, and *T*ime.

The following presents the four Rs with some sample questions for you to consider for each "R," allowing you to comfortably and confidently make major commitments and decisions:

Return on Risk (ROR): How risky does this seem? Is it super success or super failure with no in-between? Is there any gray area to land in if things don't quite go as planned? How all-or-nothing is it? Can I afford this risk at this point in my life? How sweet is the upside? And what is the potential worst-case, down-side?

Return on Effort (ROE): How much effort is involved to make this happen? Have you considered the level of effort and stress versus the probable level of return to you? Could the effort required here be better expended elsewhere? Can you bring in others to offset the effort required? If so, can someone else really replace you? Are you passionate enough about it where the effort won't really feel so much like hard work but rather more like fun?

Return on Sacrifice (ROS): Sacrifice might be one of the hardest elements of rest to grasp. As you contemplate your own sacrifices, consider the following: What will you be giving up to do this? Will you jeopardize other areas of your Ideal Life? Is it worth those sacrifices and if so, why? Does the benefit you hope to derive make the given sacrifices really worth it? Are you helping others in need with this sacrifice? Can you handle this sacrifice financially, physically, and mentally? Who else will be affected by this sacrifice and can they deal with you moving forward with this?

Return on Time (ROT): How much time will it take for this to all pan out in a best case scenario? Probable case? Worst case? Is it worth the wait? Is there a better place to spend the time required to fulfill your obligation to this commitment? Will you consider your time wasted if things don't pan out, or will you gain valuable experience and knowledge, regardless of the outcome? Knowing that time is the most valuable, irreplaceable commodity in the world, why would you spend the time to do this?

Notice that the first letters of the last words of each acronym spell out the word "REST." A great way for you to remember these four Rs is by thinking of how much you'll be able to "rest" comfortably and confidently as you forge forward (or not), knowing that you've carefully thought through all you could without second-guessing yourself.

A SHOT AT THE BIG TIME

One of my closest friends, Larry Angrisani, was working for Universal Pictures in international marketing as a publicist—and clearly on the fast track—when an interesting opportunity presented itself. One of the top producers in Hollywood wanted him to work as her assistant. She offered to teach him the business first-hand and give him experience it would take a lifetime in the business to get. After serious contemplation, my friend told his boss about the offer and left the studio with their blessings to pursue what could be the ultimate opportunity for someone in his shoes. Unfortunately, the producer didn't end up being everything he had hoped she would be, and Larry soon quit to return to his old job, which he had always loved. The studio immediately offered him his job back, but because seven months had elapsed, he lost his seniority, and was now considered a new employee—not someone who had been with the company for almost five years. As a result, he had to endure a reduced salary, fewer benefits, and a shorter vacation. But thanks to his strategic decision making in the first place, Larry knew what could happen and, despite the temporary setback, he's proud of himself for having taken the risk to pursue what might have been a much bigger and better opportunity.

Applying REST to Your Life

These four critical elements in decision making are too often undervalued or simply not considered. The Young & Successful use REST as an assessment tool to ascertain the returns associated with the varying levels and kinds of decisions and opportunities they are considering.

Contemplating these four essential components can be especially valuable in evaluating whether the potential returns in your most major life decisions are truly worth moving forward. The following chart applies the four Rs to one of the more common major life decisions many of the Young & Successful face out in the real world.

	Should I Change My Career Completely?
RISK	Can you afford this risk of changing careers at this point in your life? Can you financially afford the schooling and time to find a job? How sweet is the upside? If you leave, can you fall back on your current career if "something else" doesn't work out?
EFFORT	Are you willing to put in the effort required to learn all you need to excel in another career? Can you deal with going back to school again? Do you have the patience to put in the work it will take to climb to the top?
SACRIFICE	Do you have to take on anything you didn't plan to do this, such as some other job you won't enjoy or loans that you'll need to pay back? How significant is the commitment you made to your current career, and is it worth giving that up?
TIME	How much time will it take to get trained or become skilled in something else to be employable? What can you do to expedite the time line to getting to this point? Will you be able to invest all the time necessary to do this the right way?

PUTTING *REST* TO WORK

Jonathan Kilman had worked for two years in Boston as a corporate attorney for one of the most prestigious law firms in the country before he realized that his sense of purpose and passion were being totally sucked out of him. He was in a position he previously thought he'd do anything to be in, earning high praise, a substantial six-figure starting salary with a top firm, and was off to making a great living . . . in the office, that is. The problem was, as much as Jonathan liked working at his office, he liked his wife and having a life even more. After a while, what seemed like a twenty-four-hour job became a miserable existence. For months, Jonathan stuck it out and soon dreaded waking up each morning for work. Both he and his wife, Niva, knew that he needed a major change. To top it all off, Jonathan and Niva wanted to start a family soon. They yearned for a very different lifestyle and finally, after some deep discussions, they began to seriously contemplate options for a move.

In order to decide the best course of action, they determined what was most important to them. There were many things to consider before uprooting their whole life to start a new one. After numerous conversations with friends, family, and close advisors (including Scott and me), Jonathan and Niva came up with a list of priorities for the "returns" they were looking for. They determined that they wanted to

. Move to a city with a better climate

· Enjoy more of an active outdoor lifestyle

- Live where they could afford to buy a home, instead of having to rent a small overpriced apartment

- Live in a community where a higher standard of living was possible

- Be closer to family and several of their lifelong friends

- Start a family of their own in a quiet, safe neighborhood

- Find Jonathan a better opportunity to practice law at a high quality firm within the world of politics—one of his true passions

After a lot of contemplation and investigation of other cities, cost of living, the legal community, political atmosphere, school systems, climate, lifestyle, population of younger people like them, proximity of family and friends, etc., they narrowed down the list of cities that could potentially meet their needs, and found one that offered the greatest returns and would ultimately and undoubtedly change their life in a major way. They then proceeded to apply the principles of REST to help them make their final decision. Considering all of the pros and cons, they found that the overall upside returns of moving to Florida far outweighed the risks, effort, sacrifices, and time required to make the big idea a successful reality.

Take a look at what Jonathan says happened as a result of their moving forward:

Under the peace of mind we enjoyed applying REST to some very big decisions, within less than a year we moved down

*south after I quit my job and found another one at a great firm,
Gray Harris, in a wonderful new town. As soon as Niva finished her final graduate work, we packed up all our things and
in no time bought and moved into our first home, which happens to be close to my new office.*

*From there, I buckled down and worked hard to get ac-
quainted with everyone at work while successfully studying for
and passing the Florida bar exam. I couldn't be happier at my
new firm, which is both high quality and family friendly. It has
already enabled me to do some exciting work in the political
world—the area I wanted to work in all along. To top it all off,
Niva and I recently celebrated the arrival of Maxwell, our new
baby boy! We simply could not be happier with the outcome of
our decision. Taking the time to determine our priorities up
front made all the difference.*

We All Make Mistakes

Even with REST in hand, you're going to make mistakes, but that's not
necessarily a bad thing. Phil Tirone, the mortgage banker we met earlier,
said something strange to me when I first interviewed him. He told me
that he wakes up every day, wondering how he's going to *fail* today. *What?*
I figured that I'd either heard him wrong or that he was crazy. Even after
the second and third iterations, I didn't think I'd understood. Clearly, I
was shocked to hear someone so successful sound so utterly negative, but
he quickly assured me that his intentions were quite the opposite.

Phil explained that only by making mistakes does he ever hope to
realize his greatest successes. He's not going to do absolutely everything
right along the way, but by making and learning from his mistakes, he

knows that he's getting himself out there and making progress. Again, Phil's business is one dictated by numbers: prospects he meets, clients he secures, and deals that are done. And because he's such a disciplined tracker of his progress and goals, he knows for certain that for every ten prospects he meets with, an average of three will become clients. Phil knows that he has to get through seven rejections, or you could say failures, to get to three successes. From there, it's just a numbers game. (This should be familiar for anyone in the sales business, even though the approach may seem a little radical at first.) So instead of avoiding risks and hoping to limit his exposure to failure, Phil welcomes it, because he knows that it can only lead to bigger and better things.

Remember when you used to play video games for hours at a time? (Who knows, maybe you still do.) Well, part of the thrill of the game was playing over and over again, reaching new levels and scoring higher each time. But in between each of those games, you had to lose, right? So you'd scream or grunt or grit your teeth and do what? You'd press that little "play again" button, and off you'd go without a moment's hesitation to conquer this little bleeping, beeping, electronic challenge yet again. Each time you started over, you did so with a new understanding of what you did wrong and a more enlightened, more insightful perspective that told you that you were closer to succeeding . . . if you just kept going.

Conquering the Fear

The Young & Successful have come to realize that the only way you're going to get to greater and greater heights in anything you do is by making mistakes and conquering your fears early on. The most beautiful thing about it, though, is that the younger you are the more room you have to make plenty of little mistakes that won't amount to much in the long run.

We all run into bumps in the road and rough spots that we figure we'll never get over. It's easy to be overwhelmed by all the challenges and thoughts like

I have too little time, money, or opportunities.

I'm too young, too old, too short, too big, too much of this, or just not enough of that.

Our numbers are down, boss's door's been closed all day. Could layoff rumors be true?

I lost my job and I can't see how I'm going to get another.

Sleep is impossible lately, and with everything that's going on, I'm feeling overwhelmed.

Sound familiar? One of the biggest dangers that major life challenges pose is the fear they generate in each of us. In the darkest days of the Depression, President Franklin Delano Roosevelt said that "the only thing we have to fear is fear itself." He was definitely right. It's fine to be afraid when you hit a bump in the road toward your goal, but the thing that you can't do is let fear overwhelm you. What you're afraid of—I can't get a job; I can't pay my bills; I can't face my friends or my family; can't be the only thing that you're thinking about. If that's all you're thinking, then you won't find a job or pay your bills or face your friends and family.

This is the only time in this book when we're going to use this word: STOP! When fear is eating you up the most important thing to do is stop for a moment. Run your Personal Balance Sheet and see what you have going for you. See what assets you have that you can cash in. Run TAPPS and figure out the options that are available to you. Use the 4 Rs to help you decide on a course of action. Stop thinking about your fears and start creating your solutions.

In the big picture, being willing to make mistakes and keep ploughing forward until you get better and better will earn you the chance to play in worlds that few ever get access to. The truth is that most people just give up too early.

Want proof that every great success story is littered with challenges, mistakes, and failures? Here's Phil's list of his greatest "achievements," to remind him how he got to where he is.

PHILIP X. TIRONE'S
"Greatest Achievements"

1. In my second grade reading improvement class, everybody graduated but me.

2. In grade school I was always bullied and teased about my speech impairment, my height, and my big ears.

3. Freshman year in high school, I earned a 1.8 GPA.

4. I scored a combined 800 on my SAT test.

5. I was humiliated and embarrassed at my high school graduation when in front of 3,000 people I froze at the podium, unable to speak as I was presenting an award to our school principal.

6. I was denied acceptance into all but one university to which I applied; Arizona State University accepted me just under the wire.

7. I was denied admittance into all fraternities during my freshman and sophomore years at Arizona State.

8. The woman I was going to marry left me, went to Colombia, met another man, and married *him.*

9. In 1994, I was named Arizona State University Man of the Year.

10. In 2001, I earned $758,000 in income and felt like I was in complete control of my life.

But don't think that Phil measures his success by money alone. While he continues to increase his income every year (and he even bought three buildings this past year), he is equally as aggressive in his giving. In fact, giving away 10 percent of his annual income to charity only scratches the surface. He volunteers weekly at his church and a local hospital, and he has even traveled to Mexico to help build churches in poor communities. Phil also took up the piano four years ago and now plays at public events during holidays. What's more, Phil is constantly challenging himself physically. Not only does he train in the martial arts for up to twelve hours a week, but he now is learning ballroom, swing, and salsa dancing. He even ran his first marathon in Athens, Greece. Talk about bouncing back from defeat and challenges!

If, like Phil, you want to be Young & Successful, you clearly have to put yourself out there and take a few chances and risks. But you also must be smart enough to learn from each experience (and failure) as you go and grow. Fear, failure, mistakes, and challenges are all expected and can be confronted with confidence, dignity, and aggressive actions in the pursuit of the successes that lie just beyond.

There are worlds of people and business and pleasures all around us that we never see until we reach certain levels of achievement and success. Sometimes we'll get a small taste or a quick preview, but for the most part, we reach these new playing fields by taking chances, making our mistakes, and working right through them. So don't beat yourself up when things don't work out quite as planned. Mistakes and failures happen to everyone, but to the Young & Successful, they're bright neon signs promising better things to come. So stay the course; the storm will pass.

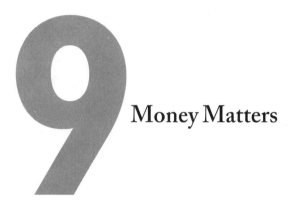

Money Matters

WITH MONEY OFTEN PLAYING THE ROLE of number-one most stressful, overwhelming, all-consuming, and life-changing component in life, it's easy to see how cash is a major issue for all of us. The Young & Successful realize that there is simply no denying the power money plays in our lives, regardless of how much we might have or how much we like it. This goes doubly for when we're still working on getting established. *Why is money so important?* Well, one of the major reasons is because the level of financial stability that Young & Successful people maintain plays such a critical role in virtually every area of their lives. The following just goes to show you how undeniably widespread the effects of money are.

Job/Career: Our earnings impact our lifestyle, freedom, respect, opportunities, comfort level, security, confidence, peace of mind, and even sometimes our health.

Pleasure Maximizers: Large or small pleasures—from trips to movies to magazines to climbing mountains to traveling anywhere and everywhere—there are few pleasures that don't cost something.

Transportation: Whether you take a bike, a bus, a car, a plane, or a helicopter to get around, it's going to cost you, even if we're just talking about spare change. Okay, maybe you can walk, but shoes need replacing too.

Home: Where and what you call home is directly tied to earned income, credit, cash flow, etc. How much space, how safe or nice an area, the proximity to important things, whether you rent versus own, are all dictated by what you can afford.

Friends and Family: Want to keep in touch? Whether it's a long-distance phone call or plane tickets, your availability of time, frequency of visits, gifts you can send, and participation in special occasions will cost you.

Education/Knowledge: Need to beef up your credentials or your bio? Many of the workshops, classes, or resources that can give you an edge can cost a pretty penny. Can you afford courses that will qualify you for a better job? Could you swing the tuition for an advanced degree? And what about down the road a bit—will you send your kids to a private or public school? Do you let them apply to the Ivy League or the state universities? Do you have money for tutors and extra books or supplies? So much of it comes down to your financial situation.

Experts and Advisors: While some advice may be out there for free, often the benefits derived from access to the high-level expertise that the Young & Successful need doesn't come cheap.

Marriage and Children: Getting married, setting up your own home, establishing your base. The mere costs associated with having, raising, and caring for children are climbing every year. Straight from conception, the costs of preparing for having kids, clothing them, buying furniture and food, educating them, child care, in addition to the free time you'll want and need to spend to be there to nurture and support them . . . this is perhaps one of the biggest financial commitments most will ever make.

Health: From affording medical insurance to a local gym membership to buying high-quality, nutritious foods to being prepared to handle large or small health "surprises," contributing to the medical needs of loved ones, or specialized housing or services to even just the luxury of having the "free time" to rejuvenate and take care of yourself can pack a hard financial punch.

Despite how much we might loathe the idea of focusing so much on it, in many ways we must (unless you do actually plan to hop in your car and move to a remote little village in Mexico . . . or some other emergency destination for that matter). As far as being Young & Successful is concerned—we have to choose whether we want to work hard and fight for what we want on the front end or suffer because we don't have what we need on the back end.

Far too many people work hard every day of their lives just to survive; and in most cases, they have every bit as much pride and desire to succeed as anyone. The whole point of this exercise, and this entire book, is to enable you to make as many right moves as you can from the beginning, and for as much of your life as possible. In fact, another big secret of the Young & Successful is just that—they give themselves every possible advantage every step of the way. There's no question that you can stack a lot of cards in your favor if you start smart and take that philosophy with you on the road.

The Young & Successful know that great benefits can arise from taking control of and pride in their financial futures. The following are some of the most significant:

- Reduced stress

- Increased focus and clarity

- Greater ability to give back

- Access to the finer things

- Freedom and control over life

- Solutions to many major life challenges

- More balanced lifestyle

- Ability to provide for your family and loved ones

So, one way or another, we all have to get our hands on enough cash to survive and do all the wonderful things we're planning with our lives. But for most, that's not such an easy task. In this department, we have any of a few options:

- Savings

- Work

- Barter

- Borrowing

- Investment (in you!)

If you don't have cash or access to it, figure out a way to get it. The bottom line is that your relationship with money will profoundly affect your success and even your perception of your own success. Your access to cash will impact not only your stress levels but also your career choices, leisure time, home, transportation, options, relationships with friends and family, your health, access to education and experts, your safety, and yes, your overall happiness.

The "Pain in the Cash" Conundrum

"Cash" is such a little word for something that can cause so much stress, isn't it?

Clearly we're all affected by money, each to very different extremes. Ever really think about how much of a hold it has on you and your future? Well here's a chance to conduct a little assessment of your own. Answer the big-picture money questions below and you too can begin to figure out the best strategy for dealing with your Money Matters, while gaining some sobering insight into how the Cash Conundrum affects you.

1 What's the golden number for you—the amount of money that would be "enough" for you to be truly satisfied that you have all you'll ever need? By what point in your life do you want to have earned it?

2 How much money do you believe you need right now to achieve and execute your immediate dreams and plans?

3 How much money would you need and how soon would you need it to be able to aggressively focus on achieving the "craziest" parts and levels of your dreams?

4 How did you come up with these numbers?

5 What would you most enjoy doing for a living, if how much you earned was not a factor? How close or far off from that ideal are you?

6 What do you typically do with the bulk of your cash when you earn it? Have you thought about why you allocate it the way you do? When you have some extra money, do you spend it right away or do you save or invest some of it?

7 Would you consider yourself to be a big risk taker with your money, or are you conservative? Are you allocating your cash in ways that align with your risk tolerance?

8 Who do you currently turn to or rely upon for financial-related advice? Do you know what their background, experience, and qualifications are? What is their incentive for helping or advising you? Are you confident you're taking advantage of the best tax-reduction strategies?

9 What type of annual return on the money you've accumulated have you enjoyed?

10 Are you satisfied with where you are now? If not, what are you prepared to do to get to that comfort zone? How long do you expect this to take?

These probing questions only scratch the surface. In the big scheme of things you'll eventually need to consider creating a comprehensive strategy and well-thought-out system to effectively take control of your financial life. Make a real commitment to creating or updating a solid financial game plan for your life, starting right now, and you will definitely set yourself apart from the masses. After all, most never really consider how to Conquer the Cash Conundrum or what to do about it until very late in the game. Daring to be different here will have an incredible impact on your ability to reach for and achieve the life you always dreamed of.

⚡ The Young & Successful CAAAAASH™ Management System

The Young & Successful CAAAAASH Management System is a great starting point for anyone looking to gain a hold on his or her financial life. It should carry you far if you make the commitment to adopt and adapt it for yourself. Keep in mind that this will also give you an excellent base of information when starting to work with a financial advisor or planner.

(You can find more financial recommendations, suggestions, and great resources on our website at www.ysn.com/CMS).

The CAAAAASH Management System is an acronym of eight essential actions for you to take to insure your finances are under control. And don't forget there are five "A"s! After all, five stars often denotes the best of the best, and that's just what we want for you here. Before we break it all down, here's a quick peek at where we're going with this and how the acronym unfolds:

Cash

Assessment

Advice

Accumulation

Allocation

Access

Six Months

Habits

Now, getting down to business . . .

CASH

Okay, we'll state the obvious: If you don't have any cash (income, savings, investments, or even credit) you don't have much to manage. Building up even just a little cash for you to work with is the first and most critical step here.

ASSESSMENT

Similar to a full physical or check-up you'd get by visiting a doctor, assessment begins with a complete "financial check-up." Start with the following questions:

- How much debt do you have? How is it all broken down?

- How creditworthy are you? Get a copy of your credit report from at least one of the credit reporting agencies online and see for yourself.

- How many months, weeks, or days of your current overhead (reoccurring monthly expenses) do you have set aside for an emergency?

- What's your personal net worth? What's the total value of all your assets?

- How liquid (easily convertible to cash) are your non-cash assets?

Whether you're deep in debt, debt free, or loaded with cash, assessing where you stand today can help you with a host of decisions. Some of the more common include whether you should (or even could) buy or rent a place to live; afford to have a child right now, and if not now, when; make a major career change or look for a new job, etc. A realistic assessment of your current situation will give you a firm grasp of what you can financially handle, greatly facilitating responsible financial decisions about both your present and your future.

Coupled with the questions above in "The 'Pain in the Cash' Conundrum," you've already begun to assess what your financial situation looks like and confronted what your personal priorities should be.

However, to take a more comprehensive approach to this, you need to jump to the next "A" . . .

ADVICE

Whether you're a financial wizard with a comprehensive assessment in hand and all your money matters totally under control, or an average Joe who can just barely manage to balance your checkbook and realizes your assessment may be a little shaky, we recommend consulting professionals to at least look over what you've put together. New laws, regulations, and creative strategies are created at such a rapid pace that it's crazy not to consult professionals who make a living by keeping abreast of the latest changes that could impact your financial well-being.

Advisors may also be able to suggest some additional options and opportunities you didn't consider or may not be aware of that could enhance your assessment and strategies moving forward. Since their job is to take into account everything that is most important to you, a great financial planner or advisor can be invaluable, but they can also be expensive. They charge for their services in various ways: fixed consultation fees, commissions on products they sell, or by taking a small percentage of the overall money that they manage and/or invest for you. They can also set their compensation plan by utilizing a combination of any of the above. Confirm that any advisors you decide to work with are very up-front about how they get paid and that you feel totally comfortable with them and certain that your interests are truly coming first.

While we recommend finding an excellent financial advisor that you can meet with in person and build a long-term relationship with, if you don't have the time or money to do so right now, there are other options available to you. For example, you can enroll in a Real World University class on personal finance by checking out some of the many resources available. There are also many products, seminars, and classes on proper money and financial management.

The absolute best book that's a must-buy for anyone who wants to get a great overview of their personal money matters is *The Wall Street Journal's Guide to Understanding Personal Finance*. Practically every issue you need to be aware of to best deal with your money is clearly and concisely presented in this surprisingly compact, visually stimulating book (with lots of great info and illustrations to help you grasp the concepts). For additional ways to find great financial advisors and create your own Real World University curriculum, check out our website (www.ysn.com).

ACCUMULATION

With your assessment completed under the influence of solid, expert advice and guidance from advisors you found that you like and trust, you are now ready to begin to enhance or adjust your strategy for actually accumulating your cash. Most of the Young & Successful we've come across over the years have not only had a primary source of income from working for a company or for themselves, but also from other vehicles as well. They've come to realize that supplementing and enhancing your primary income by having multiple sources generating cash for you is not only a smart approach, but more and more of a necessity in today's volatile economy.

For reasons ranging from simply not wanting to put all your eggs into one basket, to the potential for being victimized by corporate downsizing, to the ever-rising cost of living—establishing diversified sources of cash flow is paramount to achieving a sense of security. And in some cases, these additional streams have been known to not only supplement primary incomes but also to replace them together.

I've seen the Young & Successful repeatedly get involved in something to supplement their income only to have it wind up contributing so much cash and income that it actually overshadows what they were earning in their day job.

In no particular order, the following lists some of the more popular money accumulation vehicles that we've seen the Young & Successful use to boost their cash flow on different levels:

- Taking on an additional job during alternative hours and days of the week, such as a part-time sales or marketing associate

- Inventing or finding a new product or service to help bring to market

- Taking on some freelance work in either their field, an associated field, or a field in which they have particular knowledge or interest

- Starting an online and/or offline business, alone or with partners

- Becoming a real-estate or business investor

- Becoming a broker or agent in a variety of areas from real estate, travel, and import/export to business or other products

- Buying a franchise

- Joining a multilevel marketing company or other direct selling opportunities

- Consulting for others who could benefit from general or specialized knowledge, wisdom, or experience they possess

- Writing, editing, and/or selling a column, book, newsletter, or script

- Creating or joining a music or other entertainment group

- Coaching or managing a local sports team or entertainment talent

· Teaching part-time classes or tutoring local students in an area of their expertise

The Young & Successful don't overlook or underestimate the power of bartering, either. Any time you can exchange services or time that would have otherwise taken cash directly from your pocket is certainly worth exploration and consideration.

One thing is for sure, there are a broad range of opportunities and activities that anyone can get involved in, even with limited resources, to help maximize your accumulation of cash.

ALLOCATION

After you've figured out the best vehicles for you to accumulate more cash, as it flows in you'll then need to properly allocate it in accordance with the priorities you set earlier, thanks to your advisors or key information sources.

If you need a little help to make sure you're stashing away your cash consistently, you're in luck. Many companies and financial institutions today have begun offering "direct deposit" programs, which allow participants to automatically allocate a portion of their regular paychecks or other income sources to a savings account or other investment vehicles or plans. In the United States, 401(k)s, Individual Retirement Accounts (IRAs), Keoghs, life insurance plans, and mutual funds are some of the more popular considerations the Young & Successful look at when setting up their financial game plans.

If you don't work for a company that offers this service, we recommend pretending that you do. What we mean is, create a system of allocating your money automatically. The less you have to think about, the better. Just keep stashing money away and forget it's there. Unless you're surveying your investment options, don't touch it. Many people automate many of their allocations to reduce the natural temptation to spend it in places and on things that are not the most responsible use of the money. How many of us have had great intentions of where we "planned" to allocate our money, only to cash a check and *poof* before we knew it, that new pair of shoes or jacket miraculously appeared on our feet or in our closet. That was of course in place of the cash we actually intended to stuff under our mattress or put to some better use elsewhere.

Now don't get me wrong. I'm the first to admit that the natural impulses to spend some or all of your newfound cash on those random pleasurable purchases can become simply irresistible at times. As with a "perfect diet" that never lasts for very long, we've found that the Young & Successful often manage to overcome these urges by ensuring they allocate for a few indulgences in their budget. This strategy will lessen your temptation to "cheat" on your allocation plan. Just trust me . . . and ignore my new shoes when you meet me!

One of the great classic quick-read books that talks all about the responsible allocation of money is called *The Richest Man in Babylon* by George S. Clason. The book, among many other great recommendations, strongly suggests and logically explains why at least 10 percent *of all your earnings* should be yours to keep. Follow this suggestion by putting away even 10 percent of your own earnings, and watch your cash accumulate!

ACCESS

As your financial game plan begins to hit the predetermined levels, benchmarks, and objectives you created, you can access your cash to pay for whatever it was you were accumulating it all for in the first place!

As diligent as you were about generating cash and automating your allocations, which, in turn, enabled you to accumulate more of it over the course of days, months, or years, the Young & Successful become equally diligent about accessing their cash when the time is right. The Young & Successful recognize that the money they stockpile serves merely as a tool. While some never get past the fact that you still can't take cash with you when you die, the Young & Successful are not afraid of using what they've earned, saved, and invested as the powerful tool it is. Used properly, their funds can help tremendously in the realization of the well-thought-out plans and dreams that make up their Ideal Life.

Six months

Once you know where you stand financially, you should contemplate where you're going and how you're going to get there. We recommend running through this system and these questions at least twice a year, or every six months, for the best results. It wouldn't hurt you to review your overall financial status quarterly or monthly, though.

Habit

Successful money management is all about setting up good habits early on. And since that's the message the Young & Successful are always teaching us, you're sure to start seeing results from your efforts just by getting started.

Money Is Just a Tool

The Young & Successful understand that money is just a tool but a mighty powerful one. And it takes practice and serious insight to know how to use it properly and to the greatest advantage. Most important, you have to make sure that cash doesn't interfere more than it needs to in the execution of your plans and the achievement of your success. You also can't give it more weight than it's due and let it take over your life. Perhaps most important, you have to keep money and the role it plays in your life in the proper perspective. But based on who you are and what you're setting out to do, that can mean very different things for different people.

Lessen the Hold of Money on Your Life

One of the strange things about our culture is that for decades, people have been unwilling, even unable, to discuss money comfortably. It didn't matter whether we were talking to our friends, our families, or the people we worked with—it was often easier to chat about sex and death than money. Now, however, the boom and bust cycle of the last couple of years suddenly made it a little easier to discuss openly and frankly what we're doing both with and about our money. This increased openness can serve you as you begin to build your financial foundation. The free flow of information to your trusted advisors and mentors is crucial in our current fiscally volatile world. So, now that you're armed with the inside scoop on how many Young & Successful people deal with their money matters, we're ready to move on to the secrets of how you can leverage the incredible Power of People.

10 The Power of People™

IF YOU WANT TO GET EVERYTHING YOU WANT without waiting a lifetime, you should already know that very few things of great significance happen without the involvement and support of other people. People hire you, invest in you, include you, invite you, rally behind you, and support you along your path. And for ideas, inventions, theories, and business plans to be of use to anyone besides yourself, you must get them into the hands of the *right* people. I can't tell you who those people are, but I can certainly help you get to them.

In order to truly harness the incredible power of people in our lives, we must first build a series of solid personal and professional relationships. What this means for you is that you must begin looking at your relationships, even the very passive ones, much differently than you may currently. The people in your life have a profound effect on who you are and what you will become. Sometimes they may lead you in the right direction. But they can also stop you dead in your tracks or cause you to flee. Pay close attention to your own critical relationships, watch how they affect your behavior and your performance, and notice how you affect theirs.

One of your everyday priorities should be taking care of your relationships with the people around you. Let's begin by taking a look at your inner circle.

Your Inner Circle

The president has his cabinet, government leaders have their advisors, CEOs have their boards of directors, and you have your inner circle. Well, at least you should. No, an inner circle isn't just for politicians, business leaders, and uber-intellectual think tanks. Your inner circle is made up of the handful of people closest to you in your life—those you share your deepest passions and fears with and those who support you regardless of what you do or what choices you make. While your family, neighbors, colleagues, and friends might be *physically* around you all the time, they're not necessarily the most receptive to your wild ideas, hopes, dreams, and aspirations. And they may not always be the people who make up your inner circle. That's okay, though. They play an important role regardless. But in matters of success and achievement, it's critical that you develop or enhance your own inner circle of confidants.

Let's try to identify some of the members of your inner circle. Who are the people you trust above everyone else? Who pushes you to keep going when you falter, and who inspires you to be more and do more in the pursuit of your dreams? These are the people who "get" what you're all about. It shouldn't take long for you to identify the key candidates. In case you need a little help, here are some things to think about:

· Who do you call when you have great news to share?

· If you are on vacation and have three postcards, who do you write to?

· Who do you cc the most on funny, compelling, or important emails?

· Who do you celebrate major occasions and important events with?

- Who never forgets you on holidays, birthdays, or anniversaries?

- Who is there for you when you need to vent, let off steam, or cry on a shoulder?

- Who can finish your sentences and tell what you're thinking without speaking?

- Who do you consider family, even if they're not?

- Who could you not live without?

- Who "gets you" and what you're all about more than anyone?

Consider whether you've been doing what you need to keep your relationships up to speed. Do these people know just how much they mean to you? If not, you might want to think about picking up the phone or writing a note card. It's all too easy for us to get busy, distracted, and neglectful with even the most important things in our lives, but our closest relationships are one thing that we can't afford to take for granted.

Success might involve a lonely road, but it certainly doesn't have to be a desolate one. Your inner circle should be kept abreast of what you have going on in your life on an ongoing basis. These are the people who truly care about you and your dreams, and they are more likely to understand you than virtually anyone else. Don't shut them out. We all need great people to rely on, to talk to, to run our ideas by, to give us honest feedback, and to keep us on track. You *must* surround yourself with people who believe in you, and the key is beginning with a solid core. If you don't have an inner circle of your own, give some serious thought to doing something about it. It's not something that you can create overnight, but it's a priority that we all should work on a little bit every day. Having wonderful people in our lives is a gift. But one thing is for sure, you need people who are not only close to you, but who can help you. And that's where mentors come in.

ⅤＳ Your Mentor Mix

Mentors are wonderful people who selflessly give their guidance and expertise to people they see as having great potential. How are they different than your inner circle? Look at it this way: People in your inner circle are like family to you. Their love is more or less unconditional and they'd never turn you away if you showed up on their doorstep unannounced. Our inner circle tends to be more concerned with what happens on a day-to-day, sometimes hour-by-hour basis in our lives. They want to know who we're dating, if we're taking care of ourselves, what happened with that old friend who called the other day, and so on.

Our mentors, however, are typically concerned with the bigger picture—our future, our dreams, our grand plans. They want to know how they can help, and they do things for us that other people can't, or simply won't. Mentors typically aren't *obligated* to help us for any reason.

Their concern is making a positive impact on our lives, not just being a beloved cast member within it. They want to know that you're living up to your potential and that you've accomplished more since the last time they saw you.

Who have your mentors been? Who are the people who have taught you some of the greatest lessons of your life? Who has taken a keen interest in you and your accomplishments? Who cares about your best interest, without any obvious reason? Who looks out for you when no one else is looking? These people who you thought of, these are your mentors. They come in all shapes and sizes and can enter our lives at all different stages, from very early childhood, well on through when we're adults. And despite how old you are, you need them. In fact, I think we *all* could use a *few* of them.

Whether you're an investment banker, a teacher, a parent, a student, an athlete, a politician, or even a CEO, you need to learn from people who are smarter or more experienced than you, or hold knowledge that you don't or can't. You need people who can drive you and keep your motivation running strong. How can mentors best help you? They

- listen to your ideas and what you have to say

- act as a sounding board, giving you invaluable feedback

- share with you their hard-earned wisdom and experience

- help you understand just how far you can go

- help keep you on track

- make referrals and introductions

- sometimes introduce you to their world, inviting you in as a guest

Now this is a pretty good idea of what you can expect from a relationship with a mentor. But I use that word "expect" very cautiously, because you can't and shouldn't really expect anything from these people. In most cases, you're not *entitled* to their advice. Your relationship with them is a privilege, it's their gift to you, and if you forget that, you'll run the risk of losing it.

High-Level Help

As Young & Successful people (even in the making), we need access to specialized and sometimes top experts. So while the guy who owns the corner grocery store or your uncle Lou might give you great advice sometimes, as with everything else we've talked about, start thinking on some higher levels too. Keep your inner circle tight, but focus on properly constructing your environment and filling it with people who are going to not only like you and believe in you, but will help strategically guide you to where you need to be. I can't emphasize this enough. Mentors will help do this. But don't rely on just one or two if you can help it. Everyone brings something different to the table, yet no one person can feed a truly balanced diet of what you need to be successful. Like putting together a puzzle or going on a scavenger hunt, it's going to take a lot of pieces working together toward one goal.

Let me give you a few quick examples of my own to show you not only how mentors can dramatically improve your life, but how each one offers something very different. This is how having a mix of mentors makes all the difference in the world.

When I finally got my first big business going, the predecessor to the Young Entrepreneurs Network, I realized I needed some serious real-world mentors. Candy Brush was a professor at school who had written probably a dozen different books on women entrepreneurs, and in fact, she even helped me write my first book. She also helped introduce me to her world—the people leading the nation's top women's entrepreneurial initiatives—and she invited me to attend and even participate in a slew of different professional events that frankly gave me an enormous amount of invaluable exposure and credibility. For instance, how would I, a twenty-year-old, ever have gotten to work side by side with government leaders, drafting reports and recommendations on how to better support entrepreneurs for the president of the United States? It was Candy who opened those first doors for me.

In 1994 at a conference I walked up to a complete stranger, Steve Mariotti—whom I'd recognized from months of research on entrepreneurial education—and told him how incredible I thought he was and how I admired all the work he was doing. The next afternoon, he had invited me out to lunch and we bonded. A few years later, he wrote the introduction to my first book, then helped me get my first official certification to teach entrepreneurs. Along the way he invited me to many great events and introduced me to the heads of some of the most prestigious companies and organizations in the world. He even once bought me a ticket and invited me to join him on a trip to speak to the Harvard Club in Belgium and INSEAD University in Fontainebleau, France. Talk about an incredible mentor!

A mentor relationship can also snowball into even greater ones as you get older and your career advances. For example, Scott and I met Layne Britton through a close friend. Over the years, Layne has been heavily involved in the media and entertainment industry as a senior executive at several major entertainment companies. He has served as a close trusted personal advisor to some of the biggest people in the television industry. So why would he bother with us?

Good question. We asked him once as he was giving us his input on a television show concept that we were beginning to work on. His reply blew Scott and me away. From behind his tough, firm exterior he told us that he enjoyed sharing industry war stories with us along with his hard earned advise because of our passion for building a major company. He told us that he believed we had a real shot at eventually hitting a home-run with one of our "grand ideas". Talk about a gift from heaven! That's what Layne has always been. From making incredibly kind introductions, meeting up for a last minute lunch or dinner, acting as an important sounding board, to whipping up a batch of his famous homemade chocolate chip cookies at a moments notice, Layne is never more than a phone call or email away if Scott or I need anything. You can be sure that we'll never let go of this wonderful relationship.

◤ Getting the Mentors You Need

Many of the best mentors, like Layne, will just appear somewhere, somehow, by sheer luck, but others you'll need to do a little more work to find. If you remember what we did in Master Your Universe (Chapter Five), we walked through an exercise called "Mapping Out Your World." In it we sketched out the industry you were focused on and, in the process, figured out who all the key players are. This might be a great time to re-map, based on everything you've learned since, and come up with your ideal mentors from there. Just focus on a spectrum of people who will be able to help you through various stages of your Grand Plan. You don't have to come up with all of them at once, but knowing who and what you need will make you that much more likely to find them as you go about your business. So how do you get these people to help you?

FINDING THE MENTORS OF YOUR DREAMS

When Curtis Estes was just getting started as a financial planner in Los Angeles, he knew he needed to begin to build solid relationships with lots of successful people around the city, but he could never have expected the twist of fate to come.

Curtis decided that a great way to meet local people he had something in common with would be to get involved in his local college alumni group from the University of Kansas. Soon after joining he became president. At the first event he hosted, Curtis found himself sipping margaritas with a local alum named Dana Anderson. Before the night was through, the two had hit it off and became fast friends.

As it turns out, Dana was the vice-chairman of the Macerich Company, a real estate investment trust (REIT) and one of the largest owners/operators of regional malls in the United States. Over drinks, they realized that they both shared a similar background—both were alums of the same school, had grown up in similar middle-class backgrounds, and both were self-made men—Curtis was just getting started, though, and anxious to follow in the steps of great business leaders like Dana. In the course of their first conversation, Dana mentioned to Curtis that many of his real-estate purchases were funded by the company Curtis was just getting started with. Better yet, Dana told Curtis that he was ready to get some help with his own estate planning and in no time, Curtis had earned Dana's business and trust. As a result of the excellent job Curtis did, Dana proceeded to take Curtis under his wing and invited him to join his personal "board of directors." From there, Dana helped him build his business by introducing Curtis to other potential clients within his network—big real-estate investors, Wall Street brokers, the head of a major restaurant chain. (Let's just say that Dana gave him entrée to some seriously successful people.)

If that wasn't enough love, Dana then helped Curtis become a member of the prestigious Bel Air Country Club, where Dana was on the board. And all along the way, this incredible new mentor taught him all about his own journey from a modest start in real estate in the small town of Manhattan, Kansas, to running a public real-estate company on the New York Stock Exchange.

As you can imagine, Curtis says he was blessed to have met

Dana and has since learned so much from him over the years—particularly about philanthropy, hard work, and the power in building a trusted network of friends and supporters. Further, he says:

> *Dana has provided me with a model to follow for giving back to others in meaningful ways. His philanthropy has spanned many wonderful causes and continues to do so today. He has also shown me what it means to work hard and humbly. Even after building a hugely successful business himself and amassing a significant personal fortune, he still comes into his office regularly, quickly returns all his phone calls, and never forgets where he comes from or what he's been through along the way. He sets a wonderful example to emulate.*
>
> *I'll never forget the day Dana referred me to someone, and no matter how I tried, I could not get the woman on the phone. She continually blew me off. But when Dana got wind of this, he proceeded to call her, set up my first meeting with her, and even attended himself. When we walked in, not only was the woman I wanted to meet there, but so were her two attorneys and her CPA! All the decision makers I could ever need to close a big deal. He's simply an incredible man and mentor.*

Jeff Bloom is a Young & Successful attorney in San Diego who found his greatest mentor through networking but, in this case, by getting to know the professors at his law school. One professor in particular who had liked Jeff and heard that he was looking for a job helped set up an interview with a local superstar attorney who just so happened to be one of *his* professor's professors years before when he was in law school. She later told Jeff that he just had a feeling that they would hit it off. And she was right.

Within a few weeks of his first interview, Jeff was hired by Harvey R. Levine, one of the top trial lawyers in America. Thrilled to have the opportunity, Jeff quickly dove into his work and was soon learning from the man famous for a career of record-breaking verdicts and settlements in his field. In fact, Harvey is considered by many to be *the* national authority on his specialty, bad faith insurance litigation—when insurance companies refuse coverage to policy holders whom they insure.

While most lawyers never actually try a courtroom case in their entire career, during his first month at the firm Harvey asked Jeff to help him prepare for a large personal injury case he was working on. Better yet, he allowed Jeff to sit in on the whole trial so he could watch, learn, and become familiar with the whole process. Along the way, Harvey trusted Jeff to complete critical trial documents for presentation before the judge and jury. Jeff says that being part of the case and watching Harvey win a $6 million verdict (the largest of its kind in San Diego history) was one of the highlights of his life. Talk to Jeff, and it's not hard to see how thankful he is to have the opportunity to learn from someone like Harvey. From his experiences already, Jeff is proud to say:

> *It's very rewarding to be an advocate for those who don't have the resources to protect themselves, in a world run by corporations with very deep pockets. In my short time with the firm, Harvey has proved to me that dedication, compassion, and integrity can pay off in so many ways.*

To find mentors as incredible as Curtis's and Jeff's, you have to not only be a little lucky, but well worth the effort and investment yourself. It's your job to make that investment pay off for your mentors. Show a lot of promise, intelligence, ambition, and, most of all, your most sincere appreciation for all that they do, and the relationships that ensue are sure to reward both of you.

Building Your Board

As you start to pull people like these together in your life, consider creating your own personal board of advisors. Again, you don't have to be a billionaire or a big company to have one of these. Just think about your board of advisors as five or ten people who could make up the perfect think tank or "success committee" for you. If you could put a handful of brilliant people who believe in you in a room together so that they can all discuss how you can do better and go further, think of what you could do. Consider the level of accountability you'd have to them. Think about just how vested in your success they'd really become if they were a part of formally sculpting those plans.

Keep your board of advisors tight. Don't add people who can't contribute or whom you don't like personally. In other words, you're looking for more than an impressive résumé and list of contacts. Once you have your group together, meet live if you can, someplace where you can talk for a few hours, without interruption. Hold a big conference call. Set an agenda. Allow everyone to briefly introduce themselves to the group. Have a presentation on what you're up to and what your plans are. Get your questions ready. Let them know clearly what you need, what you're looking for, and how they can help you. And meet on an ongoing basis if you can, worst case, once or twice a year. Lastly, make sure they never forget how much they mean to you and how grateful you are to them for sharing what they know with you. And voilà! You've got your own advisory board.

⟩⟨ The Power of One

Now take all this cumulative brain power and all these wonderful people behind you, and do something profound. Just look at you! You're so pumped with brilliant ideas and ambitious plans that all you have to do now is get started. Get moving. Let all the pieces start to fall into place. It's your turn to start doing some extraordinary things.

After all, the Young & Successful believe in the power of the individual above almost all else.

Think about the people you've met or read about who single-handedly seem to change their own little piece of the world. Who are they? What have they accomplished? How did they do so much, often with so little? What motivated them? Consider the lives and careers of some of the most powerful people in our history. Gandhi, Martin Luther King Jr., Hitler, Mother Teresa, Stalin, Mao Zedong, Winston Churchill. These were all individuals who built up an enormous amount of power and influence during their lifetimes (for better or for worse) and changed the lives of millions . . . not to mention the course of history.

MAKING POLITICAL HEADS ROLL

Meredith Bagby turned quite a few heads with a self-published book that she wrote as a twenty-one-year-old senior in college. Her plan was to get to the bottom of the mystery of how the federal government spends its money . . . or should I say ours. So Meredith came up with the idea to produce an annual report, just as all publicly held corporations are obligated to do, to clearly outline where all the money goes and what the ultimate "shareholder value" is to us, its citizens. "As taxpayers," she says, "we are the shareholders of the USA, Inc. And this is the annual report from our government that we are entitled to but don't get."

Ross Perot, then presidential hopeful, couldn't have agreed more. In the midst of a highly visible campaign for office where Perot attacked the government leaders for failing to explain its practices to the people it served, he discovered Meredith's report and was quite vocal about what he found. "Only in America would a college senior, on her own initiative and on her own time, actually produce it. If the government tried, it would take two years, cost $10 million, and you couldn't read it." Within days a bound copy of her *Annual Report of the United States of America* was being waved in front of Congress and the Senate by Perot himself, demanding to know why it was that a college student could explain the federal budget better than the government itself. It was truly the moment of a lifetime. But that was just the beginning for Meredith. In addition to a torrent of media exposure that followed, including features in *People,* on *Good Morning America,* and *Larry King Live,* Meredith was asked to join CNN's Financial Network as their "Generation X Correspondent." Her on-air reports on politics and economics finally shed light on the rarely discussed issues that affect our generation and, single-handedly, her words again changed the way that millions looked at their futures.

CHANGING BODIES AND LIVES

Changing the world can happen on many different scales and be influenced by different people, supporting an endless variety of causes. By age thirty-two, Bill Phillips had achieved extraordinary success as a personal fitness trainer, magazine publisher, and founder of a nutritional products company, EAS, which produces some of the top-selling supplements, vitamins, and protein shakes in the business.

Bill was just twelve when he himself started weight training, and by high school, he was a power lifting and bodybuilding champion . . . not to mention a straight A student. At age twenty-two, he invested $185, the only money he had, into a publishing business called Muscle Media, which just a few years later would be responsible for one of the fastest growing fitness magazines, with more than 650,000 readers. But it wasn't until he began his search for a corporate spokesperson that he hit on the vehicle that would inspire hundreds of thousands of people to become "physically and mentally stronger by focusing on fitness." In the first year of the contest, 54,000 people took the famous Physique Transformation Challenge. By the next year it had grown to more than 200,000. And each year, the numbers continued to climb at a staggering rate. In 1997, at age thirty-two, Bill was honored as one of the youngest men ever to win the highly coveted Entrepreneur of the Year Award by Ernst & Young, one of the top accounting firms in the world. He also raised more than $1.5 million for the Make-A-Wish Foundation, which helps terminally ill children fulfill lifelong dreams. Today, EAS is a leading company in its industry and Bill Phillips is a symbol to millions of how inner strength can transform not only your body, but your life.

Both Meredith and Bill started out as ordinary people with extraordinary ideas that exploded, ultimately affecting more people than they ever dreamed of.

You, a World Leader?

Look at yourself in the context of some of the great leaders (and even the more infamous tyrants). If you were to become a world leader, what would you be remembered for? What would your legacy be? You don't have to be politically focused to make a difference. Just think about what you could do as a single individual to change the course of the world. What about your community? Or culture? Choose your focus and figure out how you can make your mark on your own corner of the world. Whether that's a small town or village, or your entire continent, never let your sights be limited by small thinking.

Come on, think really big. Take your personal mission, your grandest idea, your most profound dream, and let it explode in your mind. What could you do to change the way people think, act, eat, read, work, or do anything significant for that matter? Now hold on to that thought. Because you never know when you might have to write a paper, or give a speech, or take your life's work to a whole different level entirely. Exciting, isn't it?

✂ The Exponential Power of People

Since no great leader really becomes extraordinary without lots of in-credible people around them, let's talk about just that—the Exponential POP. Consider what would happen if your dream had scores of impas-sioned people behind you and your projects. Think back to your Ideal Life and the Grand Plan that you created. Imagine that, initially, a dozen people fell in love with you and your vision. What would you be able to accomplish? Now add a few zeros and imagine 1,200 or 12,000 people falling in line, eager to make *your* dream happen. What could you do then? Wait, I'll give you a few hints.

LOOKING FOR LOVE

Ken Deckinger affects many people's lives every day, in the most simple ways possible—he uses his smile, his never-ending jokes, and his crazy personality to make people happy, even if just for the moment that they pass him on the street. In fact, you can learn a lot about Ken just by his two most infa-mous nicknames: "Smiley" and the "Bald Lover." Getting a good visual there? Let me help you out. Ken's a tall, well-dressed, nicely built slim guy, with a gleaming bald head and the biggest smile you've ever seen in your life. To top it all off, when he's excited, his eyes become wild with excitement, and you just can't help but smile yourself. I've actually seen total strangers (usually intrigued women) just stop dead in their tracks to talk to him and see what he's all about.

Now Ken's a pretty smart guy, too, with an MBA and a few entrepreneurial gigs under his belt—including a small consulting firm, a publishing venture, and an events promotions company—at age twenty-eight. But it's this latest venture that really gets me. See, Ken, who's always had a knack for using the power of people to fuel his crazy ideas, has done it again . . . and this time, he brings LOVE. HurryDate is the name of his newest exploding company, and what they do is set up a big party at a local hotspot, and arrange for every single who attends to go on twenty-five different three-minute dates in one jam-packed outrageous night.

So how does he use the power of people? Well, the concept has been such a hit and Ken has infected so many people with HurryDate fever that, now, not only are clients spreading the word themselves, but they're launching new events for him all over the world. In just the first year of operation, Ken has inspired more than twenty other entrepreneurial souls to launch HurryDate Chicago, HurryDate Toronto, HurryDate London, HurryDate Amsterdam, and now, GayHurryDate, BlackHurryDate, and JewishHurryDate, just to name a few. How's that for having people fall in love with you, your cause, and your business, all in one giant love fest!

Do something profound on any subject or as part of any quest, and odds are people will start to join you in your cause, too, just like they did in Ken's quest to bring love to thousands of lonely hearts. Add a little exposure through marketing, PR, or just some powerful word of mouth (and a lot of smiling), and you're off on your own adventure, probably with a good group of supporters by your side or following close behind.

Rallying Behind a Cause

I got lucky enough to see how people rally behind causes when I started the Young Entrepreneurs Network with two friends while I was still in college. We started connecting young entrepreneurs with one another from countries around the world, because as I'm telling you here, the first thing you need is information and the second thing you need is support. We showed young entrepreneurs how they could support one another.

It wasn't until I started becoming quite vocal by doing a good deal of public speaking, teaching classes, publishing articles and books, and getting in front of a lot of people that this little quest became somewhat of a movement. If the reception wasn't enough to convince me, the fact that more than ninety students joined us as interns within five years certainly did. (Just to clarify, that's ninety people who worked for *free* to make the dream possible.) Those ninety volunteers helped us recruit members from seventy countries. How did that happen? Well, in a million different ways. For example:

- Interns would constantly tell us about other organizations that they heard about, and in a lot of cases, we forged relationships with them and cross-promoted our work. Sometimes I'd even get asked to come speak at events and get the chance to spread word of what we were doing in person.

- People who worked with us would talk to their friends about what they were doing. This helped spread the word on several different campuses around the country, and many students ended up doing reports or writing articles on what they learned.

- One of our favorite interns, Danny Essner, helped us spearhead a major research study that was featured in *The Wall Street Journal* and dozens of other publications.

· Whenever people in our office met with anyone in the press, they'd rave about what we were doing, and often it resulted in news articles. Sometimes TV crews would end up at our door within a few days.

· We even got a few consulting clients because people who were working with us knew people starting their own businesses, executives in ad agencies, and even large corporations who were trying to tap into our market.

As for changing the way people thought about the abilities of younger people like us, well, the press alone got us in front of more than 100 million people worldwide. And that was just phase one. The really good stuff came next, as we used the exponential power concept to move millions of our peers to follow their dreams and become Young & Succesful in their own right. (Just a little update for you there.) Clearly I'm a big fan of this concept!

I have witnessed the power of the individual. And in many ways, I helped start a movement that enabled young people to gain the recognition and respect that they deserve. It all started as just another crazy idea, and when we got behind it with all our energy and all the right people, the venture just took off.

Harness the Magic of Giving

While we're on the subject of causes and action, here's an important concept to mention. Why should giving be a concern of yours now? Because if along the way to your dreams you're able to harness the magic of giving, you have a powerful opportunity to do so much more. Young & Successful people know how important and rewarding giving is, and they realize that it's something that all of us need to do, regardless of who we are or what we have. There's a lot more than meets the eye here, too.

I want to encourage you to do what you can to help others, whenever you can, not only because it's the right thing to do but because you're going to need the help of others in one way or another yourself. Think cyclically. Like viral marketing, giving is also infectious. If you become more generous, other people around you will be, too. And they'll pass the urge on to others, and so on and so on. I'm sure I don't need to tell you this again, but no one gets anywhere big in life without the support of other people. With that said, don't you think we all need as much love and compassion floating around as possible? See what I have to say on this level, and I promise to show you a whole other realm of how *your* giving to others can end up giving *you* more than perhaps anything else you may be doing.

When we say "giving" we're not just talking about charity—we're talking about everyday life, business, and, in particular, personal relationships. This is what turns the people and the power in your life now into the most rewarding opportunities of your lifetime.

Everyday Opportunities

By taking advantage of everyday opportunities to do a little something special for someone else—whether a friend, colleague, or total stranger—you'll no doubt become a little more aware, compassionate, and even likable. If you think about it, there's really no downside to being a nicer, more giving person. And the upside of that is, if you spend any time you can giving, you will probably end up with a bunch of people in your life ready to spring into action when you need a helping hand yourself.

Here are a few examples of how simple this really is:

- Surprise a friend by asking if there's anything you can do to help her

- Run an errand for someone who's busy or sick

- Save an article that would be of interest to someone you know

- Refer new business

- Show up with coffee, bagels, or even flowers

- Write a letter commending someone for great service or a job well done

- Pay a compliment to someone's boss on her performance

- Let someone who's in a rush go before you in line

- Smile at strangers. Be nice and courteous

- Ask someone you normally wouldn't talk to how he's doing

While the value of pure, unadulterated charitable giving is undisputed, there may be other ways to look at the concept of doing good for others. To put it bluntly, giving can be of enormous value to us, too. Giving makes us better people, gives us a greater sense of self-worth, opens up unexpected opportunities, builds leverage, and earns respect. Not all the time but often. But that's not why we should do it. It's nice to know that there are some possible perks involved. For many Young & Successful people who have achieved an impressive sense of balance in their lives, there's often a very strong commitment to giving back in both their current and Ideal Lives. What did you include in your Grand Plan about giving back?

Making Your Mark

Have you ever raised a dollar for a charity? Hung up a poster for a politician? Volunteered for an event or a special cause? Sold raffle tickets? Then you know the power of rallying behind a cause. When you add your effort to that of others, the results can be immediate and often immense. What happened because of the group's collective involvement? Odds are, your exponential power created greater progress, change, and improvements.

Find ways to engage other people in your efforts, and your ability to advance will become exponentially greater. What could you really do if you harnessed the power of people for a cause you were passionate about? How much could you accomplish? Think about a cause that's important to you. It could be

- children's literacy

- voter apathy

- religious persecution

- planting trees or saving the rainforest

- feeding the homeless

Or even think about something more personal, closer to home, like

- cleaning up a local park

- starting a local sports league

- building a community center

• recognizing a teacher or someone who's made a big impact

• helping local kids with a lemonade stand or bake sale

Whatever mission you might choose to adopt, create a plan for how you could bring together as many people as possible to make an impact. How many people could you get to rally behind this cause? How would that translate into tangible results? All this altruism will help you. Want to know how? I'll show you right now.

The Big Picture of Giving

Ever wonder why very wealthy people spend so much of their time involved in charitable activities? It's not all about the tax write-offs. And the cause itself is just the tip of the iceberg for them. Now I certainly don't want to make any giving—especially on the more grand levels—seem insincere, because I don't believe that at all. But when you enter the world of some of the larger nonprofits, charities, fund-raisers, and community events, you may be stepping in to a world of contacts, influence, and power that, under normal circumstances, you might still be years away from being a part of yourself.

Remember the story in Take a Taste (Chapter Six) of Jennifer Iannolo, the woman who was passionate about making it in the food industry? Remember how she recounted her experience of working at the Bon Appetit charity event as a volunteer, decked out in a ball gown, drinking Champagne, eating caviar, and working side by side with the most highly respected celebrity chefs in the business? Well, may I remind you that she could barely pay her own rent at the time, let alone afford the $500-a-person ticket price. (Thankfully a friend of hers had a ball gown and evening shoes she could borrow!) And the best part was that she was just trying to get some experience and help out wherever they'd let her. This event, where she had written programs, moved chairs and tables, and handed utensils to chefs during cooking demonstrations, changed her life forever while contributing greatly to its cause.

By volunteering with great organizations and by helping out with events like this, you can often find yourself in situations that you'd only dreamed were possible. All those big, powerful people who you've always wanted to meet are often there, trying to have some fun and help out like you are. Some of the less talked about but most profound benefits of getting involved in charitable causes include, but are definitely not limited to, the following:

- valuable experience and exposure

- amazing social and professional contacts

- new, rewarding relationships

- greater fulfillment through contribution

- increased sense of value and self-worth

- personal recognition for you and your work

- the chance to spend time with very hard to reach people

- some fabulous stories to tell

- and often, a totally different perspective

So, while you probably can't volunteer to put a computer in thousands of schools like Bill Gates and Michael Dell did, by offering your time to some of the same charities that they do, you might just find yourself chatting with them or other high-powered, influential people at a cocktail party. And when it's all over, you'll probably have gotten the chance to do work that you haven't had the opportunity to do on your own. That also means getting the chance to show what you are really capable of, and having the proof and an incredible experience under your belt, to show for it. So take your people skills, sales and marketing expertise, and graphic design abilities, your knack for accounting and bookkeeping, or whatever you may have to offer, and find a worthy organization that you can help. Before you know it, you might find yourself heading up committees, sitting on boards, lunching with industry moguls—and all the while, doing more good than you ever thought possible. What an incredible win-win situation!

Vicarious Living Through Giving

Ever wonder why some very successful people take the time to help someone who appears to have little or nothing to offer them? While they may look as if they have everything they need and are already living their Ideal Life at the highest levels, they can often receive more than you think.

Sometimes other people see a spark of greatness in you and want to help where they can. (This speaks so directly to the mentoring we were talking about above.) A few reasons powerful or important people may go out of their way for you might have a lot more to do with them wanting to live vicariously through you than anything else. For example, you may intrigue them or remind them of themselves when they were your age. (How do you think I got my first commercial office space when I was twenty-two? It had a lot more to do with my reminding the landlord of his daughter than with my qualifications as a good prospective tenant!) They may be curious to see what happens to you. They may want to be around when you get closer to "their level." They might be recruiting future clients, friends, or contacts who could benefit them down the road.

Four Steps to Meeting Virtually Anyone

Now that we've explored the why, let's look at the how. How can you cultivate the most rewarding and powerful relationships? The following four secrets to meeting virtually anyone will show you how you too can have access to practically anyone or anything you may need.

Step 1: What's Your Goal?

The first step to targeted, high-level networking is figuring out whom you want to meet. In many cases you may not be thinking of one or two people in particular but perhaps of some exclusive group or organization. That makes your job so much easier and the rewards often greater. The bigger your initial list of targets is, the more likely you are to score one. You never really know when and if an opportunity will arise with one particular person. So having a range of different people you'd like to meet allows you to position yourself strategically enough so that at some point you just start running into them! So, to create your list, think about the people you admire:

- people who have contributed significantly to society

- industry titans who are the creators, controllers, or legends

- executives who can put you on the fast track

- entrepreneurs who can put you into your own business or make you a part of theirs

- educators at the forefront of modern thought

- writers who are highly acclaimed and widely read

- politicians who run the government

- entertainers who top the charts

- mentors who can take you under their wing

- investors who can fund your dreams.

Once you have your list, you have to find them. You've already learned a lot about how to do this in Master Your Universe (Chapter Five) and Take a Taste (Chapter Six). But the Young & Successful still have a few secrets you can learn.

Step 2: How Do You Find Them?

Once you have your targets, the smartest thing you can do is some intensive research on them. (This is where all those years of homework and research papers pay off.) Go back to The Grand Plan (Chapter Four) if you need to and employ the strategies you used for finding these people. Here are a few more things to keep an eye out for that can start to focus your radar:

- the company they own or work for

- people on their board of directors

- what city they live in

- their websites, fan clubs, or online profiles

- their clients

- biographies on their family and friends

- what social activities or hobbies they engage in

- their charitable activities

· their religious affiliations

· where they went to school

· any speaking engagements or conferences they attend

· what networks, fraternities, or organizations they are a part of

Follow these trails through the Internet, the library, word of mouth, friends of friends, the media, or any sources you can find. And remember, you're not supposed to creep anyone out by stalking his or her every move. Nothing will blow your chances of a meaningful encounter more. At the same time, if you can reasonably and professionally start to piece together what people do with their time, you will absolutely begin to find opportunities to meet them in person.

FROM INTERN TO AGENT

As a top national racquetball champion, Mark Bloom had been obsessed with sports his whole life. There wasn't a day that passed without watching ESPN, a week without *Sports Illustrated*, or a month when he wasn't reading a book written by some huge athlete or industry executive. More than anything, Mark wanted to be a sports agent some day. He knew that getting an internship with a big agency would be his best chance at getting in the game . . . but he had no idea where to start.

Since Mark was already such an active researcher (I'm sure law school didn't hurt that tendency), he already knew a lot about the top agencies. One day when he was reading about one in particular, he spotted a familiar name on one of the client rosters. He started to scream for his brother. To their great surprise, someone they had grown up with back home— who had become a top pro football player—was on the list! This was his chance. Remembering that he had been friendly with the player's father many years before, he picked up the phone and tracked him down. When Mark asked for a possible reference or suggestion on how he could talk to someone at his son's agency, the father graciously offered to call on his behalf. The father picked up the phone, got Mark a meeting, and lo and behold, he landed an internship for one of the top sports management agencies in the business. And now, a year later, Mark is a sports agent himself at Synergy Sports Management, a hot new firm that represents football players, basketball players, and coaches.

Step 3: Assume the Position

To best understand positioning, let's break it down in two ways: strategic positioning and day-to-day positioning. Day-to-day positioning is a series of seemingly insignificant decisions that we make every day yet can give us a better chance at being in the "right place at the right time" for something great to happen. You may not have any idea when or what that may be, but if you go to a basketball game, for example, and decide to spring for the better seats, your chances of sitting next to someone interesting are far greater. If you opt for the floor seats, you're almost guaranteed to be a few feet away from a celebrity or big industry mogul. That's what day-to-day positioning is all about—getting close to the power.

Strategic positioning is about deliberately getting right up to the people you want to meet or the companies you want to do business with. Say you wanted to meet the founder of Starbucks, Howard Schultz. All you need to do is watch out for one of the national food and beverage conferences. He's almost certain to be there, speaking or walking around, pushing his product or announcing his latest plans. Have your business card ready and something to say. (This is where your story comes in hand). If you can't get to the show, run a search online and see where he's speaking or even attending the opening of another Starbucks in a new market.

Or imagine you wanted to meet Kay Koplovitz, the founder of USA Networks, CEO of the Working Woman Network, and the co-founder of Springboard 2000, the first series of women's venture capital conferences. As an active member of the business world, she's always out making speeches and attending fund-raisers, but you can be sure to run in to her if you attend any of the three Springboard conferences a year in various parts of the country.

Most moguls like Kay will always attend certain functions. It's up to you to figure out what those events are. That's strategic positioning.

Every day we make choices that affect our positioning in some significant way. What we usually don't think about is being a little calculating in these decisions. Who we talk to, where we go, what we read, and how we look when we venture out all play a part in what happens to us in the course of everyday life. Want to be better prepared? Keep reading.

Don't Be Shy—Talk, talk, talk

Think about something as simple as getting a cup of coffee. You can probably pop in to any convenience store and get a cup with as much caffeine as you would in one from Starbucks. But where are you more likely to bump into someone more interesting? What are you doing when you're standing there waiting for your latte? Talk to people! Randomly talking to strangers is something your mother always warned you not to do, but as an adult, you'd be amazed at all the people you're missing out on just because you keep silent.

Planes are some of my favorite places to meet people. Now, I'm not one to talk people's ears off on a long flight, but I almost always try to say hello to anyone I'm sitting next to for hours at a time. Just by observing what he's wearing, carrying, or reading, you can tell a lot about a person. If they look interesting, a few quick comments like, "Can I help you with that bag?" or "Do you think we're going to get in on time? I have a meeting I've got to get to" or "I'm so glad the weather cleared up here, it has been miserable all week" can often spark more dialogue. Be brief with what you say in the beginning and keep the conversation going back and forth until you sense any real interest or disinterest. If the person seems bored, annoyed, or anxious to move on to his reading or sleeping, let him. If not, you may have the beginnings of a great plane trip or even a new friendship that never would have happened if you'd kept silent.

Once you get good at the art of talking to strangers, a whole new world can open up. Just pick the people you talk to with some discretion. Handled the right way, the sky's the limit.

Hang out in the right places

Talking to strangers works best at

· small parties

· conferences

- charity events

- political fund-raisers

- restaurants

- on long lines

- airport lounges or on airplanes

Or anywhere that you can get a better sense of what someone is all about. One little secret, which you probably know but haven't done much about, is that the absolute best places to meet major players are in exclusive airport clubs, first-class cabins, country clubs, posh hotels, top spas, expensive salons, the most exclusive restaurants and bars, golf courses, and definitely the trendiest shopping spots. In these places you can't go wrong, but you can go broke!

Get the gossip by reading

Taking it a step further, the challenge of day-to-day positioning is not only figuring out which places are the best for you to go but how you can get access to some of them. Believe it or not, a recent articles in *Los Angeles* magazine talked about this very thing—"Where to Meet the Most Powerful Women in the Entertainment World." It proceeded to list pages of favorite hangouts, offered an inside peek at each of the scenes, and threw in some juicy gossip on who specifically you could find frequenting these places. While we're on the subject, go get copies of your city's top magazines, business journals, who's-who trades, and any local papers that cover people in the community. You should be reading these religiously to stay abreast of who's who in your industry.

Check your mirror

The last, but perhaps most important thing you have to concern yourself with in this kind of positioning is being prepared. This can mean a lot of things. How you look, what you're wearing, your overall attitude, and even what you're carrying with you can all have a huge impact on your chances of something *happening*. Think I'm being too vain? Wander into Barney's or a hot nightclub in a pair of sweatpants and old sneakers and see how attentive people are to you. Or try to go to a big meeting without combing your hair or pressing your clothes. These are extreme examples, but I mention them because when you are first meeting someone, the only way they can get a sense of who you are is by your appearance.

One thing I've learned over time is to always try to look my best. Now, sure I get lazy and wander out in flip-flops, no makeup, and my hair in a bun more often than I care to admit, but so many times I've thought, "You know, Mom was totally right." It's always when I find myself a few feet away from someone I'd love to talk to that I realize I should have made more of an effort to put myself together. It could be a drugstore, Staples, or even more likely, Kinko's in the middle of the night. Point is, you've got to make the most out of any situation and way too many of them, we just don't plan for.

Strategic positioning is all about applying your research and finding a way to get in front of the people and companies you want to meet or work with. The goal of strategic positioning is to get your targets on your radar screen. Think of an air traffic controller whose monitor covers a ten-mile radius. Lots of planes will cross his or her screen (just like you'll come into contact with many different people) but what he's most concerned with are the ones coming into his airport. (Just like you're focused on your targets.) Once he knows exactly where the planes are, navigating the best way to bring them safely to the landing strip is easy.

So imagine you've figured out that one of your targets is going to be at a certain conference. Showing up at that conference is like you meeting the plane when it arrives on the landing strip. Only one major step to go from there! The introduction . . .

The concept of strategic positioning can be summed up easily: Find out exactly where your targets are and go there yourself. What you say from there is answered in Step 4.

Step 4: Take a Calculated Approach

All right, you're in position. You're looking at your target from across the room. Or maybe you did some digging and got the direct number of her office. Perhaps you found something that you both have in common and got the address to write a letter. What do you say? Let's break it down to four scenarios: in person, over the phone, via email, or snail mail.

In person

This is where you'll thank God you did your research or want to die because you didn't. In person you may only have one shot at meeting someone. If you thought getting the courage to talk to her was hard, catching her at the wrong time is worse.

While this is totally subjective, there are some general rules of etiquette. Don't bother someone

- as he's preparing to give a speech

- when he's mobbed with people

- when he's on the phone or engaged in a private conversation

- when he looks grouchy

- when he's in the middle of eating at a restaurant or function

- if he's in the middle of an argument

- if he's clearly trying to avoid people (reviewing notes, averting his eyes or attention, intentionally standing off to the side)

- when he is in the restroom

Ultimately, it is up to you to decide when someone is most approachable, but here are a few general tips on when might be best:

- when you can get someone to introduce you personally

- when you can pay a meaningful compliment ("I loved your article in *Fortune*")

- when someone he is with seems bored—and you can talk to him

- when he's casually walking

- when he's alone

- if he looks lost or lonely

- if it looks like he's waiting for something or someone

- if he mentions anything publicly that you want to follow up on

- when you can first chat with his assistant or spouse and get their blessings

One of my tried and true methods of getting to speakers at a function is to find them when they first arrive and introduce myself quickly, letting them know that I'm there to hear them speak and am looking forward to their comments or thoughts on something in particular. So many times, I've then become the only familiar face to them in the room. Then, they point their comments toward me, smile at me, choose me for questions first, and even sometimes work something I've said into their speeches.

Familiar faces put speakers more at ease and give them more confidence. When I'm speaking, I'm also more likely to seek out that same person at the end and ask for his or her opinion of how I did. They love that I'm coming to them, and I love the immediate feedback. Try this technique sometime yourself. You're sure to get some great one-on-one time with someone you might not have had the chance to really talk to otherwise. It's something few people ever do, but it can work like a charm!

When you finally approach them, have some good idea about what you want to say, but you don't have to blurt out your purpose right away unless you are likely to get interrupted quickly. If possible, you want to engage them in conversation and show them that you're someone they wouldn't mind getting to know more. Buy them a drink. Try to mingle with their friends or colleagues. Find things you have in common and opportunities to contact them again. Sometimes meeting someone doesn't go as planned. That can be pretty disappointing, but turning it around is often possible with a little follow-up work. In these situations it's important to remember that you accomplished your goal, and that one encounter, however brief, was only your first contact. If it's your last, that's your fault.

Any good salesman will tell you that it usually takes several contacts before you begin to build a relationship with a potential customer. So, once you've met someone big, you have to get right into a relationship-building mode. Follow-up from the first encounter can take many forms:

- bumping into her again later at the same event and talking some more

- getting her business card

- following up with a really nice, sincere "nice meeting you" note: "think what you said on _____ was brilliant."

- sending her an article she may find interesting

- making sure you are at another event you know she'll be at

- inviting her to something she would probably enjoy

Over the phone

If you're trying to reach someone for the first time on the phone, be prepared to deliver a short, smart pitch. This could be your one and only shot to pitch this concept, so you have to be able to act fast and grab her attention. Because, just like entrepreneurs who have to plan for that sixty-second elevator ride with a potential investor that could be their one and only shot to pitch the concept, you have to be able to act fast and grab their attention. Most likely an assistant will answer the phone and your task will be to convince him or her to pass you on to a personal voice mail or the boss directly. Never forget that these are the "gatekeepers." They wield enormous control. So be very nice and direct about why you're calling and why their boss may want to talk to you.

If you get voice mail, notice whose voice is on the message. If it's the person you're trying to reach, he or she probably retrieves the messages. If someone else recorded the message, then be aware that the message could be screened and never heard by him or her at all. Be nice but get right to the point. "I'm calling because . . . And I'd like to . . . If you could call or email me back . . . I really appreciate your time . . .

Here's my info again . . . Hope to hear from you soon . . . If I don't hear from you, I'll try you back in a few days."

If you get them live, you're on the spot and have to learn to take the clues from their voice, their background, and their response to your call. Same rules apply as before.

Via email or snail mail

I personally have learned to love email as a point of first contact because it gives you a better chance at reaching people when they're in a mail reading mode and open to new information and people. With email you're usually getting your message to people when they've allocated some time—maybe first thing in the morning or late at night when they're alone and can concentrate. The best part is that it gives you the chance to start a back and forth dialogue, even if it's a few sentences at a time . . . like so many busy people use as their writing style these days. Never be offended by this, or if someone seems not to read part of a lengthy email. Some people are just in the habit of scanning for important pieces of information, especially if they get more than a hundred emails a day, which many important people actually do.

Put yourself in their shoes and respond accordingly. Follow the approach that you'd use on the phone. Be specific and brief. "Dear Bill . . . Wanted to write you because . . . and to say . . . I would love the chance to talk with you briefly . . . Or get your opinion if you have a minute to chat or write back . . . I've heard that you've been a great help to others . . . Hope to hear from you soon . . . Here's my contact info . . ." That's a good skeleton to follow. But try a few approaches.

Chris David, a programmer I've worked with, carefully crafts every email to make his entire point in one brief paragraph at the top, then expands on it in subsequent comments below. "That way," he says, "you're somewhat guaranteed they'll at least make an attempt to understand what you're looking for." Noting the enormous amount of junk mail that is out there now, he stresses that this technique gives your emails a fighting chance of being looked at, when so much unsolicited mail is quickly being trashed. If it looks too much like a sales pitch, your email could end up in the same place as the rest of them!

If your email message is a really important one, write a draft before you send it. Save the email and reread it a day later before you send it to make sure you're comfortable with it. Forward it to a friend whose opinion you trust and see what he or she thinks before it goes out. Whenever possible, get a referral and mention that so-and-so suggested you get in touch and include that in the beginning. When something comes from someone they already know, your message will carry more weight and stand a better shot at getting a response.

If you're opting for the old-fashioned letter writing approach, make sure it's a personal one. The more standard or generic it looks, the more likely it won't be read at all. I've heard a lot of people suggest hand writing your notes (if it's legible) to give letters a more personal feel. I have to agree that they definitely do get opened more often. After all, any secretaries or personal assistants who might normally screen incoming mail are more likely to think it is a personal letter from a friend, and thus not pry it open. Another trick is to write "Personal & Confidential" on the envelope or send your letter in an unusual package or envelope, or even an urgent-looking overnight package. They tend to get opened first and treated more seriously.

Doug Mellinger aspired to build a large company and approached building his network strategically. Sifting through the Fortune 500 in search of CEOs from the biggest companies in the world, Doug made a list of dozens he wanted to meet, then wrote them all letters. He told them about himself, made sure to let them know what he admired about them, requested a meeting or phone call, and mentioned that he was looking to build a powerful board of advisors. Within months,

Doug built up one of the most powerful boards anywhere with chief executives from more than a dozen Fortune 500 companies. Just a few years later, Doug was featured on the cover of *Inc.* magazine with a caption that read "The Next Bill Gates?" With an upside like that, what are you going to do to build your network?

Few people I've come across have mastered the art of leveraging the Power of People quite like Michael Bronner—a true Young & Successful legend—as far as I'm concerned.

LEVERAGING THE POWER OF PEOPLE

Michael Bronner's outstanding success in both life and career can best be attributed to his extraordinary ability to build and manage relationships with powerful people and corporations, and then deliver their messages, services, and products into the hands of the masses. You could also say that it all started with a little college business, but now that would be an understatement. That little college marketing company he created to distribute coupon books on campus reached 14,000 students at Boston University in one day, and within a few months of that, more than 100,000 other students throughout the city. So as you can see, he's always had a gift when it came to marketing. But Michael was just getting started.

With a keen understanding of the true Power of People fast developing into some serious real-world expertise, Michael created a string of marketing programs that targeted students, then city office workers, then high-end customers of American Express—which happened to be his first major corporate client. From there, he pitched AT&T on yet another marketing initiative and secured a $100 million marketing budget to implement it. Fast forward a few years and Michael's corporate bio compounds to include relationships with everyone from Coca-Cola to Exxon Mobil to McDonald's. After a successful career as a master marketer, Michael sold his business for more than $100 million.

Now, Michael has another brilliant idea—it's called Upromise. It's a new loyalty program that helps parents create college funds for their children in time to cover the rising costs of higher education. All they have to do is set up a college savings account, register it with Upromise, and use their regular credit cards the way they always do at major vendors (who are program partners) around the country. For every purchase they make, a small percentage of that amount is deposited into their college fund and left to accumulate.

This time, despite all the contacts, credibility, experience, and marketing prowess that Michael would have to leverage to make this idea a reality, it involved starting a new company, with a very different mission than his previous ventures. As he explained his idea to *Fast Company* magazine:

> *About 40 million people have an American Airlines AAdvantage frequent-flier account . . . But how many have a college-savings account? A little more than 1 million. What does that tell you?*
>
> *I've been working with companies for eighteen years, helping them spend billions of dollars in marketing money for one purpose—to improve customer economics, to acquire customers at a lower rate, to keep customers who are more profitable. If I could just get a small percentage of those billions to go into col-*

lege-savings accounts, we could begin to change the economics of paying for college.

Michael knows about this problem intimately, because despite his best efforts and early success in business, his own money for college dried up prematurely, forcing him to drop out and lose his chance at earning a degree. But with Upromise, he has committed to helping parents avoid this potential problem by helping them start saving earlier. Through it he's developed a customer loyalty program that automatically deposits a percentage of money they spend while shopping at their favorite merchants, into college savings accounts.

On top of the $90 million he raised in start-up capital, he's also built an advisory board that any entrepreneur would die for. Check this out—Michael is now getting his advice from the dean of Harvard Business School; the chairman of Eastman Kodak; David Rockefeller; the former governor of Vermont; and the legendary venture capitalist John Doerr of Kleiner Perkins. And he couldn't have bigger companies involved either. How's this for corporate partners: GM, AOL, Toys "R" Us, Borders, Exxon Mobil, Century 21, Staples, Starwood Hotels & Resorts . . . and the list goes on and on.

Behold, the power to reach, communicate with, and influence people is perhaps the most powerful ability any one of us can hope to have. Just ask Michael.

The House on the Hill™

IMAGINE YOU'RE READING ONE of those magazines that profile celebrities, business leaders, or politicians. You're looking at glossy multipage spreads packed with photos of the who's-who. They're dressed to impress, laughing, snacking on hors d'oeuvres, shaking hands, and having a great time. Your mind absorbs the pictures as you look for familiar faces. There's a constant stream of people coming and going, many of whom you recognize by face or name, but have never had the chance to meet. These people are fascinating to you, and you find yourself wishing more than anything that you could be a fly on the wall, if not there standing among them yourself. In the context of your life and your dreams, this is the big party, with the people who impress and inspire you the most, and this is where you want to be.

Now picture this gala taking place in a huge compound or estate with a long driveway, a towering set of wrought iron gates, a guard station at the base, and the most beautiful landscaping you've ever seen. Captivating, isn't it?

This is what I call the House on the Hill. Most people only learn about it from the pages of tabloids, fashion magazines, and segments on entertainment news shows. But this house has real significance for a lot of people. *This is where the power is.* The House on the Hill represents the place where deals are made that shape the lives of hundreds, and sometimes millions of people. This is networking at its finest.

It doesn't really matter which house we're talking about because there are many of them. Some exist in the entertainment world, others in politics, and many, many more within specific industries like corporate finance, real estate, the restaurant business, the art world, and publishing. They're spotted all around the globe, but the really big ones, the ones with the biggest players (for lack of a better word), are in the many places you'd expect to see them—New York, Los Angeles, London, Milan, Zurich, Tokyo. You get the picture. Sure, there are incredible people who wield great influence and power in almost every city, and they can range from the mayor of a small town to the CEO of a billion-dollar company to a world leader, for that matter. The trick is in finding the areas that the people you want to do business with are in, then getting in the front door to join the party yourself.

How Does This Apply to Me?

If you think about this elitist world as the place where decisions that affect all of us are made, it can take on a different meaning for you as an individual. If you're organizing a nonprofit, this is where your funding may come from. If you're climbing a corporate ladder, this is where the promotions, division layoffs, and profit sharing plans are decided. If you're running for political office, this is where your biggest supporters and contributors may come from. If you're looking to get attention for your work, this is where the articles are written, the large events are held, and the big endorsements come from. If life is in fact a game, this is where the high-stakes game is played. And it's the place where, if you can get into it yourself, *you* can be a player.

As far as I'm concerned, this is the ultimate test that makes the Young & Successful who they are and sets them apart from the rest. It's their ability to make things happen. The most powerful secret we know is, after all, access.

Six Degrees of Separation

Have you heard of that game called Six Degrees of Kevin Bacon? It's kind of a joke in the entertainment industry that came from a little research someone once did to figure out who was the most connected person in the business. They ran through hundreds of examples and believe it or not, the person who turned out to be more connected than anyone else was Kevin Bacon. You know, he's the guy from the movies *National Lampoon's Animal House, Footloose, My Dog Skip, Diner, A Few Good Men* . . . Strange, huh? So, over the years, countless tabloids have made jokes about this game and have found other ways to connect him with everyone who's ever acted in any major movie, television show, or theatrical production. If you want to check this out for yourself, just go online to www.cs.virginia.edu/oracle/, a little site put together by the department of computer science at the University of Virginia to prove this point once and for all. You can't help but laugh after playing with it for a minute or two. Type in any star and the computer will tell you in a second how they are connected to Kevin Bacon and by exactly how many degrees, or acquaintances. The average I found was about 2 or 3 degrees, even when I typed in the most random people, like high school friends who were small-time actors. I know at first this whole thing sounds ridiculous, but it proves a really interesting point: We're all a lot more connected than we think.

Pick a few people you might want to meet . . . really big people . . . and see how many degrees of separation you are away from any one person. Here's an example. Say you wanted to get to the president of the United States.

0   You . . .

1   have a friend named Jesse . . .

2   Jesse's wife, Susan . . .

3   has a sister who works for . . .

4   this big organization, whose chairman . . .

5   knows the president's brother . . .

6   and he clearly can get you to the president.

That would put you 6 degrees away from the most powerful person in the world. If you know Susan yourself, then you're only 5 degrees away. Meet Susan's sister, and you're now 4 degrees away. See how it works?

Now apply that concept to just about anyone else you want to get to and you might find yourself a lot closer than you think! I personally love this game and use it all the time to make sure I'm staying connected in the industries I need to focus on. Over the years I've met such an insane amount of people and made friends in so many places that my average is down to about 2 or 3 degrees. And that I just happen to find really cool. (Okay, call me strange.) It tells me that I can manage to get access to and have my crazy ideas heard by just about anyone.

Six degrees of separation may apply to the average person, but since you haven't settled for being average yet, this, along with the House on the Hill concept, can help you slash that number significantly. You may be six people away from anyone in the world right now, but when you read the rest of this chapter and put even a small amount of what you learn to work for you, I'll bet you can get as close as two or three people away from anyone, too.

Who's in the House?

Few were born into the House and its world of influence, power, and privilege. Most had to work their way into the House one way or another.

There are a lot of ways to get into the House yourself, and just as some say "it takes money to make money," without a doubt, it takes people to meet people. So, let me introduce you to a few. In the House on the Hill there are Owners, Part-Timers, Visitors, Workers, and the Public. ·

Owners

The people at the top of the power food chain are the Owners. They have the ultimate control over who comes and goes from the House, the most coveted place to be. Think about it this way: If the entertainment world is one neighborhood, Oprah may own the biggest house. Actually, she may own one of the biggest houses in the world because, after all, she is one of the richest women in the world and certainly one of the most powerful. But Oprah built her own house from scratch, after starting out as just another person in the Public. Like most of us starting out, she too was a whole lot of degrees away from power of any kind. In fact, she had challenges that far exceed what most of us will ever have to contend with. And not only did she work her way into the House, but all the way up the proverbial food chain, until everyone around seemed to be working for her. As for the degrees of separation concept, Oprah is now one or two degrees away from anyone, because after all, anyone will take her call! That's access. That's ownership.

If Oprah invites you into the House, you might as well be the guest of honor, because you can get in front of anyone. Just think about how Dr. Phil got started. They met, he impressed the heck out of her, she put him on her show, introduced him to the world, endorsed his work, and *BAM,* he became a powerhouse in his own right.

I'm sure I don't have to say much more on this. Oprah is the ultimate owner.

Part-Timers

These are the people who come and go from the House regularly. They may be family, business partners, neighbors, close friends, or anyone in the Owner's close inner circle.

My friend Suzanne Marx is the ultimate Part-Timer. She's one of those who's-who people you actually do see pictures of in glossy magazines. And she knows more Owners than just about anyone I've ever met. Her closest friends are some of the most influential people in the worlds of philanthropy, politics, education, and the arts. Suzanne is a high-level professional fund-raiser whose work includes some of the biggest private building projects in the country. For one, she helped raise $40 million to build the Ronald Reagan Presidential Library in Simi Valley, California, which now houses more than 50 million pages of government records and documentation from Reagan's political career and more Reagan memorabilia than you'll find anywhere. She also worked on the highly publicized Walt Disney Concert Hall, the new home of the Los Angeles Philharmonic. This $274 million effort enabled the building of a 293,000-square-foot state-of-the-art center that takes up a full city block downtown and is said to be one of the most acoustically sophisticated concert halls in the world. (Impressive stuff, huh?) The Reagan and Disney families just scratch the surface of who she knows, too.

As you can imagine, Suzanne is a serious socialite who's constantly on the move. Her work on behalf of various social and political causes calls for her to float in and out of the House in an endless array of breakfasts, lunches, dinners, benefits, and intimate gatherings. All day, every day, she plays an instrumental role in networking Owners, Part-Timers, and even introducing a few Visitors into the mix.

There's another important group of Part-Timers, as well. Personal assistants, secretaries, and business managers, who are virtually inseparable from the Owners, also fall in to this category as the "gatekeepers" who can determine whether you get in or not. Their power to deny you access means little if the Owner has already granted it, but if you don't know the Owner yet, Part-Timers can be like the pit bulls who guard the gates or the sweet old lady that answers the front door when you ring.

THE BIG HOUSE

Speaking of gatekeepers, have you ever considered who actually controls access to the most powerful person in the free world? (Interesting question, isn't it?) Her name is Ashley Estes, and if you can believe it, she's only twenty-six. Ashley is the personal secretary to George W. Bush, the president of the United States, and she herself is probably the most powerful gatekeeper in the world. It's Ashley's job to know everyone the president knows or needs to know, and keep track of anyone the president ever meets or speaks with on a tight schedule. As she describes it, "You play traffic cop, coordinate with the first lady's office, help get people up to Camp David, and of course, if he's ever running late, he wants us to get him back on schedule." To do her job, Estes must know who Bush's friends from Austin are, which members of Congress he actually wants to talk to, and which members of the White House staff are allowed to glide into the Oval Office without having to cool their heels by her desk.

But Ashley isn't the only gatekeeper. There are many people who, in the big scope of things, control access to the president. But the only other gatekeeper with maybe even greater access than Ashley is twenty-seven-year-old Logan Walters (who incidentally still gets carded when he goes out with friends in Georgetown). Logan is the personal assistant to the president, and he goes absolutely everywhere with him. Meeting President Bush at 6:30 every morning and staying with him until he retires each night, Logan even goes to black-tie events with him, which can keep the two of them out and about until almost midnight.

During one fascinating television special that took cameras into the "Real West Wing" for the most unprecedented access ever granted to the public, Tom Brokaw talked to Ashley and Logan. Standing with them, just a few feet from the Oval Office himself, he called them "the young gatekeepers that even the most senior officials must go through to get to the president." Talk about being Part-Timers. And talk about being Young & Successful!

Just as a side note (because I know you're wondering this yourself!), Ashley and Logan got their jobs in pretty much the same way. As students at the University of Texas, both landed internships in the governor's office and apparently made quite an impression. (Logan, by the way, grew up working summer jobs as a fence builder and pumping gas at his grandfather's gas station.) So when George W. Bush, then governor of the state of Texas, was elected president, he took his most trusted aides with him, and, well, the rest is history.

Part-Timers can often be your best bet to getting into the House. After all, they have the best access themselves and are among the most trusted in any Owner's inner circle. Just think about the friends you're closest to, who you call a few times a week, who you have dinner with on a pretty regular basis. It's like that kind of access.

Visitors

Now pay attention carefully, because this is the easiest and best route into almost any House . . . as a guest. Visitors are either invited over by Owners or Part-Timers, but may also be given entrée by other Visitors who are friends or even casual acquaintances of the Owner. Ever get invited to a party, benefit, or performance where you couldn't believe the people who would be there? Whoever invited you had received an invitation and either wanted you as a date or figured you'd really appreciate the offer. If you took him or her up on it, you've already been a Visitor yourself.

I got to see this firsthand on one unforgettable VIP trip through New York with Suzanne, the Ultimate Part-Timer. And for what it's worth, observing Suzanne was actually what helped me formulate this theory in the first place. After all, she first showed me how access worked at the highest levels when she walked me right in to meet Ronald Reagan himself one day. But that was just a teaser for my introduction to how the House really works.

On one of her frequent business trips to New York from Los Angeles, Suzanne invited me to come along as her guest. Having always been fascinated with her and her work, I couldn't have been more intrigued, and I jumped at the chance. She promised we'd meet some really great people and have a lot of fun in the city, but that was about the biggest understatement I'd ever heard.

We had a packed schedule ahead of us. Because as I'd soon learn,

Suzanne never travels without a carefully planned agenda. I soon learned that with fund-raisers come lots of people to meet, introductions to make, catching up to do with friends, updates on latest projects to be given, and support to be offered. On the surface, it looks like a lot of social visits, but they are business meetings too. If you ever thought you understood the term "too many places to go, and people to see," you haven't yet met Suzanne. Fund-raising isn't just about asking people for money, you see, it's about building and maintaining relationships. And as we've talked about the whole way through, Suzanne is an expert in knowing how to leverage the power of people to make incredible things happen.

Arriving in New York, we headed with our bags right to the Pierre, an elegant hotel (where she knew practically everyone) on the edge of Central Park. The Pierre rolled out the red carpet for her and after a few minutes of chatting with the general manager, we were upgraded to one of their top suites and escorted upstairs.

For breakfast we met with one of Suzanne's oldest friends, Didi Burke. Her husband, who was golfing in the Hamptons, was the ex-chairman of Johnson & Johnson. (To this day, I still rely on some of Didi's tricks for packing without crushing everything you own while on business trips.) Later that afternoon, we lunched with perhaps the most stunning and elegant women I've ever met: Marion Davidson, the vice president of marketing for Hermès, one of the world's most exclusive apparel companies. In that hour or so we learned all about how she climbed to the top of this great company and lived a virtual fantasy life commuting back and forth between New York and Paris every other week.

Then we were off to meet more people for drinks. Back at the Pierre lounge we hooked up with Khaki & Max, the official interior designers for the Clintons, who had followed them from their home state of Arkansas all the way to the White House. With them we had a blast.

They were no less colorful than the magnificent tapestries they described placing in the White House just a few weeks before. For dinner, Suzanne and I grabbed some down time and a few caesar salads at the world famous Cipriani's, a posh little restaurant next door. Then we went back to the suite and crashed for the night. And that, my friends, was just day one.

The next day (after waking up early and quickly scanning *The New York Times, Los Angeles Times,* and *The Wall Street Journal*) we met up with the senior vice president of Tiffany's, who said something to me that just about any girl would die to hear. At the very end of our meeting, this incredibly dressed man, whom I will never forget, shook my hand good-bye and said graciously, "Jennifer, if there is anything that Tiffany's can ever do for you, let me know." I could have melted right there. Audrey Hepburn, eat your heart out!

One last visit, which I'll end my two-days-in-the-life-of-Suzanne story with, would give me more strength and confidence in who I was and what I was working toward over the next few years than perhaps any single meeting ever would. On the way to a big Broadway show on our second night we met up with Tina Brackenbush who told us we had a stop to make. So off to a big high-rise apartment building overlooking the Hudson River we went. Next thing I knew, we were ushered up to a huge penthouse apartment (with 360-degree views from balconies that wrapped all the way around the building!) and were met at the door by a casually dressed but obviously very powerful woman. Her name was Charlotte Beers, and as I'd come to learn, she was known as the highest ranking, most powerful woman in the advertising business. Today she is the only executive to have served as chairman of two of the top ten worldwide agencies: Ogilvy & Mather and J. Walter Thompson. When I met her she was the CEO of Ogilvy & Mather Worldwide, a $5.4 billion agency with more than eight thousand employees. She had been credited with bringing in accounts like IBM, Gillette, and Jaguar and increasing agency billings by $2 billion, all the while making famous some of the best known advertising campaigns in history.

And there I was, sitting on her couch, in her home.

I still remember the thrill of hearing all about the party she had just thrown, and how her friend Martha (yeah, Martha Stewart) popped in to her kitchen to have a look around (as she *usually* did) and ended up whipping up a little culinary masterpiece of fingerfoods she couldn't even pronounce in a matter of minutes. Luckily the conversation turned to Suzanne and her latest projects, so I could take a few deep breaths and slow my head from spinning. But before we left, Charlotte wanted to know about me. Somehow I found the words to tell her all about my adventures in business thus far, and how I was on a mission to help young people like me start their own companies. I still can't believe how interested she was and how many questions she asked. Then she said something I'll never forget. "I really think you're on to something there." Here was a woman whose ideas moved millions of people to action. She had a golden touch, not to mention a golden Rolodex, and even *Fortune* had heralded her as one of the most powerful women in America, putting her picture right on the cover of the magazine.

As a struggling young entrepreneur, desperately trying to get on the right path and affect as many lives as I could, that was just about the greatest validation I could ever get. *Charlotte thought I was on to something.* The rest of that trip is just a blur.

All and all, my trip with Suzanne not only introduced me to some of the most amazing people I'd ever met, but it helped me conceive of this concept now called the House on the Hill. But even beyond learning how this whole other world of power and influence works, I learned that I, an everyday person, could not only gain access, but be accepted in it. Thanks to my friend Suzanne, the Part-Timer, I attained a new level of confidence and self-esteem that to this day still drives me to conquer new worlds, new opportunities, and even pursue relationships I once considered out of reach.

And that was my adventure with Suzanne . . . my trip to the House. I was the lucky Visitor, who was accompanied by a serious Part-Timer, who introduced me to big-time Owners. Those two days gave me an extraordinary and unforgettable firsthand look inside the House on the Hill.

Workers

Then there's another group called the Workers. They make up the bulk of the support team behind the scenes. While being a Worker is definitely a form of serious access to the House, it also comes with very strict rules of conduct and requires extensive references and often a stellar reputation to get in. This group includes the people who offer their services to maintain the House and keep the people inside of it going.

Workers in general are probably not invited into the House as guests, but they nevertheless get in through the side door. And while they may be at the parties, they're rarely hanging out by the pool with the Owners, sipping a martini.

Don't let this discourage you, though. You can still have a lot of fun, and some amazing opportunities can open up for you by taking this route. Don't believe me?

THE VIEW FROM 40,000 FEET

Patrick Canzares spends his whole life working with people at the highest levels and gets to see how this world works every day. In fact, for Patrick, the House is his whole world . . . well, actually it's the private plane that takes people to and from the House, whenever they hop houses or traverse the world for business or pleasure. Need a little clarification? Patrick is a corporate flight attendant who flies full-time for a private, extremely wealthy family and for a major basketball team that his boss, the Owner, also owns.

Patrick is one Young & Successful guy who has *the life*. See, when Patrick goes to work, he climbs aboard a $35 million private Boeing business jet (not to mention the $15 million interior work), and enters a world few will ever see, let alone practically live in. Allow me to explain. When he's not home at the airport hangar stocking up the plane with delectable food and drinks, a serious minibar of snacks, and piles of new movies and music, he's jetting all around the world with his boss. And if you wonder where he goes, well, don't worry, I already asked that one. When I talked to Patrick, he was prepping the G4 Gulfstream Jet he manages for a little trip to Scotland, so the owner and his family could play a few rounds of golf the next day at St. Andrews, one of their more frequent hangouts. But for Patrick, I guess you could call that *just another day at the office*. In case you were wondering, other recent excursions have included trips to Peru, New Zealand, France, Spain, Morocco for lunch one day, and even dinner in the Amazon jungle with a bunch of Indians one night. Patrick says he can't believe he's paid for this either. Talk about loving life as a Worker!

Go ahead, ask the question again, *How did this guy get here* (or get this job)? Well, not unlike most of the Young & Successful we meet, he started at the bottom. He grew up in Mexico City, and his family was fairly well off until his father's business failed while he was still young. Suddenly the family was thrown into poverty, just like so many others in his country. Without speaking a word of English, they moved to Florida when Patrick was thirteen and made a new life for themselves. All the while, Patrick's mother promised him that anything he wanted in life could be his. So finding a way to travel the world was something that he never accepted as out of his reach.

After college, Patrick went to work in the hospitality world and fell in love with the art of customer service. He started out at the Dolphin Hotel in Orlando and quickly got promoted to VIP guest services, where he catered to the property's most important clients. It was there that he first started meeting Owners, and he discovered an intriguing niche—special services for the rich and famous. His new dream, in addition to traveling the world, was eventually to start his own business catering to the special needs of this exclusive clientele. But first, he needed the right experience. So with top recommendations from the hotel, he went to work on a private yacht that was owned by a big corporate CEO. For a year, he worked as its steward, managing the housekeeping functions of the boat and traveling up and down the east coast and all around the Caribbean. The next step was experience in the air. Luckily, the person he worked for was thinking the same thing and suggested that Patrick get some flight training as well. That led him to his current job—the last step before he strikes out on his own and forms his own consulting company in a few years. But for now, what makes him most proud is being one of the only Mexicans on the planet with his type of job. And of course, he now travels everywhere, just as he always dreamed of doing. (Bet he didn't expect to travel in this kind of style, though!)

And as if spending all your time hanging around with a billionaire and his major league sports franchise isn't great enough, I had to know more. I had to know what Patrick thought about working with Owners and being in the House. In response, he assured me that the House is definitely the place to be.

All of us want to be up in the House. And while it takes a tough character to be an Owner, once you're at the top, you don't have to play the game anymore. People are always going to try to bring you down when you are that wealthy, but my boss is really just like us. He's a regular guy who likes his steaks cooked medium rare and just wants him and his family to be happy. That's all that really matters anyway. But as far as the House on the Hill concept goes, the most important thing to remember is that the House is reachable . . . and the view is fabulous.

I asked Patrick to send pictures.

As with Part-Timers, there is a wide range of Workers, too. There are some who have access to the House, yet very minimal exposure to or contact with the Owners and guests. They include the housekeepers, baby-sitters, and grounds keepers, but also the caterers, florists, messengers, etc. Their job is more to maintain the House, than to attend to the Owners. Then there are Workers like Patrick, with a much higher form of access and much more intimate contact with the Owners, as they serve them directly. These are the personal trainers, masseuses, hairdressers, stylists, nannies, even full-time drivers. Because these people spend so much one-on-one time with Owners, friendships can often develop, and it's not uncommon for them to build on that experience and move quickly up the ranks.

If you have some sort of business or service that could be of interest to Owners, present it to them. Be creative with your approach, too. Send them something, talk to other people who work with them. Talk to people they respect, if you can. Find creative yet nonobtrusive ways to get yourself and your expertise in front of those you covet. And follow the advice in the last chapter on how to get to anyone you want to meet. Just remember that referrals are the absolute best way to get in the door, whoever you may be. Countless careers have taken off because people who started out as Workers won the admiration of the Owners. The greatest thing about gaining access this way is that Owners talk to other Owners. Like any good neighbors, they gossip, chat about their lives, and make recommendations to one another for all sorts of things.

The Public

If you're not an Owner, Part-Timer, Visitor, or Worker, you're the Public. Sorry, Charlie. That means you can drive by the House all you want or read everything you get your hands on, but if you don't take certain proactive steps to change your status now, chances are you never will. The Public is totally on the outside, with only a vague sense of what really goes on inside the House, virtually no access to it, and little, if any, ability to influence what happens within it.

In the Public, you live at the mercy of countless decisions that are made by others, many of whom you will never meet. Without any power or influence of your own, your neighborhood, community, government, the educational system, justice system, health care system, financial world, corporate enterprises, and even the small businesses around you will affect you at will and at their own discretion. Not simply because they seek to control, but because someone has to.

It's your choice, though. Who you are in this picture is up to you. If we've taught you anything by now, it should be that you *can* do anything, go anywhere, meet anyone, and accomplish practically anything you want to. You just have to first decide who you want to be and where you want to go.

⋈ The Keys to the House

Barbra Streisand said it best (and painfully often) when she sang about people needing people. I sometimes laugh when I hear people introduce me as, "Jennifer, the one who knows everybody." Actually, I don't know everybody, but I now know I can get to almost anyone. And since we're all an average of six degrees away from everyone, so can you. It doesn't matter if they're Owners, Part-Timers, Workers, or other members of the Public. By now you should be able to communicate your story, your dreams, your plans and ideas to anybody you want to.

At first glance, the House on the Hill may seem to be a fortress. It is my hope that you come to understand that it's more open to the Public than you've ever imagined. Put this concept to use yourself and it will increase your personal access, opening huge doors for you in life.

When I discovered this hidden world myself some years ago, and one night came up with the House on the Hill concept to explain it to others, my life changed forever. I now have an invaluable network of people, and everyone I work with seems to know it.

As you've seen above, the difference between those who are standing on the sidelines and those who have been invited into the party is whether or not they've bridged those six degrees of separation. Now, you know how to make the move across the gap. You know that it's not all about the money, it's not all about what or who you know—the most important thing is how you use what and who you are and what you have to offer to make the leap.

Kick In the Front Gate

You thought you were done, didn't you? Well, there's one more thing you should know: *You can throw the rules out the window.* Look, the House is all about access, one of the most important commodities in business and life. It's not all about power, fame, and money. The access can be yours by coming in through the front door as a guest, entering through the side door as a worker, or jumping the fence and crashing the party. You can also be a Part-Timer who just moves in and refuses to go. Or you can ignore the game entirely.

RALLYING THE PUBLIC

Rich Thau saw the House and all the people in and around it and decided that the game wasn't for him. In essence, he kicked down the front gate. How? He figured out a way to create an organization for his generation—the twentysomethings—that created a unified voice that allowed them to be counted and heard, the same way Boomers are.

See, Rich realized despite the great power that could be found in the House, to make change happen you don't necessarily have to be in it. Because what's most powerful in this world? The Power of People. And there are certainly more people on the outside, in the Public, than there are in the

House, in those often far removed, small, concentrated circles of power and influence.

The challenge this strategy posed was in mobilizing the Public, bringing them together to fight for a single cause. And despite how complex and overwhelming a concept as *that* was, it's the one that Rich chose when he decided to ensure the younger generation found its own voice in the political world. Amid what he called the "grand constellation of generations," young adults needed to start taking more interest in the longer term issues that were facing the nation. Debt, crime, the environment, education, race relations, and the economy were all being discussed without the input of the very generation that would be inheriting these very challenges. Clearly something had to be done to engage them on a higher level. After all, the younger generation was barely even voting, let alone becoming active in developing and shaping new policies that affected them.

Rich explained to me how, in the big scheme of things, power in politics worked. The senior citizens (in the Public) are well organized because AARP (formerly called the American Association of Retired Persons) is actually the largest membership organization in the United States. Baby Boomers are at the age where their chosen leaders are running the country, and young adults . . . well, they were nowhere to be found . . . at least at the decision-making tables. Young people needed to vote on the issues that affected them. According to Rich, the situation was simple to explain. The only reason the things younger people care about don't get fixed in this world is because they don't vote. They don't speak up. (See why we love Rich? He's practically singing the Young & Successful theme song!)

So at twenty-eight, Rich set up a nonprofit organization called Third Millennium and set out to earn a place in the House—not by, should we say, the more "political routes," but by chorusing members of his generation in the Public. Rich set up a think tank that focused on the issues that he thought were most critical to address. The first? Aging in America. It obviously didn't sound that interesting at first. But there was a serious crisis at hand. The Baby Boomers, the largest generation in history, were getting ready to retire. At stake was the Social Security system, which people pay into their whole lives via taxes so that when they retire, there's money there to take care of them. The problem was, this generation was so large that they were about to wipe the funds out, leaving future generations (particularly the youngest, so called Generation Y, who even outnumbered the Boomers) with nothing for when they grew old and retired. Even more disconcerting was the idea that younger generations just entering the work force would have to pay into this black hole fund for the next forty or fifty years, when that money might never be returned to them.

When Rich started making calls to the House, the lawmakers who answered weren't listening because the young people weren't voting and didn't seem to care. Rich had to make them care. But first, they needed to be reached and convinced of how important politics were to their future.

Third Millennium thus set out into the Public and began asking a lot of questions through major research initiatives. What he found was not only startling, but brilliantly positioned. In what would soon be the most cited poll study of the decade, Rich riled up the mass media, and thus the members of the House, with some juicy news. More young people believed that UFOs were more likely to exist than Social Security when they retire. Essentially this said that people had more faith in a visit from space aliens than a government system that worked in their favor. His next study showed that our generation believed the TV soap opera *General Hospital* would outlast Medicare.

The House started to listen, and the young Public instantly wanted to know more.

Government doors began to fly open and Rich went from a member of the Public to a Visitor with increasing access, and a lot of attention. The work that he was doing was featured by hundreds of newspapers around the world. He was invited to testify in front of Congress (and before the nation via CSPAN) more than twenty times. Third Millennium was being invited to meet with the nation's most prominent leaders and represent young Americans at White House summits and conferences. Soon, not only were the most powerful people in the country quoting his research on a regular basis, but the Secretary of the Treasury was initiating private get-togethers for them to chat and start to find solutions. At one point, the president's office even called after Bill Clinton delivered the annual State of the Union address, just to see if Rich had any questions on what was being proposed.

In what was dubbed "Neglection 2000," Rich and a number of other groups banded together to study and publicize the fact that politicians were neglecting the needs and issues of the young. By attacking this issue head-on, Rich finally made it clear that the problem was more a lack of communication from the politicians than a lack of caring on the part of the young. There's still much more work to be done, but now at least, Rich has kicked the doors open.

Rich said that someone once explained politics this way: "Politicians are like reeds in the wind. Blow on them and they sway in one direction. Shift the winds entirely and they'll get up and move." Rich said his interest was on the outside of the House, and he encouraged his peers to consider what they can do from the outside too. "You can create more change by mobilizing the masses. Inside you can have a great career, learn the inner workings of the House, and have a very different experience than I did, and probably an easier time." But Rich heeded the advice of yet another great mentor, a college professor who once said, "Go where the great minds aren't going. Forge your own path." And so he did, and in the process, he encouraged the young Public to speak louder and the House to listen more closely.

The Young & Successful know that getting to the House is the goal. And even though Rich wasn't interested in staying inside, he did want access to come and go, and thus be recognized and heard by the people inside.

Whether your aim is to own it yourself one day, just have the opportunity to hang around it, access it when need be, or to overthrow it entirely, you now know what can be done to get there. It's up to you. You have the option to have this kind of access and influence. And that translates into the ability to make big and important things happen. You decide whether you want to play by the rules, change them, or make up your own.

You now know who the Young & Successful are. You've met them. You've begun to tell your own story. You've thought about your Ideal Life. You've sketched out your Grand Plan. You've made a map of your new world and started to take a taste of it. You've learned about Real World University and how to equip yourself with any information, skills, or expertise you need. You've given thought to your Major Life Challenges and started to think strategically about the choices and major decisions you make. You've learned to harness the incredible Power of People and cultivate powerful and rewarding relationships. You've seen how important and beneficial it is to give back yourself. And most important, you now have a new understanding of how you fit into the world and how you can use that knowledge to your greatest advantage. This information is your ticket to the party going on in the House on the Hill.

It is important that you understand how this world, the real world, works, and what role you truly do fill in it. Because we are all someone here, even if we're just the Public. Understand that, and you'll start to see how you can be a player in life . . . just like the Young & Successful. They may not be Owners yet, but they can get in to the House and get done what they need to do. After all, they know what they want and know how to get it. They take responsibility and control of their lives and their circumstances. And this is how they make extraordinary things happen.

These are the Young & Successful. And now you know their secrets.

Index

ysn.com
your success network

for the stuff
they never taught
us in school

CONTACT US:

Nothing is more inspiring to us than hearing your personal stories.
To share your success, email us at yourstory@ysn.com

SPEAKING ENGAGEMENTS:

For information on booking Jennifer Kushell for a speaking engagement please email us at: speaking@ysn.com

YS Media Corp. • 4712 Admiralty Way #530 • Marina del Rey • CA • 90292

ysn.com

Go to ysn.com today and subscribe for the **FREE** YSN Weekly newsletter, filled with:
Profiles • Tips • Tricks • Tools • Insights • Resources

Each week you'll receive timely, cutting-edge information, with contacts
and short-cuts to achieve rapid success. Best of all, it's FREE!!!

ysn.com

DRIVE SMARTER

**Secrets of the Young & Successful
now available as an audio book**

THE *NEW YORK TIMES* BESTSELLER

secrets of the
young&
successful

how to get everything you want
without waiting a lifetime

with FREE online self-assessment at
ysn.com

JENNIFER KUSHELL   SCOTT M. KAUFMAN